REPUBLICANISM, RHETORIC, AND ROMAN
POLITICAL THOUGHT

Republicanism, Rhetoric, and Roman Political Thought develops readings of
Rome's three most important Latin historians – Sallust, Livy, and Tacitus –
in light of contemporary discussions of republicanism and rhetoric. Drawing
on recent scholarship as well as other classical writers and later political
thinkers, this book develops interpretations of the three historians' writings
centering on their treatments of liberty, rhetoric, and social and political
conflict. Sallust is interpreted as an antagonistic republican, for whom elite
conflict serves as an outlet and channel for the antagonisms of political life.
Livy is interpreted as a consensualist republican, for whom character and its
observation help to maintain the body politic. Tacitus is interpreted as being
centrally concerned with the development of prudence and as a subtle critic
of imperial rule.

Daniel J. Kapust is Assistant Professor in the Department of Political
Science at The University of Georgia. He is the author of several published
or forthcoming articles and book chapters on Sallust, Livy, Tacitus, Cicero,
Machiavelli, Hobbes, political fear, republicanism, and Friedrich Hayek.
Professor Kapust received his PhD from the University of Wisconsin,
Madison, in political science.

REPUBLICANISM, RHETORIC, AND ROMAN POLITICAL THOUGHT

Sallust, Livy, and Tacitus

DANIEL J. KAPUST

University of Georgia

CAMBRIDGE
UNIVERSITY PRESS

CAMBRIDGE
UNIVERSITY PRESS

32 Avenue of the Americas, New York NY 10013-2473, USA

Cambridge University Press is part of the University of Cambridge.

It furthers the University's mission by disseminating knowledge in the pursuit of
education, learning and research at the highest international levels of excellence.

www.cambridge.org
Information on this title: www.cambridge.org/9781107425279

© Daniel J. Kapust 2011

First published 2011
First paperback edition 2014

A catalogue record for this publication is available from the British Library

Library of Congress Cataloguing in Publication data
Kapust, Daniel J., 1976–
Republicanism, rhetoric, and Roman political thought: Sallust,
Livy, and Tacitus / Daniel J. Kapust.
p.   cm.
Includes bibliographical references and index.
ISBN 978-1-107-00057-5 (hardback)
1. Political science – Rome – History.   2. Republicanism – Rome – History.
3. Sallust, 86-34 B.C.   4. Livy.   5. Tacitus, Cornelius.   I. Title.
JC83.K37   2011
321.8´6–dc22   2010043977

ISBN 978-1-107-00057-5 Hardback
ISBN 978-1-107-42527-9 Paperback

CONTENTS

Acknowledgments   *page* vii

1   Introduction   1

2   An Ambiguous Republican: Sallust on Fear,
    Conflict, and Community   27

3   Channeling Conflict through Antagonistic
    Rhetoric in the *War with Catiline*   53

4   Exemplarity and Goodwill in Livy's *From
    the Founding of Rome*   81

5   Tacitus on Great Men, Bad Rulers, and Prudence   111

6   Tacitus' Moral Histories   141

Epilogue   173
Bibliography   177
Index   191

v

ACKNOWLEDGMENTS

This book's origin is in a doctoral dissertation of a different name and slightly different topic, *Rereading Republicans: Roman History and Liberal Dilemmas,* defended at the University of Wisconsin, Madison, in 2005. I began to write *Republicanism, Rhetoric, and Roman Political Thought* in the fall of 2006, and continued to work on it through the spring of 2010. During that time, portions of the book were presented at meetings of the American Political Science Association, the Midwest Political Science Association, and the Southern Political Science Association, as well as at a workshop sponsored by the Politics Department at Fairfield University.

I would not have gone to graduate school, let alone have written this book, if it were not for the interest and encouragement of many remarkable teachers of political theory, history, and the classics that I had the benefit of working with at the University of Maryland: Charles Butterworth, Arthur Eckstein, Stephen Elkin, Jessica Dietrich, Lillian Doherty, Judith Hallett, Hugh Lee, Steven Rutledge, Greg Staley, and Eva Stehle. They inspired my love of classics and political theory and encouraged me to pursue graduate studies.

My dissertation committee members – Richard Boyd, Victoria Pagán, Patrick Riley, Howard Schweber, and Bernard Yack – each played integral roles in the formation and completion of this project. Richard Boyd went above and beyond the call of duty, reading draft after draft of my dissertation and providing valuable advice on this book, while Victoria Pagán always made sure that my argument – whether in the dissertation or the book – was on solid footing. Howard Schweber pushed me to clarify and sharpen my thinking, and Patrick Riley, through his kindness, generosity, compassion, and immense knowledge, was a source of constant encouragement.

I especially wish to thank Bernard Yack, who not only convinced me to write a dissertation on Roman political thought, but who, despite having taken a new position while I was still writing my dissertation, was generous with his time and comments, and always willing to offer his guidance, professional and personal, both during and after graduate school.

Since I began writing *Republicanism, Rhetoric, and Roman Political Thought*, I have benefited from the comments of many scholars, and I wish to thank each of them as well: Jocelyn Boryczka, Richard Boyd, Daniel Cordes, Bryan Garsten, Stephen Kelts, Eric MacGilvray, John McCormick, Daniel O'Neil, Victoria Pagán, John Parrish, Gary Remer, Patrick Riley, Vin Rosavich, Giovanni Ruffini, Stephen Rutledge, Arlene Saxonhouse, David Williams, Andrew Wolpert, and Bernard Yack. I wish to thank Brandon Turner and John Lombardini in particular, as each of them read complete drafts of the manuscript and provided me with generous comments on it.

Eric Crahan, the Cambridge editor with whom I have dealt, has been helpful, patient, and supportive, and I cannot thank him enough for his encouragement and assistance; I also thank the two anonymous referees who read my manuscript for Cambridge University Press and gave me careful and thorough comments that were also of great help. Answering their criticisms made the manuscript immeasurably stronger. I am grateful to The University of Georgia and the School of Public and International Affairs for research support, which greatly assisted my writing of this book, and to two graduate students in the Department of Political Science, Elliot Slane and Brandon Gorman, each of whom provided editorial and research assistance. My colleagues in the Department of Political Science at The University of Georgia supported and encouraged me in this project, and for that I thank them as well. More friends than I can count have provided me with support throughout the course of this project, and throughout my graduate and scholarly career, my family has been tremendously supportive. I owe them in particular my gratitude.

Finally, I thank my darling wife, Eunsook Jung, for her patient, kind, and loving support while I was working on this book. I dedicate this book to her.

Nam simul te aspexi, nihil est super mi.
– Catulus 51

I

INTRODUCTION

I. SETTING THE STAGE

In his dialogue *Brutus*, written in 46 BCE, Cicero describes the deep pain he experienced at the death of Quintus Hortensius four years earlier. Hortensius was not only a friend, but like a father to Cicero: A distinguished man of like political sympathies when there was a "great dearth of wise and patriotic citizens," he passed in a time of grave public danger.[1] Hortensius was also "a comrade and fellow-worker in the same field of glorious endeavor" – namely, the endeavor of eloquent speaking. Hortensius had been one of Rome's leading orators; the young Cicero "had to outdo him, if he wished to take over this position" – and he did in the trial of Gaius Verres in 70 BCE.[2] Yet despite his grief at the passing of his friend, Cicero suggests that he passed "opportunely"; had he lived longer, he would have been "able only to lament the fate of his country, not to help it."[3]

Had Hortensius lived to the time in which Cicero wrote *Brutus*, he, like other "good and loyal men" – *bonis et fortibus civibus* – would "mourn the loss of many things."[4] In particular, Hortensius would be saddened at "the spectacle of the Roman forum ... robbed and bereft of that finished

---

[1] Cicero, *Brutus*, trans. G.L. Hendrickson, *Cicero: Brutus and Orator* (Cambridge: Harvard University Press, 1952), 2. In citing English translations of Latin or Greek texts, I generally cite the translations noted throughout, though I frequently provide key Latin phrases and terms, and occasionally paraphrase or loosely translate the Latin text.

[2] Manfred Furhmann, *Cicero and the Roman Republic*, trans. W.E. Yuill (Oxford: Basil Blackwell, 1992), 26.

[3] Cicero, *Brutus*, 4.

[4] Ibid., 6.

eloquence worthy of the ears of Rome or even of Greece," emptied of eloquence by the rule of Caesar. For it is this eloquence and its weapons, suggests Cicero, "which are the peculiar and proper resource of a leader in the commonwealth and of a civilized and law-abiding state" – *bene moratae et bene constitutae civitatis.*[5] Eloquence and its weapons were of little use now that Caesar had taken power.

The passages cited from Cicero are striking in their beauty and sentiment. But their importance for my discussion does not lie in their illustration of Cicero's emotional state or even their possible effect on the work's recipient, Marcus Junius Brutus, the future participant in Caesar's assassination. Rather, Cicero is articulating the close connection between the freedom of the Roman republic and the practice of oratory, a connection seen in the loss of eloquence and the emptying of the forum with Caesar's displacement of republican politics. This is a common theme in Cicero's later writings, especially *Orator*, *Brutus*, and *On Duties*: The perils facing the republic and threatening its demise were the perils facing eloquence and threatening its demise as well. With Caesar's victory in the civil wars, the status of eloquence had – so it seemed – been altered profoundly. We may note, in this regard, a passage from *On Duties*, written in 44 BCE, where Cicero contrasts his leisure with that of P. Scipio Africanus: "my leisure was determined by scarcity of business, not by my eagerness to rest; for when the senate has been suppressed and the lawcourts destroyed, what is there worthy of me that I can do in the senate house or in the forum?"[6]

The reality was, to be sure, more complex; Cicero, as is well known, has a penchant for exaggeration. Cicero was still giving speeches, though some were of a different sort, especially his two so-called Caesarian speeches, the speeches *For Marcellus* and *For Ligarius*, each of which praised Caesar's clemency. Indeed, in *On Duties*, he refers to "the interruption – not to say the destruction – of eloquence."[7] Eloquence was not finished just yet, and Cicero would soon put it to use, though with tragic results, in his *Philippics*. Yet the danger Caesar posed to eloquence and liberty was real, for Cicero, and the relationship between Roman liberty and the practice of oratory was strong in his writings.

[5] Ibid., 7.
[6] Cicero, *On Duties*, ed. M.T. Griffin and E.M. Atkins (Cambridge: Cambridge University Press, 1991), 3.2.
[7] Cicero, *On Duties*, 2.67.

Cicero is our entry point; he provides a glimpse into the link between liberty, the participatory politics of the Roman republic, and oratory. We may now step forward nearly 150 years to Tacitus, whose *Dialogue on Orators* also centers on rhetoric and its relationship to liberty and order. In this dialogue, the interlocutors debate a number of issues – the relative merits of rhetoric and poetry, the training and ability of the orator, and the usefulness of rhetoric, past and present. The character Maternus, who early in the dialogue defends poetry and attacks oratory, makes an intriguing argument at the end of the dialogue, one that echoes and yet seems to subvert Cicero. He agrees with Cicero in linking oratory to liberty, though with a twist. What for Cicero was liberty is for Maternus license: "great and famous oratory is a foster-child of license, which foolish men call liberty, an associate of seditions, a goad for the unbridled people."[8] Rhetoric is thus linked to liberty, but to liberty misconceived, and the practice of rhetoric is not characteristic of the peaceful and well-ordered imperial present of Maternus and his interlocutors, since it "does not grow under a well-regulated constitution."[9] The irony is profound: Maternus's *bene constitutis civitatibus* recalls Cicero's *bene constituta civitas* and denies eloquence its place, suggesting that Cicero's past in which eloquence blossomed was not well constituted, and that Cicero, champion of the free republic, misunderstood liberty itself.

In these texts, we see two poles of thinking about liberty and rhetoric – and Roman liberty and rhetoric in particular. One pole emphasizes the centrality of rhetoric to Roman liberty and the Roman republic itself. So close is the connection that in his classic article, "*Libertas* in the Republic," Brunt remarks that the absence of a Latin equivalent to the Greek term παρρησία (frank speech) does not indicate that free speech was not valued in Rome; rather, free speech was so important "that the word *liber* can be used *tout court* to mean 'speaking one's mind.'" For Romans – or at least *elite* Romans – free speech meant speaking what one "felt without being subject to fear or pressure."[10] The internal conditions of liberty – peaceful and free republican government – could, then, be conceived as linked to the practice of oratory, a point that we will see Cicero making in subsequent discussions of *On the Ideal Orator*.

---

[8] Tacitus, *A Dialogue on Oratory*, trans. W. Peterson and M. Winterbottom, *Tacitus: Dialogus, Agricola, Germania* (Cambridge: Harvard University Press, 1958), 40.2.

[9] Ibid., 40.2.

[10] P.A. Brunt, "*Libertas* in the Republic," in *The Fall of the Roman Republic and Other Related Essays* (Oxford: Clarendon Press, 1988): 281–350, 314.

This is not to say that Rome was a democracy, as Fergus Millar has argued.[11] Indeed, much recent scholarship shows that while Rome was participatory, it was not a democracy, at least not in the sense that classical Athens was a democracy.[12] Yet while the Roman republic was no democracy, and was also a highly inegalitarian society, the liberty of the republic pitted the *libertas* of the people against the *auctoritas* of the Senate.[13] It was antagonism between the people and the Senate, the many and the few, that was the stuff of republican politics, and it was partly the practice of rhetoric that set "limits on the arbitrary exercise of authority … by figuring it as a practice constrained in part by 'natural law,' in part by the consensual standard of public approval."[14]

If rhetoric and liberty were linked in one pole of thought about rhetoric and the Roman republic, the prior can also be understood as paving way for the latter's destruction. As Hamilton wrote in *Federalist 1*:

of those men who have overturned the liberties of republics, the greatest number have begun their career by paying an obsequious court to the people; commencing demagogues and ending tyrants.[15]

It is as if Hamilton were paraphrasing Cicero's speech *On the Agrarian Law*, where Cicero describes:

the hypocritical pretences of certain individuals, who, while attacking and hindering not only the interest but even the safety of the people, are striving by their speeches to obtain the reputation of being supporters of the people.[16]

---

[11] See Fergus Millar, *The Crowd in Rome in the Late Republic* (Ann Arbor: University of Michigan Press, 1998).

[12] See, e.g., K.J. Hölkeskamp, "The Roman Republic: Government of the People, by the People, for the People?," *Scripta Classica Israelica* 19 (2000): 203–23; Robert Morstein-Marx, *Mass Oratory and Political Power in the Late Roman Republic* (Cambridge: Cambridge University Press, 2004); Henrik Mouritsen, *Plebs and Politics in the Late Roman Republic* (Cambridge: Cambridge University Press, 2001). For a recent synthesis of this discussion, see Allen M. Ward, "How Democratic Was the Roman Republic?," *New England Classical Journal* 31, no. 2 (2004): 101–19.

[13] See Joy Connolly, *The State of Speech; Rhetoric and Political Thought in Ancient Rome* (Princeton: Princeton University Press, 2007), 64.

[14] Ibid., 4.

[15] Alexander Hamilton, *Federalist 1* in *The Federalist Papers*, ed. Clinton Rossiter (New York: The New American Library of World Literature, 1961), 35.

[16] Cicero, *De Lege Agraria*, trans. John Henry Freese, *Cicero: Pro Publio Quinctio, Pro Sexto Roscio Amerino, Pro Quinto Roscio Comoedo, De Lege Agraria* (Cambridge: Harvard University Press, 2000), 2.7.

Eloquence – and especially the deceptive eloquence of demagogues – could be destructive to liberty and undermine the practice of rhetoric itself insofar as it undermined political liberty. Cicero, for instance, has Scaevola describe the Gracchi in *On the Ideal Orator* as having "shattered the State … by eloquence."[17] Roman history abounds with stories of demagogues seeking *regnum* – seeking to make themselves kings.[18] The great Roman historian Ronald Syme termed Caesar a "patrician demagogue," and the point is clear: Sweet-talking leaders courted the people into the destruction of their liberty.[19]

In these texts by Cicero and Tacitus – *Brutus, On the Ideal Orator, On Duties*, and the *Dialogue on Orators* – we see, then, two themes, and two rival ways of interpreting these themes, whose contested relationship was of great importance in Roman political thought: liberty and rhetoric. Maternus and Cicero agree that rhetoric and liberty are connected, but what was a desirable phenomenon for Cicero was, it seems, undesirable for Maternus. For the latter, the tumult and turmoil of liberty and the play of eloquence was more trouble than it was worth; for the former, eloquence was symptomatic and productive of peace and liberty, rather than discord.

II. THE "ROMAN TURN" IN POLITICAL THEORY AND THE HISTORIANS SALLUST, LIVY, AND TACITUS

These two themes and their problematic connections, important as they were in the thought of Rome, are of great importance to contemporary scholarship in political theory. Indeed, Roman liberty – or republican liberty – has been of much interest to contemporary political theorists, as have the theory and practice of oratory – whether under the name of persuasion or rhetoric. Scholars such as Pettit, Skinner, and Viroli have sought to revive and reinvigorate a Roman-rooted conception of republican politics centered on

---

[17] Cicero, *On the Ideal Orator*, trans. James M. May and Jakob Wisse (Oxford: Oxford University Press, 2001), 1.38.

[18] See Andrew Lintott, *The Constitution of the Roman Republic* (Oxford: Oxford University Press, 1999), 36.

[19] Ronald Syme, *The Roman Revolution* (New York: Oxford University Press, 1939), 25. See also Andrew Lintott, "The Crisis of the Republic: Sources and Source-Problems," in *The Cambridge Ancient History, Volume IX: The Last Age of the Roman Republic, 146–43 B.C.*, ed. J.A. Crook, Andrew Lintott, and Elizabeth Rawson (Cambridge: Cambridge University Press, 1994): 1–15, 9–10.

a distinctive conception of liberty, one that rivals the more dominant liberal tradition. Other scholars, such as Allen, Garsten, and Remer have looked to classical rhetoric to enrich and broaden contemporary debates over democratic citizenship and deliberation. In the background of both discussions looms the liberty and rhetoric of republican Rome.

As its title, *Republicanism, Rhetoric, and Roman Political Thought: Sallust, Livy, and Tacitus*, indicates, this book is concerned with these contemporary discussions, and more broadly with rhetoric and liberty. This book explores rhetoric, liberty, and their relationship to social and political conflict in Roman thought of the first century BCE and the first century CE. My primary concern is not with the works of Roman philosophers such as Cicero or Seneca or with Roman rhetorical writers such as Quintilian, though recent scholarship, with which I engage, has focused on these writers.[20] Rather, my concern is with the ways in which conflict, liberty, and rhetoric were depicted and theorized by Rome's three greatest Latin historians: Sallust, Livy, and Tacitus. To be sure, other Roman writers (such as Pliny, Quintilian, and Seneca) and scholarly engagements with them will feature in my discussion; this is especially true of Cicero, who will often serve as a point of comparison to the historians, and whose writings – especially *On the Ideal Orator, On Duties, Orator*, and *Brutus* – will serve as crucial sources of ideas and themes in my analysis of the historians.

My focus, however, is on the Roman historians themselves. Why turn to Rome's historians to write about conflict, liberty, rhetoric, and the Roman republic? A possible answer is simply to point to the diverse and broad influence exerted by these historians on subsequent figures in the history of political thought who dealt with a wide array of problems. The Roman historians served as key sources for Augustine and other medieval thinkers, such as John of Salisbury and Christine de Pizan; their importance in Renaissance political thought is hard to exaggerate; their status as key sources and influences in early modern thought, ranging from Lipsius to Hobbes, to eighteenth-century thinkers such as Rousseau, Madison, and Burke, to nineteenth-century thinkers such as Mill, and to twentieth-century thinkers such as Arendt, have all been the subject of scholarly inquiry.[21] The historians

---

[20] See, for instance, Connolly, *The State of Speech*; Bryan Garsten, *Saving Persuasion: A Defense of Rhetoric and Judgment* (Cambridge: Harvard University Press, 2006); Dean Hammer, *Roman Political Thought and the Modern Theoretical Imagination* (Norman: University of Oklahoma Press, 2008).

[21] For overviews of each historian's influence on subsequent thought, see Neal Wood, "Sallust's Theorem: A Comment on 'Fear' in Western Political Thought," *History of*

were received and interpreted in many different ways by these writers: Sallust provided ammunition to Augustine in his critique of Roman ideas and practices and to humanists in their conflicts with Italy's ducal cities, whereas Hobbes would cite him in his own struggles with the practice of rhetoric and the admirers of the Roman republic.[22] Livy provided Machiavelli with themes for his *Discourses*, and was a key source for Montesquieu. He has been read as an Augustan, in that he seems to back Augustus' agenda; he has also been read as a champion of the Senate and a critic of autocracy.[23] Tacitus, for instance, was viewed as both teacher and critic of tyrants — that is, as a "black" Tacitus or "red" Tacitus.[24] An exploration of these historians in their own right is thus a useful contribution to the study of the history of political thought.

A second reason — and one of more contemporary concern and directly linked to my topic — centers on their role in contemporary discussions of republicanism and rhetoric. Pettit, Skinner, Viroli, and other scholars of republicanism discuss Sallust, Livy, and Tacitus; political theorists such as Saxonhouse, Boesche, and Fontana have looked to Tacitus and Sallust as resources for exploring rhetoric and liberty, respectively.[25] The Roman

Political Thought XVI, no. 2 (1995): 174–89; Sheila M. Mason, "Livy and Montesquieu," in *Livy*, ed. T.A. Dorey (London: Routledge and Kegan Paul, 1971): 118–58; J.H. Whitfield, "Machiavelli's Use of Livy," in *Livy*, ed. T.A. Dorey (London: Routledge and Kegan Paul, 1971): 73–96; P. Burke, "Tacitism," in *Tacitus*, ed. T.A. Dorey (New York: Basic Books, 1969): 149–71. For a discussion of the role of the historians in Renaissance thought in particular, see Quentin Skinner, "Machiavelli's *Discorsi* and the Pre-Humanist Origins of Republican Ideas," in *Machiavelli and Republicanism*, ed. Gisella Bock, Quentin Skinner, and Maurizio Viroli (Cambridge: Cambridge University Press, 1990): 121–41.

[22] See Skinner, "Machiavelli's *Discorsi* and the Pre-Humanist Origins of Republican Ideas." I will discuss Hobbes' reading of Sallust in more detail in Chapter 2.

[23] For a reading of Livy as Augustan, see T.J. Luce, *Livy: The Composition of His History* (Princeton: Princeton University Press, 1977). For a reading of Livy as a champion of the Senate, see P.G. Walsh, *Livy* (Oxford: Oxford University Press, 1974).

[24] On "red" and "black" readings of Tacitus, see Burke, "Tacitism," 162–6.

[25] See Roger Boesche, "The Politics of Pretence: Tacitus and the Political Theory of Despotism," *History of Political Thought* VIII, no. 2 (1987): 189–210; Benedetto Fontana, "Sallust and the Politics of Machiavelli," *History of Political Thought* XXIV, no. 1 (2003): 86–108; Philip Pettit, *Republicanism: A Theory of Freedom and Government* (Oxford: Oxford University Press, 1997); Arlene W. Saxonhouse, "Tacitus' Dialogue on Oratory: Political Activity under a Tyrant," *Political Theory* 3, no. 1 (1975): 53–68; Quentin Skinner, *Liberty before Liberalism* (Cambridge: Cambridge University Press, 1998); Skinner, "Machiavelli's *Discorsi* and the Pre-Humanist Origins of Republican Ideas."; Quentin Skinner, "The Republican Ideal of Political Liberty," in *Machiavelli and Republicanism*, ed. Gisella Bock, Quentin Skinner, and Maurizio Viroli (Cambridge: Cambridge University Press, 1990): 293–309; Maurizio Viroli, *Republicanism*, trans. Antony Shugaar (New York: Hill and Wang, 2002).

historians are thus of continued importance because of their influence on contemporary scholarly developments in political theory.

Yet these writers do not merit attention simply because they have been read by other authors or feature in the genealogies of political concepts; they are worthy of attention in their own right because they wrestled in psychologically rich ways with tensions and problems in the practice of rhetoric, its place in the political community, its relationship to conflict, and its associations with liberty and participatory government. It is on these problems and these relationships that the present study will focus. Before we move further, however, I turn to a discussion of republicanism, rhetoric, and Roman historiography in particular.

III. REPUBLICANISM AND POLITICAL THEORY

It is no exaggeration to say that interest in Rome and Roman thought has not been center stage in political theory for much of the twentieth century, though recent years have seen renewed interest.[26] Indeed, Rome has been much in the air of late; some have drawn comparisons between the American republic and the Roman republic, or between Roman imperialism and American power.[27] My starting point is with two threads of recent scholarship, behind each of which lies Roman thought: the republican revival in history and political theory, on the one hand, and recent scholarship exploring the relationship between rhetoric and its practice and democratic theory and practice.

Republicanism has been an important focus of inquiry among political theorists and historians since the late 1960s.[28] This scholarship emerged in

---

[26] On the fate of Roman political thought in the twentieth century, see Hammer, *Roman Political Thought and the Modern Theoretical Imagination*, chapter 1. On this renewed interest beyond the republican and rhetorical scholarship discussed in this section, see, e.g., Connolly, *The State of Speech*; Fontana, "Sallust and the Politics of Machiavelli"; Benedetto Fontana, "Tacitus on Empire and Republic," *History of Political Thought* XIV (1993): 27–40; Daniel J. Kapust, "Between Contumacy and Obsequiousness: Tacitus on Moral Freedom and the Historian's Task," *European Journal of Political Theory* 8, no. 3 (2009): 293–311; William Walker, "Sallust and Skinner on Civil Liberty," *European Journal of Political Theory* 5, no. 3 (2006): 237–59.

[27] For a discussion of both topics, as well as the general status of matters Roman in American culture, see Cullen Murphy, *Are We Rome? The Fall of an Empire and the Fate of America* (New York: Houghton Mifflin Company, 2007).

[28] See, for instance, Bernard Bailyn, *The Ideological Origins of the American Revolution* (Cambridge: Harvard University Press, 1967); Caroline Robbins, *The Eighteenth-Century*

part as a reaction to the perceived dominance of liberalism in both political theory and intellectual history, a dominance that seemed both overstated and illegitimate.[29] This concern began to shift from historical to normative inquiry with the waning of the liberalism/communitarianism debates, especially in the scholarship of Quentin Skinner and Philip Pettit.[30]

Skinner and Pettit's discussions of Roman liberty and republicanism were, at least in part, reactions to a perceived false dichotomy in the debates between liberalism and communitarianism. By way of illustration, MacIntyre argued in *After Virtue* that "the crucial moral opposition is between liberal individualism in some version or other and the Aristotelian tradition in some version or other."[31] In "The Republican Ideal of Political Liberty," Skinner challenges this dichotomizing view, seeking to navigate the gap between liberals whom he views as "sweeping the public arena bare of any concepts save those of self-interest and individual rights" and those who hold an Aristotelian view of public life based on a conception of humans as "moral beings with certain determinate purposes."[32] There is instead a third way, Skinner argues, and a key historical resource for Skinner's argument is Roman political thought.

In making this argument, Skinner also challenges the view – linked to Isaiah Berlin – of political liberty as either a primarily negative or primarily positive concept.[33] Skinner describes a view of liberty he associates with "classical republicans" – seventeenth-century English opposition figures, Machiavelli, and ultimately Roman writers such as Sallust – a view that sees a free state as "one that is able to act according to its own will, in pursuit

Commonwealthman: Studies in the Transmission, Development and Circumstance of English Liberal Thought from the Restoration of Charles II until the War with the Thirteen Colonies (Cambridge: Harvard University Press, 1959); Gordon S. Wood, *The Creation of the American Republic 1776–1787* (Chapel Hill: University of North Carolina Press, 1969).

[29] Especially important in this regard was Louis Hartz, *The Liberal Tradition in America: An Interpretation of American Political Thought since the Revolution* (New York: Harcourt, Brace and World, 1955). For a discussion of republican scholarship in American history, see Daniel T Rodgers, "Republicanism: The Career of a Concept," *The Journal of American History* 79, no. 1 (1992): 11–38.

[30] For a good summary of these debates, see Stephen Mulhall and Adam Swift, eds., *Liberals and Communitarians* (Blackwell: Oxford, 1996).

[31] Alasdair MacIntyre, *After Virtue* (Notre Dame: Notre Dame University Press, 1984), 259.

[32] Skinner, "The Republican Ideal of Political Liberty," 308, 306–7.

[33] See Isaiah Berlin, "Two Concepts of Liberty," in *The Proper Study of Mankind: An Anthology of Essays*, ed. Henry Hardy and Roger Hausheer (New York: Farrar, Straus and Giroux, 1997): 191–242.

of its own chosen ends."[34] To be free is to be independent of the will of another, and to follow one's own will in one's actions. Such a view of liberty entails collective and individual benefits: "civic greatness and wealth," along with "personal liberty."[35] The latter concept emphasizes that each citizen remains free from any elements of constraint (especially those that arise from personal dependence and servitude) and in consequence remains free to pursue her own chosen ends.[36]

The crucial opposition, then, is not between liberty and interference, as with Hobbesian negative liberty, but rather between liberty and servitude – a *liber* (a free person) is not subject to a *dominus* (a master).[37] By this account, the individual cannot be free unless she lives in a particular kind of community: a self-governing community. This account was not burdened by moral perfectionism, but it still enabled citizens to share in a public life founded "on common meanings and purposes," as opposed to the calculations of instrumental reason.[38] The departure from Berlin is clear: Rather than view liberty as a dichotomous concept, entailing positive (illiberal) and negative (liberal) poles, republican liberty views certain kinds of interference as undesirable and other kinds as beneficial, combining aspects of both positive and negative liberty (though republican liberty is itself largely negative in locating liberty in the *absence* of slavery).[39]

Skinner's account of republican liberty – rooted in the world of republican Rome and transmitted, via humanist and prehumanist Italian thinkers, to English commonwealthmen – was primarily historical.[40] Philip Pettit, by

---

[34] Skinner, "The Republican Ideal of Political Liberty," 301.

[35] Ibid., 301, 302.

[36] Ibid., 302.

[37] See *The Digest of Justinian*, ed. Theodor Mommsen, Paul Krueger, and Alan Watson, vol. I (Philadelphia: University of Pennsylvania Press, 1985), 1.5.3; 1.6.1, 4.

[38] Skinner, "The Republican Ideal of Political Liberty," 308. On this distinction, see Paul Weithman, "Political Republicanism and Perfectionist Republicanism," *Review of Politics* 66, no. 2 (2004): 285–312.

[39] To be sure, Berlin was aware that the idea of political liberty as a negative concept entailed difficulties; he notes that while "all coercion is, in so far as it frustrates human desires, bad as such ... it may have to be applied to prevent other, greater evils; while non-interference, which is the opposite of coercion, is good as such, although it is not the only good." Berlin, "Two Concepts of Liberty," 200. Other values might intervene to trump the good of non-interference.

[40] See, for instance, Quentin Skinner, *Hobbes and Republican Liberty* (Cambridge: Cambridge University Press, 2008); Quentin Skinner, "The Italian City-Republics," in *Democracy: The Unfinished Journey, 508 B.C. to A.D. 1993*, ed. John Dunn (New York: Oxford University

contrast, has focused less on the historical foundations of republicanism than Skinner and more on the conceptual structure of the tradition itself, and made normative arguments in its favor – though he, like Skinner, emphasizes the roots of republicanism in "the ancient Romans," such as Sallust, Livy, Tacitus, and Cicero.[41] Like Skinner, Pettit describes republicanism as moving beyond the liberal emphasis on "certain negative liberties," focusing instead on "being ensured in a suitable measure of having them."[42] Pettit describes the republican conception of freedom as emphasizing the undesirability of *arbitrary* interference as opposed to *all* interference. Restraint and nonfreedom are thus not identical: "the restraint of a fair system of law – a non-arbitrary regime – does not make you unfree."[43] For Pettit, republican freedom is "non-domination"; he argues that "freedom consists in an absence, as the negative conception has it, but in an absence of mastery by others, not in absence of interference."[44] One is subject to arbitrary interference if in one's actions there "are others who can interfere at their pleasure."[45] To be dominated is, literally and figuratively, to be like a slave – subject to a *dominus*, and to live "at the beck and call" of another.[46] After all, one was not a slave insofar as one always *was* interfered with arbitrarily; rather, one was a slave insofar as one always *could* be interfered with arbitrarily.

If the key value around which the republican tradition coheres is a distinctive conception of liberty, then other values central to the republican

Press, 1992): 57–69; Skinner, *Liberty before Liberalism*; Skinner, "Machiavelli's *Discorsi* and the Pre-Humanist Origins of Republican Ideas"; Quentin Skinner, "On Justice, the Common Good and the Priority of Liberty," in *Dimensions of Radical Democracy: Pluralism, Citizenship, Community*, ed. Chantal Mouffe (London: Verso, 1992): 211–24.

[41] Philip Pettit, "The Freedom of the City: A Republican Ideal," in *The Good Polity: Normative Analysis of the State*, ed. Alan Hamlin and Philip Pettit (Oxford: Basil Blackwell, 1989): 141–67, 158.

[42] Ibid., 158. In addition to this chapter, see Philip Pettit, "Discourse Theory and Republican Freedom," in *Republicanism: History, Theory and Practice*, ed. Daniel Weinstock and Christian Nadeau (London: Frank Cass Publishers, 2004): 62–82; Philip Pettit, "Keeping Republican Freedom Simple: On a Difference with Quentin Skinner," *Political Theory* 30, no. 3 (2002): 339–56; Pettit, *Republicanism*; Philip Pettit, "Reworking Sandel's Republicanism," in *Debating Democracy's Discontent: Essays on American Politics, Law and Public Philosophy*, ed. Anita L. Allen and Milton C. Regan, Jr. (New York: Oxford, 1998): 40–59; Philip Pettit, *A Theory of Freedom: From the Psychology to the Politics of Agency* (Oxford: Oxford University Press, 2001).

[43] Pettit, *Republicanism*, 5.

[44] Ibid., 6, 21–2.

[45] Ibid., 26.

[46] Ibid., 32.

tradition may be understood by reference to this conception. For instance, a key concern of republican political theorists across time has been civic virtue.[47] Whereas a civic humanist conception of public life entails a view of virtue as political cum ethical, Skinner and Pettit argue that the republican tradition does not. The virtue of the republican citizen – civic virtue – was not perfectionist in nature, but largely instrumental.[48] Skinner describes republican virtue – and its antithesis, corruption – thus:

> To be corrupt … is to forget – or fail to grasp – something which it is profoundly in our interests to remember: that if we wish to enjoy as much freedom as we can hope to attain within political society, there is good reason for us to act in the first instance as virtuous citizens, placing the common good above the pursuit of any individual or factional ends. Corruption, in short, is simply a failure of rationality, an inability to recognize that our own liberty depends on committing ourselves to a life of virtue and public service.[49]

The virtue of the citizen is thus not linked to a conception of the human good or the perfectibility of human beings, but to the flourishing and well-being of a particular political society, centered on a particular kind of liberty. The proper orientation of the citizen to the community is thus embedded in a nonperfectionist account of civic virtue.

In addition, in the republican conception of politics, the public sphere centers on a conception of the common good. Skinner has described what we might call a thick conception of the common good, by which maintaining our individual and collective liberty requires that we place "the ideal of the common good above all consideration of individual advantage."[50] This ideal is strongly substantive: It entails citizens being devoted to public service and not placing their own liberty over the liberty of the community as a whole. Those who do not value the common good of the community, placing their own interests and liberty above those of the whole, are corrupt. We might also describe the common good in a thinner way, as that

---

[47] For a broad discussion of republican views of civic virtue across the history of thought, see Iseult Honohan, *Civic Republicanism* (London: Routledge, 2002).

[48] On this point, see Weithman, "Political Republicanism and Perfectionist Republicanism." I take up this issue in more detail in the following chapter.

[49] Skinner, "The Republican Ideal of Political Liberty," 304. Compare to Pettit, who writes that "people enjoy a higher degree of non-domination under a regime where there are norms to support republican laws." Pettit, *Republicanism*, 246.

[50] Skinner, "On Justice, the Common Good and the Priority of Liberty," 217.

good which all citizens hope to derive from republican government: republican liberty. Pettit, for example, argues in *A Theory of Freedom* that "The definition of common interests ... holds that a certain good will represent a common interest of a population just so far as cooperatively admissible considerations support its collective provision."[51] By far the most common of goods is freedom as nondomination, which he here identifies as "freedom as discursive control."[52]

For both Pettit and Skinner, then, Roman political thought is the primary source of subsequent republican political thought, especially an account of republican political thought understood in opposition to civic humanism and to liberalism. Roman political thought provides an historical and conceptual framework from which subsequent republican political thought derives, and also provides a rich variety of ideals and figures, historical and literary, on which subsequent republicans would draw. The location of the tradition's origins in Rome, and its transmission across time through later writers, provides an important resource for critiquing and challenging liberalism.[53]

IV. RHETORIC AND POLITICAL THEORY

Just as republicanism rooted in Roman political thought has emerged in recent years, so too have the practice of rhetoric and its relationship to

---

[51] Pettit, *A Theory of Freedom.*

[52] Ibid., 136.

[53] It is worth noting, in this regard, the argument of Eric Nelson, who suggests that we can distinguish two different threads of republican political thought: one Greek and one Roman. Beginning with the observation that "the extant Roman historians ... bitterly attack the agrarian laws and their sponsors, while the ancient Greek historians of Rome almost uniformly praise them," Nelson argues, drawing on Hegel, that Greek political thought and Roman political thought differ in fundamental respects. Plato and Aristotle do not conceive of freedom as nondependence, but instead conceive it as "the condition of living according to nature" insofar as they "depend upon their intellectual and moral superiors." This is a departure from both the Roman value placed on the ideal of nondomination. Furthermore, the Greek conception of justice as "an arrangement of elements that accords with nature" could quite easily conflict with the priority given to property in Roman thought. Writers influenced primarily by the Greek tradition, such as More and Harrington, might found their political theories "on the abolition of private property or on some mechanism designed to secure its egalitarian distribution." Eric Nelson, *The Greek Tradition in Republican Thought* (Cambridge: Cambridge University Press, 2004), 7, 11, 16. Though I find Nelson's thesis to be plausible, I focus in this work on the Roman historians, rather than on Greek republicans.

legitimacy and deliberation received increased interest. As republicanism may be viewed as a reaction to liberalism, this development, in turn, may be viewed as part of a reaction to theories of democracy – elite, economic, and pluralist – which view democracy's ability to reach the common good via speech through skeptical lenses. Schumpeter, representative of the elitist approach, famously argued in *Capitalism, Socialism, and Democracy* that "the democratic method is that institutional arrangement for arriving at political decisions in which individuals acquire the power to decide by means of a competitive struggle for the people's vote."[54] In such a conception, "the deciding of issues by the electorate" is less the focus of democracy than "the election of the men who are to do the deciding."[55] Downs, representative of the economic approach, argued in *An Economic Theory of Democracy* that "democratic governments act rationally to maximize political support."[56] The voter is akin to a consumer, and the government to a firm in this understanding; indeed, political ideologies are not rooted in parties' desires to promote "a better or an ideal society" but rather in the means by which parties seek support to attain power, though he adds that "The competitive struggle for office compels parties ... to be both honest and consistent in formulating policies and ideologies and developing them over time."[57] Representative of a pluralist approach, Dahl writes in *A Preface to Democratic Theory* that "the making of governmental decisions is not a majestic march of great majorities united upon certain matters of basic policy. It is the steady appeasement of relatively small groups."[58] This is so because of the power of even small groups to make themselves heard in a democratic society – especially America.

Theorists of deliberative democracy, by contrast, view deliberation not as an exercise in choosing ruling elites, interest aggregation, or interest group competition but instead as a process of "political justification."[59] By way of illustration, both because of his prominence and because he has been

---

[54] Joseph A. Schumpeter, *Capitalism, Socialism, and Democracy* (New York: Harper and Row, 1950), 269.
[55] Ibid. 269.
[56] Anthony Downs, *An Economic Theory of Democracy* (New York: Harper and Row, 1957), 20.
[57] Ibid. 96, 97.
[58] Robert A. Dahl, *A Preface to Democratic Theory* (Chicago: The University of Chicago Press, 2006), 146.
[59] Joshua Cohen, "Deliberation and Democratic Legitimacy," in *Deliberative Democracy: Essays on Reason and Politics*, ed. James Bohman and William Rehg (Cambridge: MIT University Press, 1997): 67–91, 81.

criticized by scholars sympathetic to the classical rhetorical tradition, we may briefly turn to Habermas's discourse theory. Habermas's understanding of deliberation is a rejection, in part, of what he terms the liberal conception of democracy; by this conception, "politics ... has the function of bundling together and pushing private interests against a government apparatus," and citizens "pursue their private interests within the boundaries drawn by legal statutes."[60] By contrast, Habermas's deliberative (or "discourse-theoretic") conception of democracy "insists on the fact that democratic will-formation draws its legitimating force not from a previous convergence of settled ethical convictions but both from the communicative presuppositions that allow the better arguments to come into play in various forms of deliberation and from the procedures that secure fair bargaining processes."[61]

Discourse within such a framework displays three qualities: "claims to truth, claims to sincerity, and claims to normative rightness."[62] Discourse uttered in such a context would fulfill the following procedural parameters:

Under the pragmatic presuppositions of an inclusive and noncoercive rational discourse among free and equal participants, everyone is required to take the perspective of everyone else, and thus project herself in to the understandings of self and world of all others; from this interlocking of perspectives there emerges an ideally extended we-perspective from which all can test in common whether they wish to make a controversial norm the basis of their shared practice; and this should include mutual criticism of the appropriateness of the languages in terms of which situation and needs are interpreted.[63]

The outcome of Habermas's conception of agreement is a situation in which "*all* participants harmonize their individual plans of action with one another and thus pursue their illocutionary aims *without reservation*."[64] Arguing, in such a conception, entails the production of "cogent *arguments* that are convincing in virtue of their intrinsic properties," and excludes "all motives

[60] Jürgen Habermas, "Three Normative Models of Democracy," in *Democracy and Difference: Contesting the Boundaries of the Political*, ed. Seyla Benhabib (Princeton: Princeton University Press, 1996): 21–30, 21, 22.
[61] Ibid., 24.
[62] Elizabeth Markovits, *The Politics of Sincerity: Plato, Frank Speech, and Democratic Judgment* (University Park: The Pennsylvania State University Press, 2008): 17–18.
[63] Jürgen Habermas, "Reconciliation through the Public Use of Reason: Remarks on John Rawls's *Political Liberalism*," *The Journal of Philosophy* 92, no. 3 (1995): 109–31, 117.
[64] Jürgen Habermas, *The Theory of Communicative Action, Volume 1: Reason and the Rationalization of Society*, trans. Thomas McCarthy (Boston: Beacon Press, 1981), 294.

except that of a cooperative search for the truth."[65] This could also exclude the emotional appeals of the classical rhetorical tradition, and the artful proofs of *ethos* and *pathos* in particular, whose persuasive value is distinct from the persuasive value of the argument (*logos*) itself.[66]

Theories of deliberative democracy such as Habermas's are different, however, from classical understandings of rhetoric and deliberation. Manin's "On Legitimacy and Political Deliberation" is of great importance in this vein, as he helped to articulate grievances with prior theories of deliberation and because he recognized the distinction between aspirations to unanimity through deliberation and ancient conceptions of deliberation.[67] According to Manin, thinkers such as Rousseau and Rawls aim at unanimity because of their conception of the individual "as the possessor of a completely determined will."[68] What Rousseau meant by a will was something very distinctive: A will had to be one's own will and free to be moral, since "to deprive one's will of all freedom is to deprive one's actions of all morality."[69] Thus, political deliberation entailed that one *not* deliberate insofar as deliberation is conceived as the give and take of information and argument and the play of emotion among those making decisions, since this risked having a will that was not one's own; rather, "If, when an adequately informed people deliberates, the Citizens had no communication among themselves, the general will would always result from the large number of small differences, and the deliberation would always be good."[70]

As Manin notes, because Rousseau views the individual as entering deliberation with "a completely determined will," it follows that "if a collective decision does not conform to the sum of individual decisions, democratic

---

[65] Ibid., 25.

[66] On this point, see Arash Abizadeh, "On the Philosophy/Rhetoric Binaries: Or, Is Habermasian Discourse Motivationally Impotent?," *Philosophy and Social Criticism* 33, no. 4 (2007): 445–72.

[67] Also noteworthy is Jon Elster, "The Market and the Forum: Three Varieties of Political Theory," in *Foundations of Social Choice Theory*, ed. Jon Elster and Aanund Hylland (Cambridge: Cambridge University Press, 1986): 103–32.

[68] Bernard Manin, "On Legitimacy and Political Deliberation," *Political Theory* 15, no 3 (1987): 338–68, 347.

[69] Jean-Jacques Rousseau, *Of the Social Contract*, ed. Victor Gourevitch, *Rousseau: 'The Social Contract' and Other Later Political Writings* (New York: Cambridge University Press, 1997), 45. For a discussion of Rousseau's concept of will, see Patrick Riley, "Rousseau's General Will: Freedom of a Particular Kind," *Political Studies* XXXIX, no. 1 (1991): 55–74.

[70] Rousseau, *Of the Social Contract*, 60.

individualism will no longer be respected."[71] Manin suggests that the same mechanism is evident in Rawls's original position, in which the individual "already possesses the criteria for evaluation that will permit him to appraise all possible alternatives."[72] Such an understanding of deliberation is quite different from classical understandings of deliberation, in which the will is not determined but becomes so through the give and take of argument.[73] Based on a classically oriented understanding, Manin argues that the criterion of a legitimate decision should not be unanimity, or that the decision represents "the *will* of all," but instead should rest on the inclusion of all in processes of deliberation.[74] Outcomes are thus legitimate as a function of the formation of wills in the deliberative process; nor does deliberation aim at elucidating necessarily true propositions, but merely persuasive arguments.

The rhetorical turn in contemporary political theory – and especially democratic theory – has in large part been directed against theories of deliberative democracy, which aim at potential unanimity, eschew emotional appeals, and emphasize rationality; as Fontana, Nederman, and Remer put it in describing the deliberative approach, "the *logos* it recognizes is that of speech and language informed by reason and argument; it relegates all other forms of talk (such as rhetoric) to the extrarational or non-rational sphere."[75] Fontana, Nederman, and Remer point to Kant's *Critique of Judgement* in making this claim, and in particular to Kant's discussion of rhetoric:

Rhetoric, so far as this is taken to mean the art of persuasion, i.e. the art of deluding by means of a fair semblance (as *ars oratoria*), and not merely excellence of speech (eloquence and style), is a dialectic, which borrows from poetry only so much as is necessary to win over men's minds to the side of the speaker before they have weighed the matter, and to rob their verdict of its freedom.[76]

---

[71] Manin, "On Legitimacy and Political Deliberation," 347.

[72] Ibid., 349.

[73] On this point, see Bernard Yack, "Rhetoric and Public Reasoning: An Aristotelian Understanding of Political Deliberation," *Political Theory* 34, no. 4 (2006): 417–38.

[74] Manin, "On Legitimacy and Political Deliberation," 352.

[75] Benedetto Fontana, Cary J. Nederman, and Gary Remer, "Introduction: Deliberative Democracy and the Rhetorical Turn," in *Talking Democracy: Historical Perspectives on Rhetoric and Democracy*, ed. Benedetto Fontana, Cary J. Nederman, and Gary Remer (University Park: The Pennsylvania State University Press, 2004): 1–25, 8.

[76] Immanuel Kant, *The Critique of Judgement*, trans. James Creed Meredith (Oxford: Clarendon Press, 1952), 192.

Rhetoric and rhetorical appeals to and from emotion are thus opposed to both freedom and reason. Moreover, rhetoric – though not necessarily bad – is unnecessary in speech, for Kant:

the simple lucid concept of human concerns of this kind, backed up with lively illustrations of it, exerts of itself, in the absence of any offence against the rules of euphony of speech or of propriety in the expression of ideas in reason … a sufficient influence upon human minds to obviate the necessity of having recourse here to the machinery of persuasion, which, being equally available for the purpose of putting a fine gloss or a cloak upon vice and error, fails to rid one completely of the lurking suspicion that one is being artfully hoodwinked.[77]

In this regard, deliberative theories that eschew rhetoric are closer to Plato's understanding of rhetoric than to that of Aristotle and Cicero, both of whom try to "save rhetorical discourse from Plato's critical attacks by showing the rational and logical structure of rhetorical persuasion."[78]

Scholars sympathetic to the classical rhetorical tradition have criticized Habermas and other deliberative democrats for their apparent hostility to the rhetorical tradition. Allen, for example, focuses on the "conceptual side effects of Habermas' insistent focus on unanimity," arguing that Habermas views agreement as solely an illocutionary phenomenon.[79] That is, Habermas focuses on Austin's concept of illocution – the "performance of an act *in* saying something as opposed to performance of an act *of* saying something" (that is, *locution*) – to the exclusion of perlocution.[80] Austin explains perlocution thus:

Saying something will often, or even normally, produce certain consequential effects upon the feelings, thoughts, or actions of the audience, or of the speaker, or of other persons: and it may be done with the design, intention, or purpose of producing them.[81]

Austin, Allen argues, viewed perlocution as less subject to rational explanation than illocution. Perlocution, insofar as it stirs and moves auditors,

---

[77] Ibid., 193.

[78] Fontana, Nederman, and Remer, "Introduction: Deliberative Democracy and the Rhetorical Turn," 14.

[79] Danielle S. Allen, *Talking to Strangers: Anxieties of Citizenship since Brown v. Board of Education* (Chicago: University of Chicago Press, 2006), 54.

[80] J.L. Austin, *How to Do Things with Words*, ed. J.O. Urmson and Marina Sbisa (Cambridge: Harvard University Press, 1975), 99–100.

[81] Ibid. 101.

is very much in the domain of rhetoric. In this regard, Austin was more a Platonist than an Aristotelian on questions of rhetoric, in that Aristotle held that "the elements of intersubjectivity involved in persuasion could indeed be conventionalized and subject to art."[82] What this means is that when Habermas makes agreement a function of illocutionary speech alone, Habermas "justifies treating agreement as perfectible by defining it entirely as a matter of conventional signs."[83]

Allen argues that such a view is flawed, neglecting a central role of rhetoric and its relationship to democratic citizenship – namely, the creation of trust. Democracies are composed of distinct individuals, and are the loci of conflict and division. Trust can lead to coherence without erasing difference through an emphasis on uniformity and identity. "Disappointment and resentment," in turn, at the losses entailed in democratic life can diminish trust.[84] Given distrust, difference, and conflict, speakers do not come to the public sphere "already mutually well-minded toward one another."[85] Just as persuasion involves both illocution and perlocution – that is, both the act of persuading and the act of being persuaded – perlocution's particular strength, and the aspect of persuasion that many deliberative theorists seek to minimize, is treating distrust through its engagement with affect. This, for Allen, is precisely the task of the orator and the domain of rhetoric.

A critic might reply that even if rhetoric can create trust, it may yet be quite dangerous. The dangers of rhetoric are well known; central to the so-called quarrel between rhetoric and philosophy, they have been discussed since Plato's *Gorgias* and are certainly evident in the writings of the Roman historians, as we will see.[86] For Plato, part of the risk of rhetoric conventionally understood was its dangerous effect upon the emotions of an audience. As Gorgias and Polus hold in *Gorgias*, the art of rhetoric could produce political power and could enslave the other arts through persuasion. For Socrates, by contrast, rhetoric a knack, and not an art, merely capable of "producing a certain gratification and pleasure," deploying emotional appeals rooted in the orator's sense of her audience's beliefs.[87] Because the rhetorician aims not at what is best but at the "most pleasant at the moment," she achieves her ends

---

[82] Allen, *Talking to Strangers*, 61.
[83] Ibid., 62
[84] Ibid., 47.
[85] Ibid., 56.
[86] On the quarrel, see George A. Kennedy, *The Art of Persuasion in Greece* (Princeton: Princeton University Press, 1963), 321–8.
[87] Plato, *Gorgias*, trans. Donald J. Zeyl (Indianapolis: Hackett, 1987), 462c.

through the manipulation of those who lack knowledge.[88] The rhetorician is little more than a flatterer, able to produce conviction in her audience not because of her knowledge but instead because she "guesses at what's pleasant with no consideration for what's best."[89] Thus, she stands in relation to the true statesman, as does the maker of confections to the physician: Both may win their cases if competing against experts before audiences of non-experts, but only because they utilize pleasures that appeal to those without knowledge.

Based on Plato's argument, then, the dangers of rhetoric may be placed in two broad categories: manipulating and pandering.[90] As Garsten puts it:

When we persuade, we want to change our listeners' minds by linking our position to their existing opinions and emotions. In our desire to change their minds lies the danger of manipulating, and in the effort to attend to their existing opinions lies the risk of pandering.[91]

Yet despite the risks of rhetoric, Garsten argues that the desire to displace and suppress rhetoric – and hence judgment – can "produce new and potentially more dogmatic forms of rhetoric."[92] Moreover, despite theorists such as Rawls, Cohen, and Habermas, who emphasize discussion and deliberation and view deliberation "as a discourse of justification rather than one of persuasion," they reproduce the central tensions of theories that seek to displace controversy.[93]

Garsten turns to Aristotle and Cicero to develop a conception of persuasion that does not displace the emotional give and take of rhetoric, or its appeals to common beliefs. He reads Cicero, in this regard, as developing an account of Roman politics and institutions rooted in his desire to do "what was necessary to protect the influence and sustainability of the practice of persuasion."[94] Though the practice was certainly central to his conception of the republic, Garsten argues that Cicero also viewed the practice of persuasion as relying upon "a certain capacity for moral and political judgment," a judgment rooted in moral convictions.[95] Cicero's skepticism

---

[88] Ibid., 464d.
[89] Ibid., 465a.
[90] Garsten, *Saving Persuasion*, 2.
[91] Ibid., 2.
[92] Ibid., 175.
[93] Ibid., 189.
[94] Ibid., 143.
[95] Ibid., 144.

is thus a tempered skepticism, and the limits to his skepticism derive in part from his commitment to persuasion; indeed, his embrace of natural law and his commitment to rhetoric and argument *in utramque partem* did not fade into mere sophistry, but into an adapted Stoic position well-suited to the practice of oratory and devotion to republican government.

V. REPUBLICANISM, RHETORIC, AND THE ROMAN HISTORIANS

Republican political theorists and contemporary theorists of persuasion both emphasize the close connection between the practice of persuasion and the vitality and sustainability of politics. This connection can be seen, for instance, in Pettit's *A Theory of Freedom*. Pettit argues that the difference between arbitrary interference, which is undesirable under a republican conception of liberty, and nonarbitrary interference, which is desirable under a republican conception of liberty, is that nonarbitrary interference will track common interests. He argues that:

The definition of common interests ... holds that a certain good will represent a common interest of a population just so far as cooperatively admissible considerations support its collective provision. Cooperatively admissible considerations are those that anyone in discourse with others about what they should jointly or collectively provide can adduce without embarrassment as relevant matters to take into account. They are not selfish or sectional considerations ... of the kind that some parties to the discussion would have to see as calls for special treatment and as calls that they had no particular reason to heed.[96]

The *res publica* thus exists within and is defined by the language and values of the community, and entails and resolves the conflicts of those that comprise it. The link between the individual and the whole, negotiated and constructed through the practice of persuasion, is the noncoercive contestation and deliberation that marks popular politics. As Connolly put it in a recent study, with regard to the core values of republican political thought — "political liberty, tolerance, personal commitment, and public accountability" — "these virtues may be understood as resting on communicative practices."[97] Talking to each other, and how we do so, is thus of great

[96] Pettit, *A Theory of Freedom*, 156–7.
[97] Connolly, *The State of Speech*, 10.

importance to both republican and rhetorical approaches. The project of freedom central to each is also related to persuasion and rhetoric, as is negotiating the conflicts and strains that arise in political communities. The starting point of my exploration of the historians – the two strains of contemporary scholarship discussed earlier – centers on a key concern, then: the relationship between liberty and rhetoric, and their relationship to political conflict. More broadly, my concern is with the ways in which Rome's three greatest historians – Sallust, Livy, and Tacitus – develop accounts of and can serve as resources for exploring the tensions within this relationship. I argue that each conceives of the place of rhetoric in the political community, and its relationship to liberty and social and political conflict, in distinct ways. In Sallust's writings, we will see an antagonistic conception of rhetoric and community; in Livy, we will see what I term a consensualist conception; in Tacitus, we will see a conception of rhetoric and its components – especially prudence – as tools to navigate political unfreedom.

The salience of rhetoric and the tensions it entails in their writings are no accident: These writers were themselves immersed in a rhetorical culture and steeped in the traditions and memories of the Roman republic (all three historians wrote after the death of Cicero and Caesar), a community in which the practice of persuasion was central to the institutions of government.[98] Moreover, the purposes the Roman historians themselves ascribed to their writings are moral and political. It is well known that ancient historians intended their writings to be useful, though the intended utility varies from writer to writer.[99] Thus, Herodotus, Thucydides, and Polybius each held their histories to be useful. For Herodotus, a key function of history is to ensure "that human achievements may not become forgotten in time" and also to ensure that "great and marvelous deeds ... not be without their glory."[100] Thucydides' history also aims at an explicitly practical purpose, as

[98] On the historians' rhetorical backgrounds, see Cynthia Damon, "Rhetoric and Historiography," in *A Companion to Roman Rhetoric*, ed. William J. Dominik and Jon Hall (Oxford: Blackwell, 2007): 439–50. On the memory of the republic, see Alain Gowing, *Empire and Memory: The Representation of the Roman Republic in Imperial Culture* (Cambridge: Cambridge University Press, 2005). On persuasion in the republic, see Elaine Fantham, "The Contexts and Occasions of Roman Public Rhetoric," in *Roman Eloquence: Rhetoric in Society and Literature*, ed. William J. Dominik (London: Routledge, 1997): 111–28.

[99] See D.C. Earl, "Prologue-Form in Ancient Historiography," *Austfieg und Niedergang der Romischen Welt: Geschichte und Kultur Roms im Spiegel der Neueren Forschung* 1, no. 2 (1972): 842–56.

[100] Herodotus, *The Histories*, trans. Aubrey de Selincourt (New York: Penguin, 1996), 1.1.

he writes that he hopes that "these words of mine are judged useful by those who want to understand clearly the events which happened in the past and which (human nature being what it is) will, at some time or other in much the same ways, be repeated in the future."[101] Polybius thought his history had practical implications as well, holding that his *Histories* and his narrative of the growth of Roman power in particular is "the soundest education and training for a life of active politics," along with "learning how to bear bravely the vicissitudes of fortune" by recalling the misfortune of others.[102]

Like their Greek predecessors, Sallust, Livy, and Tacitus understood their historical writings to be useful – though the specific use depended on the author, whose accounts are examined in more detail in subsequent chapters. All three, however, had explicitly moral purposes in writing their histories, not the least of which was to praise and blame individuals who displayed virtue or vice. This is reflective of the peculiar Roman concern to address *exempla*. The term had a specific usage in Rome, given "the singular emphasis within the Roman aristocratic world on the past as the source of all that was worthy of imitation and emulation, particularly in the guidance and training of the young."[103] Moral and political *exempla* are, in fact, a good part of these historians' influence on subsequent figures in the history of political thought; their attention to *exempla* and their moral value in turn reflected their rhetorical training and the role of rhetoric in elite Roman education.[104] *Exempla* also had an important role in the practice of rhetoric, serving as a stock of images and narratives to communicate key points and appeal to one's audience.

Despite their rhetorical training and the rhetorical features of their writings, I do not read the works of these historians as works of rhetoric, or as following the rules of rhetoric, per se.[105] Nor will I seek to resolve the question of the political character of the Roman republic – whether it was

---

[101] Thucydides, *History of the Peloponnesian War*, trans. Rex Warner (New York: Penguin, 1972), 1.22.

[102] Polybius, *The Histories*, trans. W.R. Paton (Cambridge: Harvard University Press, 1929), 1.1.2.

[103] Jane D. Chaplin, *Livy's Exemplary History* (Oxford: Oxford University Press, 2000), 11.

[104] Thomas Wiedemann, "Reflections of Roman Political Thought in Latin Historical Writing," in *The Cambridge History of Greek and Roman Political Thought*, ed. Christopher Rowe (Cambridge: Cambridge University Press, 2000): 517–31, 531.

[105] See especially A.J. Woodman, *Rhetoric in Classical Historiography* (London: Croom Helm, 1988). Indeed, in their recent translation of *On the Ideal Orator*, May and Wisse suggest that Woodman misinterprets Cicero on this point. For May and Wisse's view, see Cicero, *On the Ideal Orator*, 12. On the passage dealing with historiography, see 2.62–2.63.

democratic, oligarchic, aristocratic, or something else – though I will in my argument be more closely aligned to views expressed by critics of Millar, while the authors I engage – Sallust, Livy, and Tacitus – view the republic largely as a popularly sanctioned aristocracy, with Sallust maintaining a more antagonistic conception than Livy or Tacitus.

I do not read the historians as adherents to particular philosophical schools, or even as developing systematic theoretical accounts of the Roman republic and its relationship to rhetoric. These writers operated in rich and complex intellectual worlds, and drew on a wide array of ideas and values in their writings.[106] We may, for instance, find traces of Plato, Thucydides, Posidonius, Cato, and even Cicero in Sallust's writings alone.[107] We should not, then, look to these authors as developing systematic and coherent theoretical accounts of republicanism and rhetoric, per se. There may be good reason for this: As Wiedemann notes, we are more likely to encounter such theorizing in Greek works dealing with Rome – for instance, Polybius' *Histories* – than Roman works dealing with Rome, in part because these Greek writers' works draw "attention to aspects of Roman politics which surprised them."[108] Whether Wiedemann's claim is correct or not, if we do not find among Sallust, Livy, or Tacitus a systematic analysis of Rome's constitution along the line of Book VI of Polybius' *Histories*, we do find these historians wrestling in different ways with problems involving liberty, rhetoric, conflict community, and their relationship to each other, problems that are of interest today. The problems these writers grappled with as they grappled with thinking and writing about Roman history were problems that can enrich our own discussions and thinking about republicanism and rhetoric, along with shedding light on their thought.

VI. PLAN OF THE BOOK

The book is divided into seven chapters: the current introductory chapter and a summarizing epilogue, as well as five chapters dealing with the authors in chronological order. Chapters 2 and 3 focus on Sallust, Chapter 4 focuses on Livy, and Chapters 5 and 6 focus on Tacitus. In Chapter 2, "An Ambiguous

---

[106] On the intellectual context of Sallust and Livy, see Elizabeth Rawson, *Intellectual Life in the Late Roman Republic* (London: Duckworth, 1985). On Tacitus, see Ronald Syme, *Tacitus*, vol. I (Oxford: Oxford University Press, 1958), esp. chapters 1–5, 8.

[107] See P. McGushin, *Bellum Catilinae: A Commentary* (Leiden: E.J. Brill, 1977), 8–9.

[108] Wiedemann, "Reflections of Roman Political Thought in Latin Historical Writing," 526.

Republican: Sallust on Fear, Conflict, and Community," I develop a reading of Sallust that begins with the problem of his apparent ambiguity as a republican, given Hobbes's affinity for him.[109] This affinity, rooted in what Hobbes saw as Sallust's suspicions about rhetoric, highlights the potential dangers of rhetoric in Sallust's writings, dangers that seem, on the face of it, to be contained by collective fear and originating in a lack of civic virtue. Rather than read Sallust's thought as, in some sense, proto-Hobbesian in relying on fear or upon a perfectionist account of civic virtue, I argue that his writings are pervaded by antagonism, and that this antagonism can be supportive of the common good. Sallust, then, is what I term an antagonistic republican, whose political community is characterized by latent and actual antagonisms between individuals and groups. Engaging with contemporary republican and rhetorical scholarship and classical sources such as Thucydides and Cicero, I argue that Sallust's political community may be fragmented, but the issue is not how to do away with this fragmentation. Rather, the issue is to find a mechanism to channel it given the importance and desirability of certain kinds of antagonism.

Chapter 3 – "Channeling Conflict through Antagonistic Rhetoric in the *War with Catiline*" – builds on the prior chapter. Drawing on my reading of Sallust as an antagonistic republican, I argue that rhetorical antagonism – especially in Cato and Caesar's debate in *The War with Catiline* – can serve as a vehicle and outlet for broader antagonisms in the body politic. The tensions found in the body politic might be played out and resolved through the practice of antagonistic rhetoric, rhetoric that sought to contain and to balance seemingly contradictory elements in a productive tension. Based on my reading of Sallust, and incorporating contemporary accounts of rhetoric and classical accounts of deliberation and redescription, I argue that antagonistic rhetoric is important precisely because it can channel and blend otherwise opposite elements of the political community. These elements need not be eliminated for Sallust, I suggest, since they are the stuff of political life in his writings.

Chapter 4 – "Exemplarity and Goodwill in Livy's *From the Founding of Rome*" – draws on contemporary discussions of political friendship, trust, and rhetoric, to develop a reading of Livy's writing as depicting what I term the rhetoricization of leadership. Through a discussion of Livy along

---

[109] Chapter 2 draws on research undertaken for an article previously published: Daniel J. Kapust, "On the Ancient Uses of Political Fear and Its Modern Implications," *Journal of the History of Ideas* 69, no. 3 (2008): 353–73. In addition, Chapter 3 also draws on research for an article previously published: Daniel J. Kapust, "Cato's Virtues and *The Prince*: Reading Sallust's *War with Catiline* with Machiavelli's *The Prince*," *History of Political Thought* 28, no. 3 (2007): 433-448.

with contemporary accounts of rhetoric's role in negotiating conflict and classical accounts of *ethos, pathos*, and friendship, I argue that Livy's history portrays a community that moves between conflict and consensus via the interactions between leaders and the many. Within Livy's consensualism, Rome is a moral community, made up of unequal individuals and groups, and is a fertile and frequent ground for conflict; yet it was bound together by goodwill rooted in trust and friendship, themselves the product of the observation of virtuous behavior and character. Rome's health and illness are thus a function of the relationships between leaders and led, relations of interdependence and negotiation. Livy's harmonious republic points to the priority of consensus and the contingent in rhetoric, looking to the vision and standard of the community to secure stability.

In Chapter 5 – "Tacitus on Great Men, Bad Rulers, and Prudence" – I develop a reading of Tacitus' *Dialogue on Orators* and *Agricola* in tandem with works of Cicero, Pliny, Quintilian, and contemporary republican scholarship.[110] I focus on the ambiguity of Tacitus' present in the *Dialogue* and *Agricola*, an ambiguity rooted in part in the displacement of republican politics by the rule of a single individual and reinforced by the ambiguity of an imposed peace. Reading Tacitus as neither a wistful republican nostalgic for the days of Cicero nor a realist favoring a kind of quietism in light of the principate, I argue that Tacitus is centrally concerned in these works with delineating a model of prudence that allows individuals to navigate the active life, avoiding both cooptation and foolhardy resistance.

In Chapter 6, "Tacitus' Moral Histories," I build on my argument in Chapter 5, focusing on the ways in which Tacitus deploys praise and blame in depicting the character of different emperors. Tacitus' histories serve two broad and interrelated functions. On the one hand, they serve as a sort of posthumous judgment of the character of rulers, rewarding good character and punishing bad; on the other hand, through depicting the character of bad rulers – marked by cruelty, instability, and dissembling – he provides a set of markers by which his readers might orient themselves as they engaged in the active life. Based on a reading of Tacitus along with contemporary republican scholarship and works of Cicero, Seneca, and Pliny, I argue that through Tacitus' reading of even bad rulers, Tacitus provides resources to foster the prudence of his readers.

---

[110] Portions of Chapters 5 and 6 were previously published in Kapust, "Between Contumacy and Obsequiousness: Tacitus on Moral Freedom and the Historian's Task."

2

AN AMBIGUOUS REPUBLICAN

Sallust on Fear, Conflict, and Community

I. INTRODUCTION

In the first chapter, we encountered the connection between eloquence and liberty in Cicero's thought. Closely linked, the prior was a sign of the latter, not just accompanying, but giving structure and direction to liberty.[1] Oratory arose in conditions of peace, and in turn fostered peace and unity for Cicero: As he has Crassus put it in *On the Ideal Orator*, eloquence "has ever flourished, ever reigned supreme in every free nation and especially in quiet and peaceful communities."[2] We have also seen the way in which contemporary studies of republicanism and rhetoric view the role of rhetoric and persuasion in republican political communities: They foster the pursuit of the public good; the conditions of speaking freely are the conditions of liberty; rhetoric serves as a resource for fostering engagement and trust among citizens.

For writers valuing rhetoric for these reasons, the community is not monolithic; rather, the community is the site of conflict and contestation between distinct individuals and groups, conflict and contestation that can be channeled and treated through rhetoric and checked by civic virtue. Unanimity is not the goal; rather, it is consensus in the face of conflict, potential or actual. Yet conflict and contestation always have the potential to get out of hand and to undermine the community itself, and so, too, does the practice of rhetoric. Thus, a key concern for authors in the broad republican tradition – and especially the classical tradition – is corruption,

[1] On this point, see Gary Remer, "The Classical Orator as Political Representative: Cicero and the Modern Concept of Representation." *Journal of Politics* 72, no 4 (2010): 1063–82.
[2] Cicero, *On the Ideal Orator*, 1.30.

and ensuring that particular individuals remain focused on interests and values shared with their fellow-citizens and compatible with the common good. Individuals were citizens of republics insofar as they pursued "particular goods"; their existence *qua* citizens was a function of "the common universal good."[3] Harmonizing the particular and the common – and hence preventing the corruption of the political community – was of great importance. Corruption and virtue were in opposition; the virtuous republic was best able to stave off the corruption that the play of fortune and the republic's existence in time frequently brought.

The republic itself was a fragile community, always in danger of collapse: Existing in time, it is as a result ephemeral. As Pocock writes, "the doctrine of the *vivere civile* – the ideal of active citizenship in a republic – must struggle to maintain itself."[4] Certainly this holds true of the Roman republic, whose transformation from republic to monarchy is often read as a tale of decline from a virtuous and uncorrupted past – evident, for instance, in Montesquieu's *Considerations of the Causes of the Greatness of the Romans and their Decline* – and hence as a story of the corruption of Roman virtue. "The Roman state stands upon the morals and men of old": so begins Book 5 of Cicero's *On the Commonwealth*, quoting the poet Ennius.[5] Men, morals, and community are linked – "Morality and manliness are constructed here as the distinguishing features of Rome."[6] With the decline of one came the decline of all, and the loss of political liberty followed on the loss of civic virtue.[7]

Republican citizens, then, need to maintain certain orientations toward each other and toward their public life to pursue the common good and preserve the republic itself. To the extent that virtue and corruption are

[3] J.G.A. Pocock, *The Machiavellian Moment* (Princeton: Princeton University Press, 1975), 74.
[4] Ibid., 4.
[5] Cicero, *On the Commonwealth*, ed. James E.G. Zetzel, *On the Commonwealth and on the Laws* (Cambridge: Cambridge University Press, 1999), 5.1.
[6] Catharine Edwards, *The Politics of Immorality in Ancient Rome* (Cambridge: Cambridge University Press, 1993), 20.
[7] Views vary on the degree to which corruption actually occurred. Lintott, on the one hand, suggests that "As for luxury, greed and ambition there was no question that these abounded in the second century." Lintott, "The Crisis of the Republic: Sources and Source-Problems," 7. Edwards, by contrast, views charges and countercharges of immorality – whether in rhetoric or historiography – not simply reflecting "an accurate picture of patterns of behavior in ancient Rome," but also reflecting broader concerns to define what it meant to be a Roman, and especially an elite Roman. Edwards, *The Politics of Immorality in Ancient Rome*, 11.

conceived in terms of "traits which make their possessor a good or an excellent or a flourishing member of her kind," we may speak of perfectionist republicanism.[8] As seen in Chapter 1, contemporary republicans, such as Skinner, Pettit, and Viroli, generally view civic virtue as political, or instrumental, and not perfectionist; they try to avoid identifying the life of political action or participation with the good or higher life. From a political or instrumental perspective, then, corruption leads individuals to turn away from the common good and toward their own good, a private good that may be incompatible with the common good.

The problem of maintaining focus on the common good is particularly salient because of the social and political conflicts that often characterize republican politics, the "instability, injustice, and confusion" that so alarmed Madison.[9] This is certainly true in the case of the Roman republic, as Rome itself was not a monolithic community, but a polity whose very identity was shaped by experiences with and stories of conflict and strife; as Connolly notes:

Antagonism – indeed, the necessity of antagonism, stated or implied – is a common theme in the representation of Roman political history ... The notion of politics itself is founded on division; antagonism is as essential to the survival of the republic as the peace making that cures it.[10]

Keeping this in mind, we may posit that the struggle of individual Romans for glory – their pursuit of their *particular* glory – contributed to the common good, so long as what these Romans valued and sought was consistent with the broader good of the community. For Sallust, subject of this chapter, once Rome's kings had been expelled, the energies of its people were unleashed, and they served the common good: "every man began to lift his head higher and to have his talent more in readiness."[11] We see here the connection between liberty (that is, the absence of kings in this instance) and civic greatness, a connection that would be of special importance to later humanist writers: this energy, unleashed by liberty, serves the good of the community.[12]

---

[8] Weithman, "Political Republicanism and Perfectionist Republicanism," 285.
[9] James Madison, *Federalist 10* in *The Federalist, or the New Constitution*, ed. Max Beloff (London: Basil Blackwell, 1987), 41.
[10] Connolly, *State of Speech*, 73.
[11] Sallust, *War with Catiline*, trans. J.C. Rolfe, *Sallust* (Cambridge: Harvard University Press, 1985), 7.1.
[12] On this point, and Sallust's role in humanism, see Skinner, "Machiavelli's *Discorsi* and the Pre-Humanist Origins of Republican Ideas."

Yet with these energies unleashed, something was required to keep citizens focused on the common good. For Sallust, as he is typically read, this something was fear, and especially the fear of Carthage.[13] With the fall of Carthage, fear's constraint on collective behavior was removed, and the struggle for glory ceased to operate in a way that was compatible with the common good; without the confines of a fear-rooted consensus, struggles and conflicts in Rome undermined the very existence of the polity. Moreover, the political action of ambitious and competitive Romans – when separated from an attachment to the community's good – descended into vice, as their pursuit of glory in the service of the polity transformed into their pursuit of their desires at the expense of the polity. The republic needed discipline, and as Sallust is typically read, it needed enmity to foster discipline and cohesion. In other words, for Sallust peace might *not* be a good thing; antagonism could easily get out of control without the constraining effects of foreign enmity.

This conclusion does not sit well with Ciceronian accounts of the republic, which look to oratory – and less to collective fear – to structure and guide a conflicted community. And this is a troubling conclusion for those concerned with the boundaries of republican political community and the status of virtue in republican thought writ large. Contemporary republicans avoid emphases on republican virtue as *moral* virtue along the lines of classical thinkers; they view republican virtues as being primarily civic – that is, "valuable traits of character because they make their possessors good citizens, equipping them to contribute to the public good."[14] The potential pitfall of a primarily civic, as opposed to a primarily moral, conception of virtue, as Weithman notes, is that "it makes our motive to cultivate and sustain them too heavily dependent upon our identification with our citizenship."[15] This is precisely the danger that we see in Sallust's writings: with the removal of its chief foreign threat, and the concomitant loss of identification with the political community, Rome becomes ripe for corruption because its citizens lost sight of the common good.

Rhetoric, rather than being central to healthful communities, becomes a sign of this corruption in Sallust's narrative, a point that, as we will see, Hobbes – a key critic of both rhetoric and republicanism – echoes. Indeed,

---

[13] For a representative reading of Sallust in this vein, see, e.g., Wood, "Sallust's Theorem: A Comment on 'Fear' in Western Political Thought."

[14] Weithman, "Political Republicanism and Perfectionist Republicanism," 294.

[15] Ibid., 286.

it is tempting to read Sallust in a Hobbesian manner (anachronism aside): as a critic not just of rhetoric, but ultimately of a kind of discursive republicanism, precisely because of the fragility of Sallust's conception of the republic and his apparent reliance on fear to keep Rome united.[16] Take away the restraining fear of enemies – especially Carthage – and Rome spirals out of control. Rhetoric exacerbates division; words change their meanings, reversing the normal order of things. Fear, by contrast, contains divisions and ensures that citizens maintain the right focus on the community.

Yet in the next two chapters, I develop a reading of Sallust that will not just depart from Hobbes's reading of him, but make the case that Sallust's writing, although not Ciceronian in his conception of oratory, per se, is what I describe as an antagonistic republicanism. Fear may have served to check the centrifugal energies of the people of Rome, but what this underscores is the dynamic and contested nature of the Roman political community for Sallust. This was a community that embodied competition and featured antagonism between individuals and groups, checked in part by collective fear and in part by a particularistic civic virtue. This antagonism was not, in itself, problematic; the problem was that antagonism needed either to be checked or to find a constructive outlet.

In this chapter, which lays the foundation for and is thematically linked to the subsequent chapter, I turn first in Section I to Hobbes's reading of Sallust. His reading of Sallust highlights Sallust's ambiguity as a republican for the reasons noted above. Moreover, turning to Hobbes serves to highlight certain distinctions I draw between Sallust and Cicero in Section II on the place of oratory in the political community, the relationship of peace to corruption, and Sallust's literary relationship to Cicero and Thucydides – another of Hobbes's favored classical sources – on the matter of the corruption of moral language. In Section III, I turn to Sallust's depiction of Rome's corruption following the loss of collective fear due to the destruction of Carthage. Fear's role, in this vein, was a common theme in classical thought, but it took on a special importance in Sallust's writings. On the face of it, political fear seems to ensure stability and peace in Sallust's Rome in a manner akin to its role in Hobbes's thought, even solidifying distinctions between virtue and vice.

---

[16] For a reading of Cicero as a discursive republican, see Cary J. Nederman, "Rhetoric, Reason, and Republic: Republicanisms – Ancient, Medieval, and Modern," in *Renaissance Civic Humanism: Reappraisals and Reflections*, ed. James Hankins (Cambridge: Cambridge University Press, 2000): 247–69.

Drawing on this discussion, however, I suggest in Section IV that fear's role can be overstated in reading Sallust, and that the salience of fear in his narratives underscores just how contested and antagonistic Sallust conceives the republic to be. Dichotomies break down, to be sure, as seen in Section V. Fear may serve to check Rome's centrifugal forces, but I will suggest in Sections V and VI that this shows us more about how Sallust conceives of the political community and its internal dynamics than it does to show that he is a proto-Hobbesian, seeking to eliminate conflict and to shore up political order with fear. Sallust's virtue, seemingly vacillating between instrumentalism and perfectionism, requires an appropriate context, but it need not, I conclude in Section VI, require a kind of permanent fear analogous to Hobbes's leviathan.

II. SALLUST: AN AMBIGUOUS REPUBLICAN

Thomas Hobbes knew Sallust's writings well and read him in a way that was quite different from how most humanist thinkers read him.[17] This reading reflects broader strains in Hobbes's thought, as well as his attitude toward Rome's most prominent thinker: Cicero. Whereas rhetoric could ameliorate and treat antagonism for Cicero, Cicero – as well as the republicanism and rhetoric with which he is associated – posed problems for Hobbes. Thus, in *Leviathan* Hobbes singles out for criticism those who admire "Aristotle, Cicero, and other men, Greeks and Romanes," and hold that liberty has to do with commonwealths being popular in character. This is an error on their part, and he accuses them "of favouring tumults, and of licentious controlling the actions of their Soveraigns." Hobbes concludes that "there was never any thing so deerly bought, as these Western parts have bought the learning of the Greek and Latine tongues."[18]

Hobbes's contemporary proponents of an English commonwealth foolishly seek to control and limit sovereignty in the name of liberty, but it is not the nature of sovereignty to be limited, and it is not the *source* of the law but the *silence* of the law that is liberty for subjects. Moreover, Hobbes accuses his contemporaries, who admire the writings and traditions of ancient popular

---

[17] On Hobbes's knowledge of Sallust, see Wood, "Sallust's Theorem: A Comment on 'Fear' in Western Political Thought," 174.

[18] Thomas Hobbes, *Leviathan*, ed. Richard Tuck (Cambridge: Cambridge University Press, 1996), 149, 150. Cf. Skinner, *Liberty before Liberalism*, 8–12.

governments, of favoring tumults, and in doing so seek to "solicit and stir up the people to innovations."[19] Tumultuous politics are thus linked to participatory forms of government that feature rhetoric's free play. For Hobbes, tumults and innovations are dangers to the body politic, and they are part and parcel of a conception of a politics that he hopes to defeat through his construction of a sovereign that promotes peace, in part, through fear.

Hobbes's hostility to classical (and especially Ciceronian) rhetoric, featuring in *Leviathan, On the Citizen, The Elements of Law,* and *Behemoth,* has recently been demonstrated by Allen and Garsten.[20] What is striking about this hostility, however, is Hobbes's appeal to a particular classical source in making his case: Sallust. As we have seen in Chapter 1, Sallust is a key source in the historical narratives of contemporary republican scholarship and served as inspiration for humanists and early modern advocates of republicanism.[21] Yet Hobbes reads him as a thinker of his own ilk. For in his discussion of sedition and its causes in *On the Citizen,* Hobbes refers to Sallust's *War with Catiline:*

Sallust's character of Cataline, than whom there never was a greater artist in raising seditions, is this: *that he had great eloquence, and little wisdom.* He separates *wisdom* from *eloquence;* attributing this as necessary to a man born for commotions; adjudging that as an instrument of peace and quietness.[22]

His use of Sallust as a source to support his distrust of rhetoric, and to link a politics centered on persuasion to instability and sedition, is ironic, given Sallust's own prominence as a source for republican and humanist writers.

By Hobbes's account, Sallust separated eloquence from wisdom; the move is significant, for in doing so he seems an anti-Ciceronian. Cicero recognized that the truth of an argument was part of its persuasiveness – thus one of the tasks of the orator, and one of the components of rhetorical invention, was to prove one's case – *probare.* Though the truth of one's case could only

---

[19] Thomas Hobbes, *The Citizen,* ed. Bernard Gert, *Man and Citizen (De Homine and De Cive)* (Indianapolis: Hackett, 1991), 254.

[20] See Allen, *Talking to Strangers;* Garsten, *Saving Persuasion.* Both are engaging with Skinner's analysis of Hobbes in Quentin Skinner, *Reason and Rhetoric in the Philosophy of Hobbes* (Cambridge: Cambridge University Press, 1996).

[21] In addition to Skinner, "Machiavelli's *Discorsi* and the Pre-Humanist Origins of Republican Ideas," see also Mikael Hornqvist, *Machiavelli and Empire* (Cambridge: Cambridge University Press, 2004), 38–9.

[22] Hobbes, *The Citizen,* 253.

carry so far – one also needed to please (*delectare*) and sway (*flectere*) – Cicero doubts that one could accomplish all three tasks without knowledge – he says, *in propria persona*, "that it will be impossible for anyone to be an orator endowed with all praiseworthy qualities, unless he has gained a knowledge of all the important subjects and arts."[23] The orator requires a *scientia comprehenda rerum plurimarum* – a comprehensive knowledge of very many things – for without this the speech would be an inane and laughable swirl of words – *verborum volubilitas inanis atque irridenda est*.[24]

The departure from Cicero that Hobbes finds in Sallust, then, is important: If Hobbes is right, Sallust is a like-minded thinker, hostile to rhetoric and skeptical of – if not hostile to – participatory politics. Indeed, Hobbes's Sallust seems to conceive the place of rhetoric in the political community – and the community itself – in a very different way than does Cicero. If one can be eloquent without being wise, eloquence may well exacerbate and cause division rather than treat it, and its directing role may be undermined. It would be difficult by Hobbes's account to see how an unwise speaker would be able to inform popular judgment (since the populace is also unwise), or how tumultuous politics featuring the interplay between unwise speakers and the masses could result in stability or good policy.

There appears to be a distance between Sallust and Cicero on other matters as well, in part a function of the biographical tradition of Sallust as a supporter of Caesar.[25] While Sallust was at one point viewed as Caesar's historiographic partisan, the view has gone out of favor; yet the relationship between him and Cicero still seems ambiguous, given Sallust's writings, and especially the *War with Catiline*.[26] After all, it was Sallust who wrote the history of Catiline's

---

[23] Cicero, *On the Ideal Orator*, 1.20.
[24] Cicero, *De Oratore*, trans. E.W. Sutton (Cambridge: Harvard University Press, 1987), 1.17.
[25] McGushin, *Bellum Catilinae: A Commentary*, 4.
[26] Mommsen is most representative of this hostile view. Sallust is described as one of the "street leaders of the regents' [i.e., Caesar and Pompey's] party," whom he charges with inciting a mob of plebeians to riot following the death of Clodius. Of the four literary references, three tell us little of what Mommsen thought of Sallust; in the fourth Mommsen describes him as "a notorious Caesarian" and labels him an apologist for Caesar after his death. Sallust "endeavours to bring into credit the democratic [*popularis*] party – on which in fact the Roman monarchy was based – and to clear Caesar's memory from the blackest stain that rested on it." Mommsen argues that even though "the adroit author keeps the apologetic and inculpatory character of these writings of his in the background," it proves "not that they are not partisan treatises, but that they are good ones." Theodor Mommsen, *History of Rome*, trans. William Purdie Dickinson, 5 vols. (New York: Charles Scribner's Sons 1911), Vol. 5, 145; Vol. 4, 489. For details of Sallust's biography, see Chapters 2–4 of Ronald Syme, *Sallust* (Berkeley: University of California Press, 1964).

conspiracy, and not, as Cicero desired, his friend L. Lucceius.[27] His history of the conspiracy is not what Cicero hoped for: whereas Cicero asked Lucceius by letter (since words do not blush) that his "name should gain luster and celebrity" in his proposed history, Cato and Caesar receive far more attention than Cicero, who plays a comparatively minor role in Sallust's narrative.[28] He was certainly not the central figure, and Cicero's famous Catilinarian orations receive almost no attention – Sallust simply writes that Cicero gave a "brilliant speech of great service to the state, which he later wrote out and published."[29]

Sallust's attitude toward Cicero, however, is tenser when it comes to the writing of history itself. Cicero, in *On the Ideal Orator*, saw history as the proper province of his ideal orator, armed with knowledge and eloquence and moved by love of country. The orator's abilities are especially well suited to the writing of history for Cicero. He has Antonius describe history as "witness of the ages, the illuminator of reality, the life force of memory, the teacher of our lives, and the messenger of times gone by." Antonius then asks, "what other voice but the orator's invests it with immortality?"[30]

History, continues Antonius, has its rules – say nothing false, dare to say what is true, and avoid partiality – of which all are aware.[31] Sallust himself is cognizant of the dangers of partiality and alludes to his distance from partial motives, describing his "mind as free from hope, and fear, and partisanship" in the preface to the *War with Catiline*.[32] Less well known are the stylistic requirements that Antonius describes, which include attention to chronology and topography, statements of the author's judgment of his topic and his characters, and choice of the words themselves: As Cicero puts it, "The treatment of the words and the type of language should be broad and expansive, flowing steadily with a certain smoothness, without the sharpness of a court speech and the stinging sentiments used in the forum."[33] Though attentive

---

[27] Kraus and Woodman suggest that Sallust may well have known of the letter. C.S. Kraus and A.J. Woodman, *Latin Historians* (Oxford: Oxford University Press, 1997), 46, note 56.

[28] Cicero, *Letters to Friends*, trans. D.R. Shackleton Bailey (Cambridge: Harvard University Press, 2001), 5.12.1 His role is not insignificant, and he does receive praise, having "craft and address" to escape Catiline's plots and being perceived as a "serious obstacle" by Catiline himself. Sallust, *War with Catiline.* 26.2; 27.4. So great an obstacle was Cicero that Catiline sought to have him assassinated.

[29] Sallust, *War with Catiline*, 31.6.

[30] Cicero, *On the Ideal Orator*, 2.36.

[31] Ibid., 2.62–3.

[32] Sallust, *War with Catiline*, 4.2.

[33] Cicero, *On the Ideal Orator.* 2.64. See also Cicero, *Orator*, trans. H.M. Hubbell, *Cicero: Brutus and Orator* (Cambridge: Harvard University Press, 1952), 66.

to chronology and topography and more than ready to judge the numerous characters that populate his narratives, Sallust's language is anything but
steadily flowing – rather, it is "a struggling style born of the effort to match
contemporary political turbulence in words"; Sallust's stylistic model, in this
regard, was Thucydides, himself deeply attuned to the turbulence and corruption of moral language and quite influential on Hobbes.[34]

Cicero, to be sure, spoke of Thucydides, but not always with praise. Even
though in *On the Ideal Orator* Antonius refers to him as having "surpassed
everyone in his skillful use of language," and remarks on its density, he
later notes that Thucydides' writings are "more abundant in ideas than in
words."[35] Cicero has less praise for Thucydides in the later *Orator*, engaged as
he was in controversy with the Atticists, for whose oratory Thucydides was
a model. Cicero, against his classicizing opponents, argues that Thucydides
is not a good model for orators, as his "dark and obscure" style makes him
"scarcely intelligible."[36] The import of the comment was both stylistic and
political, a reaction to the Atticists who criticized Cicero's own "Asiatic"
style.[37] As an archaizing movement, Atticists looked to the external standards of experts to evaluate oratory, elevating expert judgment over mass
approval.[38] For Cicero, by contrast, the experts and the many could certainly
agree on good oratory. Given that central tasks of the orator are pleasing his
auditor and stirring his emotions – as well as proving his claims – the *effectiveness* of the orator will be as clear to the expert as to the non-expert: "For
that reason, as to the question whether an orator is good or bad, there has
never been disagreement between experts and the common people."[39]
If this had been Cicero's aim, Thucydides would not be a useful stylistic
model; nor would Thucydides have provided the orator with the tools he
needed to engage with all audiences.[40]

Sallust's style, given his debt to Thucydides, is not that of Cicero's historian *cum* orator, but the dissimilarities do not stop here. We have already

---

[34] Thomas F. Scanlon, *The Influence of Thucydides on Sallust* (Heidelberg: Carl Winter, 1980), 53
[35] Cicero, *On the Ideal Orator*, 2.56, 2.93.
[36] Cicero, *Orator*, 30.
[37] See Emanuele Narducci, "*Brutus*: The History of Roman Eloquence," in *Brill's Companion
to Cicero: Oratory and Rhetoric*, ed. James M. May (Leiden: Brill, 2002): 401–25
[38] George A. Kennedy, *The Art of Rhetoric in the Roman World, 300 B.C.–A.D. 300* (Princeton:
Princeton University Press, 1972), 243.
[39] Cicero, *Brutus*. 185.
[40] James M. May, "Cicero as Rhetorician," in *A Companion to Roman Rhetoric*, ed. William J.
Dominik and Jon Hall (Oxford: Blackwell Publishing, 2007): 250–63, 258.

encountered Hobbes's claim that Sallust separates eloquence and wisdom, at least with respect to Catiline – Catiline had "*satis eloquentiae, sapientae parum,*"[41] eloquence without wisdom. Hobbes sees this as a crucial move on Sallust's part and supportive of a broader point that he makes in *On the Citizen*. For Hobbes, eloquence is twofold: on the one hand, it is "an elegant and clear expression of the conceptions of the mind" – Hobbes terms this logic; on the other hand, it is "a commotion of the passions of the mind, such as are hope, fear, anger, pity; and derives from a metaphorical use of words fitted to the passions" – this is rhetoric.[42] Logic stems from true principles, which is to say *sapientia*; rhetoric stems from opinions. As readers of Hobbes are well aware, he sees the latter part of eloquence as dangerous, given to causing sedition and characteristic of those "who solicit and stir up the people to innovations" – unless, of course, eloquence is regulated (if not monopolized) by the sovereign.[43] And it is this sense of eloquence that Hobbes locates in Sallust's writings and the tumults that feature in them.

To be sure, Cicero is not sanguine about the potential misuse of oratory; yet, he argues that in addition to being responsible for the foundation of civilization,[44] oratory grew with civilization, especially in free political communities, and it blossomed most in communities that were peaceful. Eloquence bloomed in Rome especially after it had conquered its enemies:

Once we had established our authority over all nations and a stable peace had provided us with leisure [*pacis otium confirmavit*], almost every ambitious young man thought he should devote himself to oratory with all the energy he had.[45]

This, for Cicero, is not a bad thing, given the relationship of oratory to freedom and political order. Yet the removal of collective fear – through Rome's acquisition of dominion, and especially its destruction of Carthage – would, as we will see in the next section, have dire consequences for Sallust. Such consequences seem to validate Hobbes's reading of him, with fear

---

[41] Sallust, *War with Catiline*, 5.4.

[42] Hobbes, *The Citizen*, 253. It is worth noting, in this regard, Hobbes's debt to Thucydides, of which he himself speaks. See Thomas Hobbes, *Of the Life and History of Thucydides*, ed. David Grene, *The Peloponnesian War: The Complete Hobbes Translation* (Chicago: University of Chicago Press, 1989).

[43] Hobbes, *The Citizen*, 254.

[44] On eloquence as formative of civilization, see Cicero, *On the Ideal Orator*, 1.30. See also Cicero, *De Inventione*, trans. H.M. Hubbell, *Cicero: De Inventione, De Optimo Genere Oratorum, Topica* (Cambridge: Harvard University Press, 1960), 1.1–2.

[45] Cicero, *On the Ideal Orator*, 1.14.

functioning to restrain the Romans and to ensure consensus in a way that seems to prefigure Hobbes himself. The persuasiveness of a Hobbesian account of Sallust would cement Sallust's status as, at best, a highly ambiguous republican and raise troubling issues about the boundaries of republican community and civic virtue.

III. SALLUST AND THE ROLE OF COLLECTIVE FEAR IN THE POLITICAL COMMUNITY

As we will see, the peaceful conditions that Cicero valorized could, ironically, pose a problem for Sallust. Indeed, they give space to the kind of struggles that Hobbes – and Hobbes's Sallust – abhorred. Struggles, for Sallust, as with Hobbes, could undermine the cohesion of the community, and for this reason a Hobbesian reading of Sallust is tempting, especially given the salience of fear as a restraining element on collective behavior in Sallust's writings. Indeed, it is striking just how central a role fear seems to play for Sallust.

Despite recent claims regarding the distinctive role of fear in modern political thought, fear was held to bring about both unity and moral energy by many ancient thinkers.[46] Indeed, Sallust's emphasis on fear as a restraint on corruption, though certainly pronounced, is not without precedent – most immediately, the idea was prominent in the writings of Posidonius, whose history began where Polybius left off in 146 BCE.[47] Posidonius seems to be the first writer to have located the decline of Roman morality in the period following Carthage's destruction in 146 BCE.[48] Posidonius' Rome was not idyllic, characterized by rule "in the hands of the wise"[49] – rather, it saw:

the beginnings of Roman exploitation of the East on a systematic basis, the servile revolts in Sicily, the devastating conflict between Rome and her Italian *socii*, the eruption of the Mithridatic war, and the Roman brutality that followed it.[50]

[46] For a recent argument concerning the distinctiveness of fear in modern political thought, see Corey Robin, *Fear: The History of a Political Idea* (Oxford: Oxford University Press, 2004). On fear's role in ancient thought, see Kapust, "On the Ancient Uses of Political Fear and Its Modern Implications."

[47] A.A. Long, *Hellenistic Philosophy: Stoics, Epicureans, Sceptics* (Berkeley: University of California Press, 1986), 218.

[48] Wiedemann, "Reflections of Roman Political Thought in Latin Historical Writing," 527.

[49] A.A. Long and D.N. Sedley, *The Hellenistic Philosophers*, vol. 1 (Cambridge: Cambridge University Press, 1987), 434.

[50] Erich Gruen, *The Hellenistic World and the Coming of Rome*, vol. 1 (Berkeley: University of California Press, 1984), 352.

Posidonius ascribes Rome's decline to the fall of Carthage and the concomitant loss of its check on Rome's energies – as Gruen puts it, "Polybius had had a foreboding; Posidonius had seen it happen."[51]

Responsible for this destruction according to tradition was (ironically) the Elder Cato, who pushed for the annihilation of Carthage for "more than two years."[52] Cato's obsession with the destruction of Carthage brought about perverse consequences given Sallust's narrative; it harms Rome and does not help it. In hindsight, the policy seems poorly chosen, given Cato's concerns with luxury and the abandonment of Roman virtues, whether from corruption or the over-eager pursuit of Greek philosophy. In Sallust's narrative, it is precisely the fall of Carthage that brings about what Cato most feared: Rome's corruption.[53]

For Sallust, it was collective fear – and especially the fear of foreigners – that might serve as a buttress of morality and foster social cohesion. The idea that fear had such a function long preceded Cato and Posidonius; it was Greek in origin, and evident in – though not of central importance to – Plato and Aristotle.[54] Closer to Sallust's time, and dealing specifically with Rome, Polybius had argued that fear helped Rome's constitution cohere in two ways. First, the collective fear of foreign enemies fostered unity among the components of Rome's constitution. In Book 6, Polybius writes of the Senate, assemblies and consul that "whenever any danger from without compels them to unite and work together," they work together with "extraordinary" strength.[55] Second, internal fear – specifically the fear each component had of the other components – constrained the components, as "any aggressive impulse is sure to be checked and from the outset each estate stands in dread of being

---

[51] Ibid., 352.
[52] Alan E. Astin, *Cato the Censor* (Oxford: Oxford University Press, 1978), 128.
[53] A fragment of Cato's *Origines* is preserved in which he expresses concern over the corruptive effects of prosperity, in the immediate context of Rome's victory at Pydna: "I know that among most men, in favorable times, the mind exults in long prosperity, and that arrogance and ferocity grow and increase." Indeed, for Cato "adversity subdues and instructs," while great prosperity might diminish right council and judgment. Cato, *Les Origines: Fragments*, ed. Martine Chassignet (Paris: Société d'Édition "Les Belles Lettres," 1986), Fr. 5.3, 43. On the context, see Chassignet, note 2, 43 Cato was aware of the possibility that peace – especially when matched with luxury – might harm Roman virtue. On the relationship between Sallust and Cato the Elder, see D.S. Levene, "Sallust's Catiline and Cato the Censor," *The Classical Quarterly* 50, no. 1 (2000): 170–91, 179–80.
[54] See Kapust, "On the Ancient Uses of Political Fear and Its Modern Implications," 358–9.
[55] Polybius, *The Histories*, 6.18.1–2.

interfered with by the others."[56] When Polybius speculates, at the conclusion of Book 6, on the future of the Roman constitution, he suggests that Rome's acquisition of "supremacy and uncontested sovereignty" could cause extravagance, making the "rivalry for office and in other spheres of activity" become "fiercer than it ought to be."[57] With this change, the constitution itself would alter, moving from its apex "to the finest sounding of all, freedom and democracy," but in fact "to the worst thing of all, mob-rule."[58]

If fear played a role in maintaining social cohesion for Plato and Aristotle, as well as Polybius and Posidonius, it sometimes played such a role for Thucydides, whose influence on Sallust we have already encountered. This role is most evident in his narration of the Corcyrean stasis. Emboldened by the approach of the Athenian fleet and the departure of the Peloponnesian forces, Corcyrean democrats began to slaughter their enemies, who were accused "of conspiring to overthrow the democracy, but in fact men were often killed on grounds of personal hatred or else by their debtors because of the money that they owed."[59] With the oligarchs' power diminished, and the democrats' fear of them thus removed, little restrained either side. The situation would be repeated through "practically the whole of the Hellenic world," with democrats seeking to bring in Athenian forces, and oligarchs seeking to bring in Spartan forces. War provided the necessary condition, as each party knew it could attract external support if it desired "a change of government."[60]

With the revolutions came changes in language: "words, too, had to change their usual meanings."[61] Thucydides summarizes the behavior thus:

In times of peace and prosperity cities and individuals alike follow higher standards, because they are not forced into a situation where they have to do what they do not want to do. But war is a stern teacher; in depriving them of the

---

[56] Ibid., 6.18.8.

[57] Ibid., 6.57.5. On this point, see Arthur M. Eckstein, *Moral Vision in the Histories of Polybius* (Berkeley: University of California Press, 1995), 264.

[58] Polybius, *The Histories*, 6.57.9.

[59] Thucydides, *History of the Peloponnesian War*, 3.81.

[60] Ibid.

[61] Ibid., 3.82. This does not mean, as Hornblower notes, that "the *meaning* of words actually changed," but how people used these terms changed "as their evaluation of the relevant actions changed." Simon Hornblower, *A Commentary on Thucydides*, vol. 1 (Oxford: Oxford University Press, 1991), 483.

power of easily satisfying their daily wants, it brings most people's minds down to the level of their actual circumstances.[62]

As cause Thucydides points to "the desire to rule which greed and ambition inspire" – these are exacerbated by the zeal of those "engaged in factious rivalry."[63] Both factions are equally guilty, each deploying "a fair-sounding name": democrats spoke of equality before the law; oligarchs spoke for moderate aristocracy.[64] Neither slogan captures reality; the warping of language was part and parcel of the tumults of civil war. Language and values thus changed with altered circumstances in the context of the Corcyrean civil war – the democrats emboldened by the Athenian fleet, fear ceased to constrain their behavior as it had done before. In certain instances, for Thucydides, collective fear could constrain behavior, while its absence brought license and corruption; the underlying causes were greed ($\pi\lambda\varepsilon o\nu\varepsilon\xi i\alpha$) and the love of honor ($\varphi\iota\lambda o\tau\iota\mu i\alpha$), let loose by the absence of collective fear.

Despite the presence of the idea of foreign fear as salutary in these writers, in choosing Carthage's fall as the beginning of Rome's decline, Sallust did not represent the consensus of Roman opinion, though he would "set a fashion" among subsequent writers.[65] For example, we can hear echoes of Sallust's account in Plutarch's first-century CE *Life of Marcus Cato*, when he relates the story of Cato and P. Scipio Nasica's debates in the senate over the fate of Carthage. Cato added "to his vote on any question whatsoever these words: 'In my opinion, Carthage must be destroyed.'"[66] Scipio opposed Cato, declaring at the end of his speeches, "In my opinion, Carthage must be spared."[67] Plutarch attributes to Scipio the belief that "the fear of Carthage should abide, to curb the boldness of the multitude"; Cato, by contrast, thought the Romans would suffer by "external threat to their sovereignty," and ridding Rome of Carthage's threat would allow the Romans to "be free

---

[62] Thucydides, *History of the Peloponnesian War*, 3.82.

[63] Ibid., 3.82.8. The Greek consulted is Thucydidis, *Historiae*, ed. Henry Stuart Jones, vol. 1 (Oxford: Clarendon Press, 1955).

[64] Thucydides, *History of the Peloponnesian War*, 3.82.

[65] D.C. Earl, *The Political Thought of Sallust* (Cambridge: Cambridge University Press, 1961), 47. According to Earl, Sallust rejected a "tradition that by the middle of the second century Rome had undergone a crisis from which she never recovered and that the processes which eventually destroyed the Republic had already begun to work." Earl, *The Political Thought of Sallust*, 42. Cf. McGushin, *Bellum Catilinae: A Commentary*, 87–8.

[66] Plutarch, *Life of Marcus Cato*, trans. Bernadotte Perrin, *Plutarch's Lives* (Cambridge: Harvard University Press, 1967), 27.1.

[67] Ibid., 27.1.

to devise a cure for their domestic failings."[68] Both Scipio and Cato, however, share the same fear – namely, that the Roman people would be too
emboldened by their power.

Like his Greek predecessors, Sallust views collective fear as salutary, especially as a check on luxury, a vice that was highly corruptive of the republic.
Like Thucydides in particular, Sallust is concerned with the corruption of
language and the gap between words and reality, a gap that can be exacerbated by the absence of fear-induced constraint. Yet Sallust does not point
to war and its effects on the psyche to explain such behavior; rather, he points
to Rome's foreign peace.[69] Indeed, Sallust's time of peace inverts his time
of war and foreign enmity, and the inversion of values took place not when
Rome was in a bad condition, but when it was in an apparently good situation: "at home there was peace and an abundance of wealth, which mortal
men deem the chiefest of blessings."[70] The point is highly ironic: Cicero –
who, as we have noted, wrote that young Romans turned to rhetoric
"once we had established our authority over all nations and a stable peace
had provided us with leisure" – is turned upside down; peace becomes a
problem, not a blessing, because of conflict and sedition.[71] Avarice – though
introduced in Sallust's *War with Catiline* through Sulla's warfare in Asia –
taught Romans vice in the context of foreign peace. Matters culminated
in the time of Sallust himself; into this context came those who "were bent
upon their own ruin and that of their country."[72] The immorality of individuals engaged in vicious behavior thus has clear public consequences.

Metus – fear – restrains, whether it is the *metus hostilis*, as in the *War with
Catiline*, *War with Jugurtha*, and the *Histories*, or the *metus Punicus* and *metus
Etruscanus*, as in the fragmentary *Histories*. For Sallust, Romans restrained
by the fear of foreigners were harmonious, and "harmony [*concordia*] makes
small states great, while discord undermines the mightiest empires."[73] So says

---

[68] Ibid., 27.2–3.

[69] To be sure, Sallust claims that Sulla had demoralized his own troops in the east with luxury, and that it was there "that an army of the Roman people first learned to indulge in
women and drink; to admire statues, paintings, and chased vases, to steal them from private
houses and public places, to pillage shrines, and to desecrate everything, both sacred and pro-
fane" Sallust, *War with Catiline*, 11.6. Yet he also notes that Sulla, on seizing power at Rome
itself, "was spurred on … by the corruption the public morals." Sallust, *War with Catiline*. 5.8.

[70] Sallust, *War with Catiline*, 36.4.

[71] Cicero, *On the Ideal Orator*, 1.14.

[72] Sallust, *War with Catiline*, 36.4.

[73] Sallust, *War with Jugurtha*, trans. J.C. Rolfe, *Sallust* (Cambridge: Harvard University Press,
1985), 10.6.

Micipsa in the *War with Jugurtha*; Micipsa himself is something of a warning figure, given his understanding of human nature: "He dreaded the natural disposition of mankind, which is greedy for power and eager to gratify its heart's desire" – an echo of Thucydides' πλεονεξία and φιλοτιμία, checked for Sallust by fear.[74] In Rome's golden age, discord had been reserved for its enemies; the Romans were bold in war and just in peace. It is only when discord replaced concord – once fear was removed – that "Fortune began to grow cruel and to bring confusion into all our affairs."[75] Whether this was due to the fall of Carthage, as in the *War with Jugurtha* and the *War with Catiline*, or the removal of the Tarquin threat (and subsequently the fear of Carthage), as in the *Histories* (in which intermittent tumults last until the outbreak of the Second Punic War), the absence of an enemy fosters vice and discord. Sallust's Rome, under the external pressure of foreign fear, maintains its harmony; Romans behave rightly in both peace and war. One is reminded, in this regard, of what Hobbes says in *Leviathan* about the role of fear in a "great Popular Common-wealth": such a society was often held together "by a forraign Enemy that united them."[76] But with the decline of the fear of foreign enemies, the discordant elements of Roman society – *plebs* and *nobiles* – began to break apart. The question we are left with is twofold: Why is this the case, and must this be the case, for Sallust?

IV. ANTAGONISM IN SALLUST'S HISTORIES

Fear plays a pivotal role in Sallust's narrative; it seems to structure and constrain society, fostering unity and harmony in a manner reminiscent of the fear of a Hobbesian sovereign. Yet this does not exhaust the possibilities in making sense of Sallust's understanding of the Roman republic, and we should pause here precisely because struggle *is* part of Rome's precorruption past, for Sallust, though it is a struggle of a particular sort: a manifestation of the energies released with political liberty, a struggle for the rewards of virtue, not for power.

In the *War with Catiline*, he describes early Romans thus: "their hardest struggle for glory [*gloriae maxumum certamen*] was with one another; each man strove to be first and to strike down the foe, to scale a wall, to be seen

---

[74] Ibid., 6.3.
[75] Sallust, *War with Catiline*, 10.1.
[76] Hobbes, *Leviathan*, 182.

of all while doing such a deed."[77] Praise was their wealth, and they desired "only such riches as could be gained honorably." Similarly, he writes at 9.2 that "Quarrels, discord, and strife were reserved for their enemies; citizen vied with citizen only for the prize of merit" – *cives cum civibus de virtute certabant.* We are faced with *certamen* – struggle – between individuals; early Rome was not marked by the absence of conflict, per se. But this is a struggle in the domain of virtue and for rewards compatible with the common good. Conflict, then, is not necessarily a problem for Sallust; the problem is unchecked conflict not rooted in the desire to benefit the community through competition for honor.

As Fontana remarks of Sallust, "Politics represented the competitive pursuit of power and glory at the service of the *res publica* – the common or public business."[78] This competition is not only between particular Romans in the service of the republic but also between social groups. We see this in Sallust's *War with Jugurtha* in a contional speech of the tribune Memmius.[79] This speech centers on the distinction between "the power of the dominant faction [*opes factionis*]" and the people's "submission" – *patientia.*[80] Memmius draws a second important contrast between the nobles and the people: The people share a "love of freedom [*libertatis curam*]"; the nobles have a "thirst for tyranny [*ad dominationem*]."[81] And it is this opposition, as Fontana notes, that "may be seen as the founding source of republican liberty," in that Memmius refers to the plebs' secession to the Aventine hill as the plebs' forefathers' assertion of "their legal rights" and "sovereignty."[82] In this sense, then, the "secession paradoxically created a public space common to both patricians and plebeians."[83] It was thus the antagonism between people and patricians that expressed itself through and gave rise to the stuff of politics: As Connolly puts it:

---

[77] Sallust, *War with Catiline*, 7.6.

[78] Fontana, "Sallust and the Politics of Machiavelli," 89.

[79] The *contio*, as opposed to assembly-meetings, referred to "meetings where nothing was legally enacted. These were summoned with little or no restriction on venue to listen to public pronouncements, including magistrates' edicts, to hear arguments in speeches, to witness the examination of an alleged criminal or even to see his execution." Lintott, *The Constitution of the Roman Republic,* 42.

[80] Sallust, *War with Jugurtha*, 31.1.

[81] Ibid., 31.16.

[82] Fontana, "Sallust and the Politics of Machiavelli," 90; Sallust, *War with Jugurtha*, 31.17.

[83] Fontana, "Sallust and the Politics of Machiavelli," 91.

While ancient families like the Cornelii and Fabii were publicly revered in statues, triumphs, and crowded funeral processions, republican culture depended no less crucially on its memory of antagonism: the plebeian struggle from noble domination, memorialized in legends of cyclical fraternal strife. [84]

Far from being inimical to Sallust's politics, then, conflict of a certain kind is constitutive of his politics.

In this regard, multiple elements in Roman society – individuals and groups – could harm the community precisely because the community was not homogeneous and was the locus of conflict. Once corruption had set in, few are innocent in Sallust's narrative – even the plebs, for whom Sallust is often held to have sympathy, are not without fault: he notes, in *propria persona*, that "the whole body of the commons through desire for change favored the designs of Catiline," acting "as the populace usually does; for in every community those who have no means envy the good, exalt the base, hate what is old and established, and long for something new, and from disgust with their own lot desire a general upheaval." The demagogues who agitated the populace, playing on their passions and inflaming them "still more by doles and promises" to increase their own visibility, were met by nobles.[85] Neither side was forthright:

all who assailed the government used specious pretexts, some maintaining that they were defending the rights of the commons [*populi iura*], others that they were upholding the prestige of the senate [*senatus auctoritas*]; but under pretence of the public welfare each in reality was working for his own advancement.[86]

All of this was, ironically, in the very period of peace that Cicero valorized and consequent to the removal of the fear of Carthage. With the loss of *concordia*, as the result of the fall of Carthage and the removal of its restraining fear, the best of states became the worst of states. Why this should be the case, however, is not quite clear.

One possible explanation is to see *concordia* as the pivotal value for Sallust, holding together his conception of the republic and ensuring moral order. Sallust certainly places great value on *concordia*, so much that he seems to value it above all else, to the point, perhaps, that through his concentration "on

---

[84] Connolly, *The State of Speech*, 35.
[85] Sallust, *War with Catiline*, 38.1.
[86] Ibid., 38.3.

concordia Sallust has produced an over-generalized and idealistic account."[87] If *concordia* is of great value, its absence would be harmful; that conflict can be harmful is evident in *The War with Jugurtha*, in a digression on "the institution of parties [*partium*] and factions [*factionum*]" at Rome with the destruction of Carthage, the fear of which "preserved the good morals of the state."[88] Two parties emerged – the nobility (*nobilitas*) and the people (*populus*); conflict between them destroyed the state.[89] In this digression, while illustrating the conflict and discussing nobles "who preferred true glory to unjust power," Sallust turns to Tiberius and Caius Gracchus as examples.[90] The Gracchi sought to vindicate the liberty of the plebs – *vindicare plebem in libertatem* – again, we see the connection between the people and liberty.[91] This liberty was asserted against the wicked deeds of the few – *paucorum scelera*.

The same conflict between different individuals, or between nobles and people, that might be symptomatic and constitutive of liberty, is exacerbated by the destruction of Carthage; prior to the fall of Carthage, "the people and senate of Rome together governed the republic peacefully and with moderation."[92] The people and senate were still distinct, however. Once Carthage was destroyed, though, both the people and the nobles are to blame: "the nobles began to abuse their position [*dignitatem*] and the people their liberty [*libertatem*]."[93] From that point onward, "the community was split into two parties [*in duas partis*]."[94]

Harmony in the past; discord in the present: This seems to capture Sallust's attitude toward Roman history. Yet his writings even on the distant past are marked by antagonism, and this antagonism is not uniformly negative. Struggle – *certamen* – was not a problem, as we have seen, so long as it was for "the prize of merit" – *de virtute*.[95] The problem was when the struggle was not in the right domain, for the right objects, and by the right methods. As he puts it in *The War with Catiline*, "the noble and the base [*bonus et ignavus*] alike long for glory, honor, and power, but the former mount by the true path, whereas the latter, being destitute of noble qualities, rely upon craft and

[87] Earl, *The Political Thought of Sallust*, 46.
[88] Sallust, *War with Jugurtha*, 41.1, 41.2.
[89] Ibid., 41.5.
[90] Ibid., 41.10.
[91] Ibid., 42.1.
[92] Ibid., 41.2.
[93] Ibid., 41.5.
[94] Ibid., 41.5.
[95] Sallust, *War with Catiline*, 9.2.

deception."[96] Commonly desired goods may be pursued in very different ways: How they are pursued, and in what domain, is of great importance.

V. DICHOTOMIES AND THEIR BREAKDOWN

The healthful antagonism of Sallust's republic is linked to, and constrained by, the fear of enemies. In this regard, it stands in contrast to Cicero, for whom the fear of enemies does not function as a boundary of community. Nevertheless, Cicero's republic was not marked by the absence of conflict; the wise orator-statesman functioned in part to heal the antagonisms that were the essence of republican politics. Deliberative and forensic oratory would have little use absent the antagonistic contexts in which they were practiced: namely, the Senate, the *contio*, and the courts.[97] Yet if peace was a good thing for Cicero, giving space to eloquence and its directive role, the opposite appears to be the case for Sallust. A striking feature of the *War with Catiline*, the *War with Jugurtha*, and the fragmentary *Histories* is Sallust's seeming insistence on the deleterious effects of Rome's unchecked dominion on Roman political life. This effect is manifested chiefly in the acceleration and deepening of political conflict and moral decline following the elimination of foreign enemies' salutary effect on Roman political life.

When *concordia* was lost due to the loss of the collective fear of foreign enemies, Rome changed for the worse. Antagonistic forces began to spiral out of control, unchecked by the restraining fear of foreign enemies. Earlier Romans were motivated by the "thirst for glory" (*cupido gloriae*); once Carthage was destroyed and circumstances changed, Rome had "lust for money first, then for power."[98] Noble qualities, such as honor and integrity, were uprooted by avarice, which replaced them with "insolence" and "cruelty." In what is surely a Thucydidean echo, Sallust likens this decline to a disease – "a deadly plague" – and like the plague-struck Athens, as compared to its valorization in Pericles' funeral oration, "the state was changed and a government second to none in equity and excellence became cruel and intolerable."[99] Indeed, the corruption of Sallust's Rome echoes Thucydides' account of the Corcyrean stasis.

---

[96] Ibid., 11.2.
[97] See Cicero, *On the Ideal Orator*, 3.81.
[98] Sallust, *War with Catiline*, 7.3; 10.3.
[99] Ibid., 10.6.

This breakdown, in turn, is evident in the breakdown of seemingly clear dichotomies, dichotomies that can be seen in both the *War with Catiline* and the *War with Jugurtha*. Sallust begins both works with sharp distinctions, chief of which is between mind and body, which together comprise human nature. Those who crave renown should use the prior, not the latter, as the prior is in "common with the Gods," and the latter in common "with the brutes." It is by the use "of the resources of the intellect" that we ought to seek fame, and not "those of brute strength," so that "we may make the memory of our lives as long as possible."[100] The body and mind, though distinct, are not unrelated; similarly, thought and action, while distinct, are also not unrelated – we need to combine deliberation and action, as each is "incomplete in itself."[101] Distinct elements must, then, function together through a productive tension if they are to function well.

Sallust's discussion in the *War with Jugurtha* is similar. The mind is the leading element in humans; when it moves by virtue to glory, "it has power and potency in abundance, as well as fame; and it needs not fortune."[102] Fortune and virtue are thus opposed, with those who are virtuous triumphing over fortune. Indeed, were we to rely on the exercise of our mind – and hence virtue – we "would control fate rather than be controlled by it."[103] Many, however, pursue things of the body, but blame human nature, rather than themselves; their vice is more remarkable given that there are so many fields in which "the highest distinction may be won" – for instance, writing history, Sallust's own activity.[104]

Just as dichotomies are firm in human nature, dichotomies seem firm in Rome's past: in the *War with Catiline*, Rome of old (that is, prior to the fall of Carthage) had "good morals;" there was the "greatest harmony [*concordia*] and little or no avarice; justice and probity prevailed … thanks not so much to laws as to nature."[105] Rome's success stemmed from the practice of two distinct (though complementary) qualities in two distinct contexts: "boldness in warfare and justice when peace came."[106] Boldness was for enemies, as were "quarrels, discord and strife"; in peace, however, "they

---

[100] Ibid., 1.2–3.
[101] Ibid., 1.7.
[102] Sallust, *War with Jugurtha*, 1.3.
[103] Ibid., 1.5.
[104] Ibid., 2.4.
[105] Sallust, *War with Catiline*, 9.1.
[106] Ibid., 9.3.

ruled by kindness rather than fear, and when wronged preferred forgiveness to vengeance."[107] These qualities are, though distinct in domain and object, productive in their tension, and not simply opposed to each other.

In the *War with Catiline*, we see that those who found "hardship and dangers, anxiety and adversity" easy to tolerate in earlier circumstances – less luxurious circumstances – found leisure (*otium*) and wealth (*divitiae*) to be far more difficult, vices which emerged once Rome had destroyed Carthage, *aemula imperi Romani* – the rival of Rome's power.[108] It is precisely when "all seas and lands were open" that Rome began its precipitous decline.[109] We find similar language in the *War with Jugurtha*: parties and factions – *mos partium et factionum* – emerged in Rome precisely because of leisure – *otio* – and "an abundance of everything that mortals prize most highly."[110] Here, too, we find that when Carthage was destroyed, and Romans "were relieved of that dread" – *illa formido* – vices emerged, specifically lust and arrogance – *lascivia atque superbia*.[111]

In the *Histories*, Sallust develops a more nuanced analysis. Rome reached its peak, from the moral perspective, between the Second and Third Punic Wars, during which "the state conducted its affairs according to the highest moral standards and with the greatest harmony [*maxima concordia*]."[112] He ascribes Rome's "first quarrels" to "a defect of human nature which, restless and unbridled, is always immersed in struggles for liberty or for glory or for power [*certamina libertatis aut gloriae aut dominationis*]."[113] Discord, avarice, and ambition – vices that grow in "time of prosperity" – were greatest after Carthage's destruction, and when Rome was at peace. But Sallust adds that social conflict and turmoil were not distinctive to this period – "the injustices inflicted by the more powerful, the resultant secessions of the plebs from the patrician class and other types of disagreement occurred in Rome from the very beginning."[114]

---

[107] Ibid., 9.5.
[108] Ibid., 10.1–2.
[109] Ibid., 10.1.
[110] Sallust, *War with Jugurtha*, 41.1.
[111] Ibid., 41.3.
[112] Sallust, *The Histories*, trans. P. McGushin, vol. 1 (Oxford: Clarendon Press, 1992), 1.9. The Latin consulted is Sallustius, *Historiarum Reliquiae*, ed. Bertoldus Maurenbrecher (Stuttgart: Teubner, 1967).
[113] Sallust, *The Histories*, 1.8.
[114] Ibid., 1.10. This is a crucial point, adding more nuance to what seemed a highly schematic account in the *War with Catiline* and the *War with Jugurtha*. Yet even in these works, his account of the past is not one of total harmony.

Such pause in conflict as there was in the *Histories* centered on the fear of the Tarquins and warfare with Etruria. After these conflicts ended and the related fear was removed, "the patricians treated the people as slaves … and acted like tyrants over the rest of the population who were now landless."[115] Sallust characterizes the conflict as discord and struggle – *discordiarum et certaminis* – which continued to the beginning of the Second Punic War, during which Rome was at its peak.[116] Yet after the destruction of Carthage following the Third Punic War, "the way was clear for the exercise of political feuds."[117] A select few strove to win power for themselves while "masquerading as champions of the senate or of the people"; and citizens were termed good or bad – *bonique et mali cives appellati* – if they helped preserve the current bad state of things.[118] The decline of the ways of the ancestors (*maiorum mores*), which had been gradually proceeding, now moved like a torrent – *torrentis*. The decline is especially evident among the young – *iuventus* – who were marked by luxury and avarice – *luxu atque avaritia*. [119]

In all three of his works, we have, then, in Rome's past – whether it be in the *War with Catiline*, the *War with Jugurtha*, or the *Histories* – not just harmony (*concordia*) but a harmony built amid and arising from conflict and difference; yet, within this tense interplay between conflict and order, we see the proper maintenance of dichotomies, constituted by the fear of foreign enemies. Conflict and poverty combined to steer the Romans toward virtue and away from vice and luxury; luxury and greed marked Rome's decline.

VI. CONCLUSION

Conflict, per se, is not a bad thing for Sallust; we should not read him as a proto-Hobbesian longing for the simple absence of noise and tumult. The coexistence of distinct elements and tendencies in Sallust's thought – mind and body, few and many – was evident in Rome's past, after all, and not always accompanied by turmoil. Yet with the fall of Carthage came the confusion of moral language and the transposition of moral categories. Language itself transformed; vice became virtue, and virtue became vice, a clear

[115] Ibid., 1.10.
[116] Ibid., 1.10.
[117] Ibid., 1.12
[118] Ibid., 1.12
[119] Ibid., 1.13.

manifestation of corruption. Prosperity tried the soul of Sallust's Romans – not an uncommon claim, to be sure, but such vices, and the political turmoil they produce, are absent in the context of a harmonious past – the times of *concordia*. What is striking, however, is that the past was not entirely harmonious, either – we are still met with struggle between individuals and groups, especially the people and the senate. Fear may have constrained conflict, but fear did not guarantee its absence, let alone unanimity.

It is when the struggle turns from glory to domination that the republic is divided. Social and political conflict, then, could be productive of liberty, and competition – so long as it is linked to virtue – could support the republic. Checking this competition could be achieved, for Sallust, by the presence of a frightening foreign other. But this competition was still there; it was simply contained and shaped by fear. The sheer competition and energy that characterizes Sallust's antagonism makes such a threat seem necessary. This makes him seem to be, at best, an ambiguous republican, and certainly not a Ciceronian republican.

As we have seen, however, tensions could nevertheless be productive for Sallust, so long as they were rightly structured, and they might find an important place in free political communities. The dilemma this poses for interpreting Sallust, and for thinking about republican political communities marked by competition and conflict, is that the coherence of the community may become linked to the existence of a dangerous foreign enemy, and that civic virtue needs to be linked to political membership through such a threat. This was partly Hobbes's point in reflecting on what held popular assemblies together, after all.

This shows further tensions in thinking about republican virtue. Weithman has argued that if "republican government really does depend upon citizens' possessing the civic virtues," political (as opposed to perfectionist) republicanism "does not adequately secure the conditions of its own success."[120] Weithman suggests that political republicanism lacks the resources required to foster those virtues that it requires citizens to have if it is to succeed because it views these virtues as valuable due to their connection to particular regimes. One way of reading Sallust, then, would be to see that attachment to the regime was strengthened by the presence of a foreign enemy; the virtues this enmity had fostered suffered when the threat faded away. As a result, antagonisms that had been contained spiraled out of

---

[120] Weithman, "Political Republicanism and Perfectionist Republicanism," 287.

control. One solution might be to develop a thicker conception of virtue to check ambition; another might be to find a way to reintroduce – and maintain – a sense of collective fear. The solution, however, cannot simply be to get rid of conflict, given that it is not always a bad thing, for Sallust; the solution, I suggest, is to channel it properly.

The problem in such a reading of Sallust, then, is to find a way to harness the antagonism that had been structured and constrained by foreign enmity such that it was compatible with free and lasting government, or else to find a perpetual foreign enemy. A solution that avoids the latter, I will argue in the next chapter, was offered by the structure and practice of rhetoric itself. Rhetoric itself is an antagonistic process, a manifestation of competition and also a way for managing and publicizing competition. In particular, the practice of rhetoric by outstanding individuals who are distinct, yet complementary, offered a possible route for maintaining communities composed of distinct and complementary individuals and groups, albeit a contingent and temporary solution. Far from seeking to do away with rhetoric, or linking it inextricably to destabilizing tumult, as Hobbes would seem to suggest, Sallust – I argue in the next chapter – holds forth a vision of antagonistic rhetoric that serves to vindicate persuasion and its place in conflicted but free communities.

3

CHANNELING CONFLICT THROUGH ANTAGONISTIC RHETORIC IN THE *WAR WITH CATILINE*

I. INTRODUCTION

In the prior chapter, we encountered Sallust's depiction of Rome's corruption – its transformation from the best of states to the worst of states, from seeming moral certainty to moral confusion. This corruption, we saw, was linked to the removal of the fear of enemies. Collective fear in general served as a buttress to social cohesion and public-spiritedness, given that beneath the surface of Roman society lay antagonism, evident in individual Romans' pursuit of advance – the struggle in virtue – and the struggle between classes, latent until the fall of Carthage in the *War with Catiline* and the *War with Jugurtha*, but dating to the early history of Rome in the *Histories*.

With the decline of collective fear came a transformation in Roman values; struggles which had been innocuous and externally directed turned inward and wrought havoc on the body politic. This, in turn, posed a threat to a politics of virtue centered on particular attachments to the political community, given that the loss of fear weakened the sense of particular attachment, contributing to corruption. Such a process seems to make Rome's decline not only irreversible, but also inevitable, if it depended on fear. This, combined with Sallust's apparent similarity to Hobbes in his view of rhetoric, made him seem at best an ambiguous republican, and certainly anti-Ciceronian. Yet we encountered evidence that matters are more complicated for Sallust, given the healthful role of antagonism in his writings.

My discussion of antagonism in the prior chapter will play an important role in the argument of this chapter, as I will focus on a kind of antagonism – rhetorical antagonism – and its role in Sallust's *War with Catiline*. As we will see, the process of political and moral corruption that Sallust describes – and its culmination in the inversion of moral language – displays an intriguing similarity to what was, in another sphere, a common practice: The purposive assimilation of vice to virtue and virtue to vice in classical rhetoric. This is the rhetorical tactic of redescription, and it was a frequently deployed tool, especially in deliberative oratory. Ironically, then, we see an apparently antirhetorical writer deploying rhetorical techniques: Once fear no longer served to constrain the passions of the Romans, these passions subverted conventional morality in much the same way that orators, in pursuing their aims, might redescribe a vice as a virtue or a virtue as a vice. This similarity, I suggest, ought to alert us to the possibility that part of Sallust's aim is to show the *importance* of rhetoric in spite of Rome's troubles.

Resolving these troubles could involve, as we have seen, reintroducing a commonly feared enemy. It could also involve revaluating vice as vice and virtue as virtue, categories whose confusion entails, as we will see, clashing conceptions of the advantageous and the honorable. The restoration of names and the reestablishment of boundaries between the honorable and the advantageous is the younger Cato's tactic in his debate with Caesar over the handling of the Catilinarian conspirators. At the same time, Cato's effort to revaluate vice and virtue – and to return them to their proper significations – cannot solve Rome's crisis permanently. There are two potential explanations for this lack of a permanent solution, depending on how Sallust's use of fear is understood – one pessimistic, and the other less so. If we accept the stronger version of Sallust's use of fear as a near-Hobbesian device, this suggests that the roots of the crisis are too deep to uproot permanently: If maintaining the right moral language relies upon the presence of an enemy, Roman energies cannot be directed against enemies – foreign or internal – indefinitely. Yet if these tensions are simply a part of political life, a life that involves the precarious and perpetual balance of different elements – individuals and groups, complementary yet distinct virtues – then the task becomes not one of directing them outward, but finding some means to channel and temper them.

Although these energies cannot be directed outward indefinitely – after all, Rome did vanquish its great rival – they could be treated and channeled through the practice of rhetoric. Drawing on Cato and Caesar's debate in the *War with Catiline*, and the practice of arguing *in utramque partem* that was central to the practice of rhetoric, I argue that Cato and Caesar's rhetorical antagonism serves as a vehicle for expressing social and political antagonism. The tensions in the body politic, rather than tear the republic apart, might be played out and resolved through the practice of rhetoric. Rectifying the situation, then, required the presence and political action of outstanding individuals who, through their rhetorical conflict, serve as a focal point of antagonistic energies and a device by which the tense dichotomies encountered in Chapter 2 could coexist in a productive relationship.

I begin in Section II with a discussion of the device of redescription, turning to its potential dangers and their presence in Sallust's analysis of corruption. I then turn in Section III to redescription's treatment – and redescription's relationship to the honorable and the advantageous – in the anonymous *Rhetoric to Herennius* and Cicero's *On Invention*. Building on this discussion, in Section IV I closely read Cato and Caesar's debate in Sallust's *War with Catiline*. This reading centers on the distinct arguments and traits of each speaker, and each speaker's relationship to aspects of Sallust's self-portrait and narrative. Drawing on this reading, I suggest in Sections V, VI, and VII that Sallust is not showing that conflict is incapable of resolution, per se, but rather that he is highlighting the need for antagonistic rhetoric. Through antagonistic rhetoric, the tensions of political life can be balanced and channeled, but not eliminated. Nor need they be eliminated, since these tensions – within proper boundaries – are the stuff of politics itself and a sign of vitality; they might, instead, be treated by political leaders engaged in the practice of antagonistic rhetoric.

II. REDESCRIPTION AND DELIBERATIVE ORATORY

My reading of Sallust's politics and rhetoric as antagonistic is informed by recent scholarship that explores antagonism and its role in the classical rhetorical tradition. Reacting to philosophers who have sought to banish or minimize the role of rhetoric in deliberation and reasoning, Allen and Garsten have sought to broaden the role of rhetoric in democratic theory. As opposed to theorists such as Hobbes and Habermas, who emphasize the importance of unanimity and unity, Allen argues that:

The real project of democracy is neither to perfect agreement nor to find some proxy for it, but to *maximize agreement while also attending to its dissonant remainders*: disagreement, disappointment, resentment, and all the other byproducts of political loss.[1]

---

[1] Allen, *Talking to Strangers*, 63.

Rhetoric is the method by which the byproducts of loss may be dealt with, as rhetoric (as opposed to sophistry) seeks to treat "distrust, and above all else" the rhetorician does "not wish to increase its reach and power."[2] The special usefulness of rhetoric, in this regard, is its ability "to work ... with negative emotions" and to develop goodwill, a positive disposition we can display even toward those with whom we are not friends.

In a similar vein, Garsten has argued that deliberation "does not have to be viewed as a means of constructing an authoritative and unitary public standard of reasonableness."[3] In making this argument, Garsten draws on the classical rhetorical tradition, and especially the writings of Aristotle and Cicero. For Garsten, deliberation ought to include "bringing to bear upon our choice whatever different sorts of knowledge and information seem relevant," and especially "particular and personal forms of knowledge and emotion."[4] Engagement with the particular fosters judgment, and draws individuals into deliberation. Indeed, appealing to the passions is part and parcel of good deliberation, as "passions play a constitutive role in the sort of practical reasoning that characterizes judgment."[5] So, too, do deliberation and the practice of judgment entail engaging with, though not necessarily reinforcing, "our existing opinions."[6] For both Allen and Garsten, then, the goal of political argument is not unanimity, per se, but finding a way to reach agreement, given plural and conflicting voices.

Despite the arguments of Allen and Garsten, and the potential for rhetoric to foster trust and to engage judgment, there is something disquieting about a key aspect of oratory, an aspect apparently well suited to sowing distrust: the seeming ease with which words change their meanings in the mouths of different speakers. This was a common rhetorical tactic – redescription – and it might be used in any of the genres of oratory, though it was quite important for the deliberative orator. Quintilian provides the following example of the figure: "When you call yourself ... brave instead of rash, economical instead of mean."[7] The device was used either to increase or decrease the apparent viciousness or virtuousness of a moral description.[8] If, for instance,

---

[2] Ibid., 92.
[3] Garsten, *Saving Persuasion*, 191–2.
[4] Ibid., 192.
[5] Ibid., 196.
[6] Ibid., 198.
[7] Quintilian, *Institutio Oratoria*, trans. H.E. Butler (Cambridge: Harvard University Press, 1963), 9.3.65.
[8] On this point, see Skinner, *Reason and Rhetoric in the Philosophy of Hobbes*, 139. In my analysis of redescription, I am indebted to and draw on Skinner's valuable discussion.

a speaker states the facts of a case in such a way that he moves the audience against his opponent – as Quintilian puts it, to "excite strong prejudice against us and made the facts seem worse than they are by the language which he has used" – one should not and cannot deny the facts altogether; rather, one should restate the facts "in a different way, alleging other motives and another purpose and putting a different complexion on the case."[9] He continues:

Some imputations we may mitigate by the use of other words; luxury will be softened down into generosity, avarice into economy, carelessness into simplicity.[10]

A skillful speaker could thus turn vice into virtue and virtue into vice; in doing so, he might turn his opponent's descriptions upside down and move his audience to his view.

That virtues might be confused with vices – and vices with virtues – seems reasonable – if troubling – in light of Aristotle's description of virtue and vice in the *Nicomachean Ethics*, a discussion that Skinner suggests is behind the tactic of redescription and merits further attention.[11] For Aristotle, a virtue of character "is a mean between two vices, one of excess and one of deficiency," yet it is not always the case that each vice is equally opposed to its respective virtue.[12] Indeed, on occasion one of the two vices opposed to a virtue may be closer to the virtue than the other. Aristotle gives the example of bravery: In this instance, the deficiency – cowardice – "is more opposed to bravery" than the excess, rashness.[13] By contrast, the excessive vice of intemperance is more opposed to the virtue of temperance than "insensibility, the deficiency."[14] Aristotle provides two reasons for this phenomenon, the first of which is that "sometimes one extreme is closer and more similar to the intermediate condition" – that is the virtue – and hence less blameworthy; by contrast, "what is further from the intermediate condition seems to be more contrary to it," and hence more blameworthy.[15] In addition, Aristotle suggests that we may have natural propensities toward one vice instead of the other, and we should thus regard the more natural extreme – for instance, cowardice or intemperance instead of rashness or

[9] Quintilian, *Institutio Oratoria*. 4.2.75–6.
[10] Ibid. 4.2.77.
[11] See Skinner, *Reason and Rhetoric in the Philosophy of Hobbes*, 153–4.
[12] Aristotle, *Nicomachean Ethics*, trans. Terrence Irwin (Indianapolis: Hackett, 1985), 1107a3.
[13] Ibid., 1109a3.
[14] Ibid., 1109a4.
[15] Ibid., 1109a6–11.

insensibility – as further from the intermediate virtue. Moderation serves as his example: "we have more of a natural tendency to pleasure," and thus "we drift more easily towards intemperance than towards orderliness."[16] Hence, intemperance is to be avoided more than insensibility.

If Aristotle argues in his *Nicomachean Ethics* that our conventional evaluations of virtue and vice display an understanding of the closer proximity – or greater distance – of particular vices to their related virtues, we certainly see him arguing that rhetoricians ought to use this proximity of virtue to vice to great purpose in his *Rhetoric*, in which he utilizes a framework similar to the *Nicomachean Ethics* when considering "excellence and vice, the noble and the base."[17] Both praise and blame are involved in the projection of *ethos*, and "finding out how to make our hearers take the required view of our own characters."[18] Though praise and blame are the subject matter of epideictic oratory, they are parts of deliberative and forensic oratory as well, as speakers in both genres might need to portray their own or others' characters well or poorly. Aristotle suggests that "when we wish either to praise a man or blame him," we may speak as if those "qualities closely allied to those which he actually has are identical with them," singling out caution, stupidity, and thick-skinnedness: "the cautious man is cold-blooded and treacherous ... the stupid man is an honest fellow or the thick-skinned man a good-tempered one."[19] Aristotle recognizes that anyone can be idealized if we "draw on the virtues akin to his actual qualities" – someone who is passionate is frank, for instance.[20] A person who displays another vice – namely, rashness – can be called courageous. Doing so is useful for speakers because it enables them to lead astray their audiences, drawing "a misleading inference from the motive, arguing that if a man runs into danger needlessly, much more will he do so in a noble cause."[21] A propensity to vice – foolhardiness – has been redescribed such that the same individual now has a propensity to virtue – in this instance, courage.

Aristotle was not, of course, the first to discuss the practice of arguing on both sides of an issue, or of redescribing virtues as vices. This is evident in

[16] Ibid., 1109a14–15.
[17] Aristotle, *Rhetoric*, trans. W. Rhys Roberts, ed. Jonathan Barnes, vol. II, *The Complete Works of Aristotle* (Princeton: Princeton University, 1984), 1366a23.
[18] Ibid., 1366a25–6.
[19] Ibid., 1367a33–6.
[20] Ibid., 1367a37.
[21] Ibid., 1367b4–5.

Plato's *Phaedrus*, in which he refers to those speaking before the law-courts and assemblies as engaging in the practice of "speaking in opposition to each other."[22] The same speaker will "make the same thing appear to the same people at one time just, but at any other time he wishes, unjust"; this was an important capacity for an orator, especially in the courts.[23] Yet while Plato seems quite comfortable with the practice in the *Phaedrus*, integral as it was to the true rhetorical art and indicative of the orator's underlying knowledge of virtue and vice, his attitude is far more cautious in the *Republic*. There, we see that words might shift in meanings for entirely different reasons. Whereas a skillful orator might redescribe actions or qualities to defeat his opponents, changes in meaning might be much further reaching than short-term rhetorical tactics, and be rooted in deeper changes and tendencies. In the turbulent soul of the democratic man, according to Plato, "beliefs and arguments that are lying imposters" jostle for prominence, displacing good arguments. Such arguments redescribe vices as virtues: "They praise them and give them fine names, calling arrogance 'good breeding,' anarchy 'freedom,' extravagance 'magnificence,' and shamelessness 'courage.'"[24] Confusion on such matters, and the transposition of values, results in moral corruption and decay, and not just steering one's audience in one direction or another.

A danger of redescription, then, was that it – if widespread, penetrating, and effecting or manifesting internal psychological transformations – might undermine conventional understandings of morality, or perhaps sever the connection between the honorable and the advantageous. After all, if a virtue became a vice, and a vice a virtue, what had once been dishonorable and disadvantageous might be transformed into the honorable and advantageous. This was precisely the phenomenon we saw occurring in Sallust's analysis of Rome, with corruption leading vicious individuals to pursue what they saw as their advantage rather than the common good. Rhetoric, in this vein, might even undermine the very trust it requires.

If, then, rhetoric has the potential to treat and channel social and political conflict, as it does for Allen and Garsten, the practice of rhetoric, and in particular the practice of redescription, may also have the potential to exacerbate conflict and to undermine consensus. Rhetoric can undermine dichotomies that seem firm, a process clearly illustrated in our exploration

---

[22] Plato, *Phaedrus*, trans. Christopher Rowe (Warminster: Aris and Phillips, 1986), 261c5.
[23] Ibid., 261c10.
[24] Plato, *Republic*, trans. C.D.C. Reeve (Indianapolis: Hackett, 2004), 560c3, e3–5.

of the transition from pre-corruption Rome (that is, Rome prior to the destruction of Carthage) to post-corruption Rome. Faced with such corruption, Sallust's Rome had lost the true meanings of words – "honor is not bestowed upon merit," he tells us in the *War with Jugurtha*; whereas in the past Romans strove to outdo their ancestors in virtue, in Sallust's time this striving is not in virtue but for "riches and extravagance."[25] Indeed, the monographs are replete with examples of confused and confusing values, in which a vice is renamed a virtue, and a virtue is renamed as a vice. The confusion is more striking given Sallust's depiction of what *seems* a morally clear Roman past.

Dichotomies had broken down, and values had been turned upside down with the corruption of Rome. What mattered most was the pursuit of desires, and as a result the youth of Rome "abandoned themselves the more recklessly to every means of gain as well as of extravagance."[26] The most powerful of these desires was *avaritia*, which taught Romans to "set a price on everything."[27] Preceding it was ambition, which, while a problematic desire, aimed at "glory, honor, and power," and drives men toward more noble actions than does avarice, which "renders the most manly body and soul effeminate."[28] Values in general were subverted: "virtue began to lose its luster, poverty to be considered a disgrace, blamelessness to be termed malevolence"; all were "thoughtless and reckless."[29] As opposed to the youths of Rome's past, the youth today are "habituated to evil practices."[30] It is as if they had been the victims of sophistic redescription, duped into pursuing what seems advantageous over what is actually honorable.

Ironically, though, Sallust himself is depicting and utilizing redescription in deploring Rome's ills; he manipulates the use of moral terms in the same way that an orator might, as do Cato and Caesar, each of whom Sallust identifies as virtuous. Nor is his past quite as clear as it seemed to be; we should recall that Sallust's Rome, even in its glorious past, did not lack conflict. Moreover, we found Sallust's early Romans to display different, but complementary, virtues in different domains: "boldness [*audacia*] in warfare and

---

[25] Sallust, *War with Jugurtha*, 3.1, 4.7.
[26] Sallust, *War with Catiline*, 13.5.
[27] Ibid., 10.4.
[28] Ibid., 11.1, 11.3.
[29] Ibid., 12.1–2.
[30] Ibid., 13.5.

justice [*aequitate*] when peace came."[31] Virtuous as they were, theirs was a virtue with multiple and complementary facets, operative in distinct spheres.

III. THE HONORABLE, THE ADVANTAGEOUS, AND DELIBERATIVE ORATORY

If, however, earlier Romans seemed to rightly grasp the relationship between the honorable and the advantageous, thus acting appropriately in different domains, matters were less clear in the time of Sallust. Indeed, this conflict – between the honorable and the advantageous – was pronounced in philosophical discussions occurring in Sallust's time.[32] May and Wisse note, for instance, that Cicero, in discussing the topics of the honorable and the advantageous in *On the Ideal Orator*, uses philosophical language given the salience of the issue in the philosophy of his day, a topic to which he devoted much of his *On Duties*.[33] The prior – the honorable – normally held pride of place for Cicero and Quintilian; Cicero and Quintilian do, as Cox notes, occasionally allow that "considerations of *utile* may outweigh the *honestum*," but this is due to "a regrettable concession to debased popular values … or as a short-term measure uneasily justified by the pursuit of an ultimately honorable end."[34] Even if Cicero's eloquent individual was not necessarily a good man skilled in speaking (*vir bonus dicendi peritus*), as was Quintilian's (and Cato the Elder's), Cicero, like Quintilian, elevated the honorable over the advantageous in deliberative rhetoric.[35]

The conflict, real or potential, between honor and advantage lent structure and import to the practice of deliberative oratory. Those faced with choosing a course of action – the subject matter of deliberative oratory – needed to balance honor and expediency given the circumstances. The most famous oratory found in Sallust's works is deliberative: the debate

---

[31] Ibid., 9.3.
[32] On this point, see Virginia Cox, "Machiavelli and the *Rhetorica Ad Herennium*: Deliberative Rhetoric in *The Prince*," *The Sixteenth Century Journal* XXVIII, no. 4 (1997), 1113.
[33] Cicero, *On the Ideal Orator*, p. 214, n. 323.
[34] Cox, "Machiavelli and the *Rhetorica Ad Herennium*: Deliberative Rhetoric in *The Prince*," 1114.
[35] Cf. M. Winterbottom, "Quintilian and the *Vir Bonus*," *The Journal of Roman Studies* 54 (1964): 90–7. On the difference between Cicero and Quintilian on this point, see Anton D. Leeman, Harm Pinkster, and Jakob Wisse, *M. Tullius Cicero, De Oratore Libri III: Kommentar*, vol. 4 (Heidelberg: C. Winter, 1981), 200–1.

between Cato and Caesar. Their argument, in part, involves the relationship between what is honorable and what is advantageous, and how to proceed given clashing understandings. Given this, it is useful to read this debate with two first-century BCE works of rhetoric in mind: Cicero's early work, *On Invention*, and the anonymous *Rhetoric to Herennius*. Cicero's *On Invention*, is, in many respects, similar to the *Rhetoric to Herennius*. There are, however, some important differences, as we shall see – namely, the *Rhetoric to Herennius* is more pragmatic toward the honorable and does not clearly locate the honorable above the advantageous.

Cicero, in *On Invention*, argues that the aims of deliberative oratory are twofold: "honor and advantage," *honestas* and *utilitas*.[36] In the prior category are two classes of goods – those which possess "intrinsic merit," which he labels the *honestum*, as well as a mixed class, which "by its own merit and worth entices us and leads us on, and also holds out to us a prospect of some advantage to induce us to seek it more eagerly."[37] Though the latter class is complex and includes elements of both *honestas* and *utilitas* in its ends, Cicero assimilates it to the honorable because it possesses honorable elements. The advantageous – "to be sought not because of its own merit and natural goodness, but because of some profit or advantage to be derived from it" – is the other end of deliberative oratory.[38] Thus, the deliberative orator, in urging the choice of a policy, may argue on the basis of honor, advantage, or a combination of the two.

The honorable consists of four kinds of virtue, which Cicero defines as "a habit of mind in harmony with reason and the order of nature"; it includes prudence, justice, fortitude, and temperance (*prudentia, iustitia, fortitudo,* and *temperantia*).[39] By arguing that one's policy displayed these properties, one might win the agreement of one's audience. As we have seen Aristotle argue, Cicero notes that the deliberative orator ought to avoid not only the opposites of these virtues, but also those vices that seem to be virtues. He explains:

each virtue will be found to have a vice bordering upon it, either one to which a definite name has become attached, as temerity which borders on courage, or stubbornness, which borders on perseverance, or superstition which is akin to religion.[40]

[36] Cicero, *De Inventione*, 2.156.
[37] Ibid., 2.157.
[38] Ibid., 2.157.
[39] Ibid., 2.159.
[40] Ibid., 2.165.

Despite the apparent clarity of Cicero's analysis – for instance, he notes in discussing necessity that nothing is more necessary than "doing what is honorable" – Cicero argues that virtue and vice need not always be clear-cut.[41] Thus, he discusses *affectio*, which he defines as a "change in the aspect of things due to time, or the result of actions or their management, or to the interests and desires of men."[42] When this occurs, and when it is reflected in deliberative oratory, we see that "things should not be regarded in the same light as they have been or have generally been regarded."[43] Instead, we must pay attention to particulars – thus it is normally vicious to go over to the enemy, but it was not so when done by Odysseus. Nevertheless, Cicero emphasizes that security should be subordinated to virtue, unless one can regain honor by temporarily turning to security. When this cannot occur, "one should take thought for honor." Moreover, Cicero links security to honor, arguing that "without security we can never attain to honor."[44]

In the anonymous *Rhetoric to Herennius*, we see a more pragmatic attitude to the honorable and the advantageous than Cicero takes. The work's author, for instance, takes a wary stance towards utilizing *sententiae* in speeches.[45] Such maxims, he suggests, should be approached with some caution: "We should insert maxims only rarely, that we may be looked upon as pleading the case, not preaching morals."[46] Whereas *On Invention* 2.169 clearly places honor above security, the *Rhetoric to Herennius* does not. And what counts as security (*tuta*) for the author of *Herennius* includes both *vis* and *dolus* – that is, force and fraud.[47]

As with *On Invention*, redescription features in the *Rhetoric to Herennius'* discussion of deliberative oratory. With deliberative oratory, and indeed oratory in general, not only must the orator be capable of discussing "those matters which law and custom have fixed for the uses of citizenship," but he must be able to lead his auditors to agree with him. For the deliberative orator, this task entails "the discussion of policy and embraces

---

[41] Ibid., 2.173.

[42] Ibid., 2.176.

[43] Ibid., 2.176.

[44] Ibid., 2.174.

[45] A *sententia* is "a saying drawn from life, which shows concisely either what happens or ought to happen in life." *Ad C. Herennium De Ratione Dicendi*, trans. Harry Caplan (Cambridge: Harvard University Press, 1964). 4.17.24. On this point, see Cox, "Machiavelli and the *Rhetorica Ad Herennium*: Deliberative Rhetoric in *The Prince*," 1117.

[46] *Ad C. Herennium De Ratione Dicendi*, 4.17.25.

[47] Ibid., 3.2.3.

persuasion and dissuasion."[48] In persuading an audience engaged in deliberation, the orator deals with questions of choosing one of two policies,
or one of many policies; his aim is *utilitas* – advantage. What is useful has
two components – security (*tuta*) and the honorable (*honestas*). The prior
topic may be divided into two categories: force (*vis*) and fraud (*dolus*). The
latter may also be divided into two categories: the right (*rectus*) and the
laudable (*laudabilis*). If one's topic is security, one's goal "is to provide some
plan or other for ensuring the avoidance of a present or imminent danger";
considerations of *vis* include "armies, fleets, arms, engines of war, recruit-
ing of manpower," while considerations of *dolus* include "money, promises,
dissimulation, accelerated speed, deception."[49] The right, by contrast, which
is "done in accord with Virtue and Duty," entails "Wisdom, Justice, Courage,
and Temperance."[50] The praiseworthy emphasizes that a policy "produces an
honorable remembrance, at the time of the event and afterwards."[51] Each
entails specific commonplaces: Wisdom involves the use of historical precedent, for instance, while justice emphasizes that "we shall demonstrate that
an action of which we are sponsors in Assembly or council is just."[52]

Just as the orator must be able to amplify the virtues he is recom-
mending, he must also be able to deprecate them if "urging that they be
disregarded."[53] The orator cannot, of course, "propose the abandonment of
virtue" – one cannot advocate vice outright.[54] But the orator might argue,
for instance, "that the virtue consists rather of qualities contrary to those
here evinced." He provides examples, illustrating the tactic of redescription:

what our opponent calls justice is cowardice, and sloth, and perverse generosity;
what he has called wisdom we shall term impertinent, babbling, and offensive
cleverness; what he declares to be temperance we shall declare to be inaction
and lax indifference; what he has named courage we shall term the reckless
temerity of a gladiator.[55]

If one was arguing for a policy by means of security (*tuta*), one needed to
be able to deprecate the virtues emphasized by one's opponent; similarly,

[48] Ibid., 1.2.2.
[49] Ibid., 3.2.3.
[50] Ibid. 3.2.3.
[51] Ibid., 3.4.7.
[52] Ibid., 3.3.4.
[53] Ibid., 3.3.6.
[54] Ibid., 3.3.6.
[55] Ibid., 3.3.6.

if one was arguing for a policy by means of the honorable (*honestas*), one needed to be able to argue that what was in fact useful was the honorable.

IV. CATO, CAESAR, AND REDESCRIPTION

A sign of confusion and decay – namely, widespread changes in evaluative language and the relabeling of virtues as vices (and vices as virtues) – was also a perfectly normal component of effective argument. This was especially the case when the issue was the status of the honorable and the advantageous, as it was in deliberative oratory. This lent itself to the blurring, or to the appreciation of blurred, virtues and vices. What differentiates the tactic from the wider social phenomenon? We can say that while a clever orator might blur the distinctions between vice and virtue in a particular case, or for a particular purpose, such behavior is relatively innocuous. After all, the orator presumably knows what she is doing, and she is doing it for a particular purpose; moreover, such speech is not likely to lead to far-reaching social and political change, but rather responds to the dictates of convincing particular audiences. By contrast, the kinds of social transformations that lead to wide-ranging and unconscious shifts in the meaning of moral words are more dangerous because they are less the product of deliberate action than they are the results of social decay and symptomatic of broader societal corruption.

Sallust's own times and the recent past are marked by the kind of confusion that redescription might cause *or* resolve, insofar as it might rectify confused language. Into this confusion step two speakers – Cato and Caesar – arguing opposite sides of an issue, each trying to persuade the Senate of a course of action, while at the same time trying to describe persuasively a particular set of actions and policy options. In this debate, we observe one speaker – Caesar – arguing for flexibility and mercy in dealing with Catiline and his conspirators, and the other – Cato – arguing for severity and inflexibility. Caesar's speech will, on the face of it, emphasize the honorable, though giving attention to the advantageous; Cato's, by contrast, will seem to center on the advantageous, though also giving attention to the honorable. They are deliberative speeches – that is, they are delivered to a decision-making body that must make decisions, based on these speeches, concerning future events with uncertain outcomes. In this regard, Cato and Caesar's speeches will echo what we saw in *On Invention* and the *Rhetoric to Herennius*; Cato's, in particular, echoes the latter. Each speaker will also echo Sallust's own words, further highlighting the uncertainty and ambiguity involved in making a decision based on deliberative oratory.

Caesar's speech echoes Sallust's own narrative and historical predilections. Caesar urges that those who deliberate on difficult matters must not be moved by hatred, friendship, anger, or pity – *odio, amicitia, ira,* or *misericordia*.[56] In doing so, he, like Thucydides' Diodotus, seeks "to smooth the waves of emotional tension and to introduce an atmosphere of cool and rational objectivity."[57] We have also seen that Sallust holds his qualification for writing to be a function of the fact that his mind "was free from hope, and fear, and partisanship [*spe, metu, partibus rei publicae animus liber erat*]."[58] Caesar's advice thus reflects a part of Sallust's self-depiction. Caesar's rightly deliberating individual, like Sallust's rightly acting individual and historian, must be able to look beyond mere passion, since "no mortal man has ever served at the same time his passions [*lubidini*] and his best interests [*usui*]."[59] By contrast, "When you apply your intellect, it prevails; if passion possesses you, it holds sway, and the mind is impotent" – again, Caesar's language echoes Sallust's at 2.5–6.[60]

To bolster his case, which entails inflicting a lesser punishment than might be inflicted – and hence his preferred virtue of clemency – Caesar points to several prior examples of Romans behaving less harshly than they might have – acting *contra lubidinem,* against their passion – in dealing with Rhodes's desertion of Rome during the war with Perses, and its relatively lenient treatment of Carthage during the Punic Wars.[61] Caesar frames the issue thus: Just as Romans, in the past, had acted less harshly than they might have to protect their dignity, so too should the Senate, to protect its dignity (*vostra dignitas*), act less harshly than it might.[62] This also echoes Sallust's earlier narrative, especially 9.1.

Caesar in his argument, then, invokes a value – *dignitas* – associated with the Senate's self-conception. Less legality than decorum is the issue;

---

[56] Sallust, *War with Catiline,* 51.1.
[57] McGushin, *Bellum Catilinae: A Commentary,* 40. Cf. Thucydides, *History of the Peloponnesian War,* 3.42.4.
[58] Sallust, *War with Catiline,* 4.2.
[59] Ibid., 51.2.
[60] Ibid., 51.3.
[61] On clemency, see David Konstan, "Clemency as a Virtue," *Classical Philology* 100 (2005): 337–446.
[62] Sallust, *War with Catiline,* 51.7.

though the Senate might legally have ordered the conspirators executed, such an action did not fit their stature, as it is more seemly to be merciful.[63] Moreover, Caesar argues that "those who hold great power" – in this case, the Senate – have little freedom when it comes to punishing the conspirators, as anger-inspired behavior was sure to attract negative attention and provide a bad example; for such men, "neither partiality nor dislike is in place, and anger least of all."[64] Here, Caesar again echoes Sallust's own language of being free from partiality or animus. For those without power, strong actions might simply be ascribed to *iracundia*; to those with power, it would be called *superbia* and *crudelitas*, vices that bring especially ill repute to those with power.[65]

The proposal of Silanus, then, who had urged that the conspirators in custody and at large be executed, was "foreign to the customs of our country," for Caesar – a "novel form of punishment" (*genus poenae novum*).[66] Beyond this, putting to death the conspirators was not much of a punishment at all: Death "puts an end to all mortal ills and leaves no room either for sorrow or for joy."[67] This is an Epicurean comment: Caesar is denying the existence of an afterlife, perhaps, suggests McGushin, because he was "counting on the Epicurean beliefs of many of the Roman upper classes."[68]

Precedent speaks to leniency; the disposition driving the Senate – anger – is inappropriate when deliberating, given that emotion should not factor into such decisions concerning matters of interest. Moreover, death itself is an insufficient punishment – to this Caesar adds the claim that were the Senate to punish the conspirators by death, a dangerous precedent would be set for "when the control of the government falls into the hands of men who are incompetent or bad."[69] Caesar musters precedents here as well: he cites the rule of the Thirty Tyrants in Athens, who at first only killed "the most wicked and generally hated citizens," but soon "slew good and bad alike at pleasure and intimidated the rest."[70] So, too, had Sulla's execution of "Damasippus and others of that kind" been celebrated; afterwards, however,

---

[63] On this point, see also Cicero, *On Duties*, 1.88.
[64] Sallust, *War with Catiline*, 51.13–14.
[65] Ibid., 51.14.
[66] Ibid., 51.17–8.
[67] Ibid., 51.20.
[68] McGushin, *Bellum Catilinae: A Commentary*, 249. Cf. Lucretius, *De Rerum Natura*, trans. W.H.D. Rouse (Cambridge: Harvard University Press, 1992). 3.670–1107.
[69] Sallust, *War with Catiline*, 51.27.
[70] Ibid., 51.29–30.

more and indiscriminate bloodshed followed, and "those who had exulted in the death of Damasippus were themselves before long hurried off to execution, and the massacre did not end until Sulla glutted all his followers with riches."[71] In short, the killing of the conspirators would prove to be not simply indecorous, but inexpedient, as it would likely harm the state in the future. Caesar exalts the wisdom of earlier Romans, and in particular the Porcian law, which allowed those condemned "the alternative of exile" – those who had passed that law were also those "who from slight resources created this mighty empire," certainly more virtuous and wise (*virtus atque sapientia maior*) than those "who can barely hold what they gloriously won."[72] Caesar concludes by suggesting that the conspirators be imprisoned, and that their case be considered closed. Caesar's argument is thus two-pronged: the execution would be both beneath the Senate's stature and disadvantageous, and not in keeping with the *mos maiorum*. And Caesar, as we have seen, echoes Sallust's own narration, as well as an aspect of Roman virtues of old.

If Caesar's speech is designed to calm, Cato's, like Cleon's in Thucydides' *History*, is designed to inflame.[73] Cato's speech, in contrast to Caesar's measured tone, centers from the beginning on the dangers (*pericula*) of the situation. In addition, Cato seeks to transfer the issue from one of punishment (*poena*) – and justice – to one of anticipating future harms.[74] The issue for Cato is thus *tuta* – security – and not *honestas*, per se. Cato's tactic, then, is similar to that of Diodotus in Thucydides' *History*: Each seems to emphasize security over the honorable in recognition of their respective audience's priorities.[75] Cato personalizes – in a pointed way – the nature of this danger to his audience, "who have always valued your houses, villas, statues, and paintings more highly than your country."[76] Should they wish to keep their goods, it was necessary for them to act, since "our lives and liberty are at stake;" he thus portrays vividly the dangers they face, evoking the emotion of fear, important in Sallust's own account, as we have seen.[77]

---

[71] Ibid., 51.32, 34. See McGushin, *Bellum Catilinae: A Commentary*, 252.
[72] Sallust, *War with Catiline*, 51.40, 42.
[73] Cf. Thucydides, *History of the Peloponnesian War*, 3.40.7.
[74] Sallust, *War with Catiline*, 52.2–3.
[75] Diodotus suggests that due to the political climate of Athens, "the state is put into a unique position; it is only she to whom no one can ever do a good turn openly and without deception." Thucydides, *History of the Peloponnesian War*, 3.43.
[76] Sallust, *War with Catiline*, 52.5.
[77] Ibid., 52.6.

Cato notes that he has often criticized Rome's luxury and avarice – *luxuria atque avaritia* – just as Sallust has in his own voice; like Sallust, who depicts himself as victimized for his moralism, Cato in deploring these vices has brought much hostility to himself.[78] His criticisms had then fallen on deaf ears, as "the state was unshaken; its prosperity made good your neglect."[79] In the present context, however, the state is in danger, and it is even more shocking that someone (*quisquam*, which is to say Caesar) speaks of *mansuetudo* and *misericordia* – mercy and pity.[80] Yet according to Cato, "we have long since lost the true names for things" – *vera vocabula rerum amisimus*; he again echoes Sallust's own voice in noting the corruption of Rome's moral vocabulary.[81] Cato describes the problem thus:

It is precisely because squandering the goods of others is called generosity [*liberalitas*], and recklessness in wrong doing is called courage [*fortitudo*], that the republic is reduced to such extremities.[82]

People have misapplied names; values have been inverted. He thus describes the breakdown of dichotomies, which we encountered in Sallust's voice in the prior chapter. For Cato, those who misuse language may desire to "be liberal [*liberales*] at the expense of our allies," and to "be merciful [*misericordes*] to the plunderers of the treasury," but this is both dangerous and misguided[83] – he again echoes Sallust at 12.1 and 38.3. To display such merciful behavior toward the conspirators, however, would "bring ruin upon all good men."[84]

The speech comes to a crescendo as Cato extols vigor to counter the ferocious enemy (*feroces*).[85] He follows this exhortation with an analysis of the strengths of Rome's ancestors and the difference between past and present. Earlier Romans possessed "efficiency at home, a just rule abroad, in counsel an independent spirit free from guilt or passion"; the passage echoes Sallust's voice at 9.3.[86] Cato is thus suggesting that Caesar's analysis

---

[78] Ibid., 52.7.
[79] Ibid., 52.9.
[80] Ibid., 52.11.
[81] Ibid., 52.11.
[82] Ibid., 52.11.
[83] Ibid., 52.12.
[84] Ibid., 52.12.
[85] Ibid., 52.18.
[86] Ibid., 52.21.

of the *mos maiorum* was in error, and that far from adhering to tradition, his contemporaries have turned things upside down: "In place of these we have extravagance and greed, public poverty and private opulence" – the transposition of values echoes Sallust's own analysis of Rome at, for instance, 10.4.[87] The reason for this is, in part, the vice of his audience: "each of you schemes for his own private interests ... you are slaves to pleasure in your homes and to money or influence here."[88]

In his peroration, Cato chastises the Senate for its *mansuetudo* and *misericordia*, which will bring misery; misunderstood and misdescribed qualities bring with them suffering, not success.[89] Such dispositions, while virtues in normal circumstances, are not in this instance – they neglect the reality of things, and reflect the corruption of language rather than prudence. In such a situation, what is called for is neither "vows nor womanish entreaties"; rather, what is called for is "watchfulness, vigorous action, and wisdom in counsel" – virtues which echo the warlike virtues of earlier Romans at 6.4– 6.7 and 9.3.[90] Cato's *exemplum* affirms this: "[Titus] Manlius Torquatus, while warring with the Gauls, ordered the execution of his own son, because he had fought against the enemy contrary to orders, and the gallant young man paid the penalty for too great valor with his life."[91] As Levene notes, the example was not normally cited for emulation; yet Sallust himself cites it as a positive example at 9.4.[92]

The speech concludes by emphasizing the danger the Senate faces, again deploying fear: *undique circumventi sumus* – we are surrounded on all sides.[93] Stressing the immediacy of this danger, as well as the wickedness of those involved (*sceleratorum*), Cato urges that "those who have confessed be treated as though they had been caught red-handed in capital offenses, and be punished after the manner of our forefathers."[94] Fear, and the importance of attaining security, are central to Cato's speech. And Cato, like Caesar, echoes Sallust's narrative and persona, seeming also to embody an aspect of Rome's past – boldness in war as opposed to Caesar's justice in peace.

[87] Ibid., 52.22.
[88] Ibid., 52.23.
[89] Ibid., 52.27.
[90] Ibid., 52.29.
[91] Ibid., 52.30–1. This, Cato's sole *exemplum*, is an error on Sallust's part, according to McGushin. McGushin, *Bellum Catilinae: A Commentary*, 266.
[92] Levene, "Sallust's Catiline and Cato the Censor," 185.
[93] Sallust, *War with Catiline*, 52.35.
[94] Ibid., 52.36.

V. THE SYNKRISIS

Following his presentation of the speeches, Sallust next turns to a comparison of Cato and Caesar's virtues, the synkrisis.[95] Cato, whose proposal wins the day, is praised for his *virtutem animi* – his greatness of spirit – and was held *clarus atque magnus* – distinguished and great.[96] This leads Sallust to want to find "out what quality in particular had been the foundation of so great exploits" that featured in Roman history.[97] His summary of Rome's history echoes his discussion of pre-corruption Rome (6–13):

with a handful of men they had encountered great armies of the enemy ... with small resources they had waged wars with mighty kings ... they had often experienced the cruelty of Fortune ... the Romans had been surpassed by the Greeks in eloquence and by the Gauls in warlike glory.[98]

What, then, had brought about Rome's distinguished deeds (*praeclara facinora*)? The answer, for Sallust, is "the eminent merit of a few citizens" – *paucorum civium egregiam virtutem*.[99] In its growth, then, individual virtues were paramount.

This seems a departure from Cicero, whose ambiguous relationship to Sallust we encountered in the last chapter. In Book 2 of *On the Commonwealth*, Cicero attributed to Scipio a statement that echoed the elder Cato:

the organization of our state surpassed all others for this reason: in others there were generally single individuals who had set up the laws and institutions of their commonwealths – Minos in Crete, Lycurgus in Sparta, and in Athens which frequently changed its government, first Theseus, then Draco, then Solon, then Cleisthenes, then many others ... Our commonwealth, in contrast, was not shaped by one man's talent but by that of many; and not in one person's lifetime, but over many generations. He said that there never was a genius so great that he could miss nothing, nor could all the geniuses in the world

[95] Batstone defines the device of synkrisis: "Essentially agonistic, it is used for competitive comparison and to praise or blame. It is said to reveal or illustrate δεικνύναι, a judgment, and consequently it makes explicit the terms of that judgment." William W. Batstone, "The Antithesis of Virtue: Sallust's *Synkrisis* and the Crisis of the Late Republic," *Classical Antiquity* 7, no. 1 (1988): 1–29, 3.

[96] Sallust, *War with Catiline*, 53.1.

[97] Ibid., 53.2.

[98] Ibid., 53.3.

[99] Ibid., 53.4.

brought together in one place at one time foresee all contingencies without the practical experience afforded by the passage of time.[100]

Rome lacked the single, wise lawgiver so valued by many ancients. As Zetzel notes, "Scipio/Cato here makes a virtue of the haphazard growth of the Roman constitution, in contrast to the systematic but imperfect work of single lawgivers"; he differs from Polybius who praised Rome's constitution, but placed it below Lycurgus' Sparta.[101]

That being said, Cicero's account of Rome's history under the kings seems both to demonstrate and *not* to demonstrate his claims about Rome's collective growth. To be sure, individual kings add to the work of their predecessors, leading to a piecemeal development by incremental adjustment – in showing how "our commonwealth ... is born, grows up, and comes of age," he seems to show the truth of Cato's claim.[102] Yet in focusing on the role of *particular* kings – that is to say, outstanding individuals – Cicero does not neglect the role of individual greatness, or of particular individuals. Thus, Romulus, because of his glory, founded Rome itself, and his "exceptional foresight" is evident in his choice of location: A non-maritime city was both easier to defend from aggressors and less liable to "corruption and alteration of character."[103] Romulus, in choosing Rome's location, then, brought the benefits of its proximity to the coast without the harms, and Rome's very location made it well suited to being the "center of the greatest empire."[104] Romulus, too, was responsible for increasing Rome's resources and size through orchestrating the seizure of the Sabine women – "the mark of a great man who looked far into the future."[105] He echoes the wisdom of Lycurgus in creating the "Fathers," as cities "are guided and ruled better under the sole power of a king if the authority of the most responsible citizens is added to the monarch's absolute rule";[106] with the Fathers in place, Romulus waged much warfare, enriching his citizens, and not himself. Romulus also showed great wisdom in his attention to auspices and his creation of the augurs.

---

[100] Cicero, *On the Commonwealth*. 2.2.
[101] Cicero, *De Re Publica: Selections*, ed. James E.G. Zetzel (Cambridge: Cambridge University Press, 1995), 159. See Polybius, *The Histories*. 6.10.12–14.
[102] Cicero, *On the Commonwealth*, 2.3.
[103] Ibid., 2.7.
[104] Ibid., 2.10.
[105] Ibid., 2.12.
[106] Ibid., 2.15.

Romulus' successor was Numa Pompilius; he saw that "the men of Rome, under Romulus' instruction, were inflamed with eagerness for war," and chose to diminish this by giving them "a love of tranquility and peace [*otii et pacis*], through which justice and trust are most easily strengthened," as well as the art of agriculture, by which the Romans might produce what they had heretofore attained by plunder.[107] Numa also gave great attention to religion, mollifying "minds that were inflamed with the habit and the desire for making war."[108] It was he, then, who "restored to human and gentle behavior the minds of men who had become savage and inhuman through their love of war."[109] Because of his wisdom, his rule was marked by "great peace and harmony" – *in pace concordiaque*, just as he brought them a love of peace and tranquility.[110] All of this would have been difficult to achieve had they remained in their savage state; Rome could only be marked by justice and faith if the negative effects of war were ameliorated.

Rome's origins and growth were, then, a collective enterprise for Cicero. The kings were different in character, but complementary, mutually contributing to Rome's greatness through the productive tension existing between their attributes and actions. In Sallust's estimation, gone is the collective enterprise of Cicero's *On the Commonwealth*, or so it seems: Cicero relied upon the complementary actions of the *few*. Rome was made great by the few who were great, and the few, as we have seen, are ambitious and competitive, though, for Sallust, neither ambition nor competitiveness is a problem so long as they are rightly directed. Yet these outstanding few were incomplete in themselves, requiring each other and different modes of virtue: Greatness emerges through rightly directed difference.

Once Rome had been corrupted by luxury and sloth, "it was the commonwealth in its turn that was enabled by its greatness to sustain the shortcomings of its generals and magistrates" – but Rome produced for some time no one of great virtue (*virtute magnus*).[111] In his own memory (*memoria mea*), however, there were two such men – *ingenti virtute, divorsis moribus* – of great virtue, and of diverse character: Cato and Caesar.[112] They were equal in many ways – birth, age, eloquence, greatness of spirit, even fame – but the

---

[107] Ibid., 2.26.
[108] Ibid., 2.25.
[109] Ibid., 2.27.
[110] Ibid., 2.27.
[111] Sallust, *War with Catiline*, 53.5.
[112] Ibid., 53.6.

difference lay in the source of their *gloria*. Caesar is characterized by *beneficiis ac munificentia magnus, mansuetudine et misericordia* – his willingness to grant benefits, his munificence, his mildness, his compassion – he was similarly characterized at 49.3 as displaying great generosity (*egregia liberalitate*); Cato is characterized by *integritate vitae*, and *severitas* – integrity of life and severity. For Sallust, "Caesar gained glory by giving, helping, and forgiving; Cato by never stooping to bribery."[113] Both attain glory by their virtues, as Sallust suggests one ought to do at 1.3. The behaviors are not antithetical; indeed, they could be complementary. Caesar was praised for his *facilitas* – his easy-going character; Cato was praised for his *constantia* – his constancy.[114] Again, there is no *necessary* conflict in these attributes.

Caesar "had schooled himself to work hard and sleep little, to devote himself to the welfare of his friends and neglect his own, to refuse nothing which was worth the giving"; he wanted *magnum imperium* – a great command – as well as an army and a *bellum novom* – that is, "a war begun by himself and for which he had sole responsibility."[115] Cato, however, pursued *modestia, decorum,* and *severitas*. He did not pursue wealth with the wealthy or intrigue with intriguers; he vied "with the active in good works, with the self-restrained in moderation, with the blameless in dignity," like the Romans of old.[116] To sum it up: "He preferred to be, rather than to seem, virtuous; hence the less he sought fame, the more it pursued him."[117] It is important to note here that Sallust does *not* say that Caesar preferred fame to virtue, or appearance to reality; indeed, he ascribes to Caesar his own set of virtues, different from, but complementary to, Cato, just as Romulus and Numa were different but complementary.

VI. ANTAGONISM AND RHETORIC

Caesar and Cato both aim at victory in argument. They seek to move the Senate to their position, persuading them that their recommended policy is advantageous. In his victory, Cato restores distinctions, and does so in a way that seems to echo Sallust's own analysis of the turmoil of Roman moral

---

[113] Ibid., 54.1–3.
[114] Ibid., 54.3.
[115] Ibid., 54.4.
[116] Ibid., 54.5–6, cf. 7.6–7.
[117] Ibid., 54.6.

language; he even hones in on the same causes and symptoms as Sallust. Yet Caesar, too, echoes Sallust's analysis. Both, indeed, seem to embody not just an aspect of Sallust, but also a distinct component of Roman virtue of old. As Syme put it:

Caesar and Cato were divergent in conduct, principles, and allegiance. Their qualities could be regarded as complementary no less than antithetic. In alliance the two had what was needed to save the Republic. That may be what the historian is gently suggesting.[118]

For Syme, however, their virtues are distinct "Caesar was splendid and lavish, clement and forgiving; but Cato, austere and inflexible, gave no favors."[119] It would appear that they, together, embody precisely the mix of virtues that characterized early Rome, albeit in sharply delineated spheres. We might note as well that Rome's first two kings – Romulus and Numa – were both outstanding individuals, though their particular virtues and contributions to Rome were quite distinct.

Batstone goes somewhat further, arguing that Sallust does not suggest a solution so much as a conceptual failure, and insofar as "Sallust offers no mutually exclusive antitheses or comparisons" in his presentation of Caesar and Cato, he "avoids the kind of divisions that create intellectually secure boundaries."[120] That is to say, except for "*severitas* opposing *misericordia* at 54.2" – the prior applied to Cato, the latter to Caesar – the contrasts between Caesar and Cato are not between mutually exclusive attributes.[121] The attributes may even be complementary, but each set of attributes represented a possible path to glory and distinction.

Batstone suggests that Sallust reveals "the cynicism and the conflict of forces which thwarted both virtue itself and the understanding and evaluation of apparent virtue."[122] Both Cato and Caesar were virtuous, and their particular displays of virtue are not antithetical. The *synkrisis* is meant to confuse, and to illustrate the difficulty of judging their respective characters, each of which had merit. Disagreement was too widespread even to agree on a moral vocabulary.

---

[118] Syme, *Sallust*, 120.
[119] Ibid., 114.
[120] Batstone, "The Antithesis of Virtue: Sallust's *Synkrisis* and the Crisis of the Late Republic," 6, 7.
[121] Ibid., 6.
[122] Ibid., 28.

But this is not the only way to think about the dissonance of the speeches and the *synkrisis*. Both Cato and Caesar seem to embody not just an aspect of Rome's ancestors, but of Sallust himself. They are antagonistic in action and quality, yes, but they are not opposites, per se. Perhaps the issue is not cynicism but rather the great complexity of moral and political life in the face of disagreement and discord; Sallust's conception of the community is certainly antagonistic, as we saw in the prior chapter. Such seemingly secure boundaries as there were stemmed from fear, and competitive energies swirled beneath Rome's surface of *concordia*.

Cato and Caesar's present is, to be sure, contested, just as history itself could be contested – each has his own understanding of Rome's past. Events might be remembered differently and interpreted differently, depending on the situation: Connolly points to Antonius' discussion of his defense of Norbanus in *On the Ideal Orator*, where he argued that not all discord was bad, and that some was both just and necessary. The incident is of interest precisely because Antonius engages in redescription to defend Norbanus from the charge of sedition; indeed, earlier in the narrative Crassus suggested that Antonius had sought "to glorify sedition itself."[123] Antonius describes his speech thus:

I surveyed all types of sedition, the harm they did and their dangers, and in this account I traced these through the whole eventful history of our State, concluding that, though all instance of sedition had always been troublesome, some of them, nevertheless, had been justified and almost necessary.[124]

Antonius noted that without sedition, the kings would not have been expelled, there would be no tribunate, and no *provocatio*.

Conflict, then, served a key purpose in Rome's development. The origin of Rome's liberties was a story of conflict: the conflict between the Tarquins and Rome's early elites, and then the Conflict of the Orders.[125] Even Rome's founding was rooted in conflict – Romulus' killing of his brother. Central to the politics of the republic, an effort to secure harmony, was discord, and one thing that rhetoric sought to do, insofar as it was "a rationally organized system," was to find resolutions to the antagonism of the republic:

[123] Cicero, *On the Ideal Orator*, 2.124.
[124] Ibid., 2.199.
[125] I discuss the Conflict of the Orders in the next chapter.

"the antagonism baked into its earliest memories, the antagonism of competition among the ruling class and between rulers and ruled."[126] As Connolly puts it – with respect to the *Rhetoric to Herennius* and *On Invention* – "Both treatises foreground the capacity of language to resolve disputes that could otherwise divide and damage the political community."[127]

In effect, so, too, does the debate between Cato and Caesar. Through their debate, Cato and Caesar guide their audience to decision. The goal in making a decision, in this instance, is not unanimity, but some kind of consensus, and the practice of rhetoric is able to achieve precisely such an end. In doing so, rhetoric helps to maintain community, bringing together different elements of the Roman community and character. This maintenance is contingent and impermanent, however, and it must be practiced again and again by outstanding individuals who, in competitive political action, embody and enact different aspects of Rome itself.

VII. CONCLUSION

The debate between Cato and Caesar is, in effect, a vivid representation of the problems inherent not just in the practice of rhetoric, but in a community like Rome, composed of different, conflicting, yet complementary individuals and groups. If the agreement of the past was partly a function of external pressures on centrifugal elements of Roman society, maintaining stable distinctions between virtue and vice might depend on external elements that might check the passionate disagreement of Roman social forces. In this sense, with the presence of a new enemy – Catiline – Cato can restore the meanings of words that have been lost. The irony is that while distinctions between friend and enemy seem to be more clear-cut in warfare, Rome's internal enemy – and especially Catiline's army – displays particularly Roman qualities: The wounds of Catiline's troops were on the front of their bodies, or they fell where they fought.[128] Rome's enemy was Roman to the core. As Levene puts it, "a genuine threat to the life of Rome has to meet a firm response. Catiline is that threat, as Carthage was before him: Removing that threat removes the moral order that made such

[126] Connolly, *The State of Speech*, 73.
[127] Ibid., 72.
[128] Sallust, *War with Catiline*, 61.1–6.

a victory possible in the first place, and instead allows Rome to accelerate into further disaster."[129] But this problem also highlights the necessity of the practice of antagonistic rhetoric. Cato restores order in *this* instance; maintaining community over time requires that individuals – especially *outstanding* individuals – keep talking, and that the antagonisms of republics' political lives find expression in rhetorical conflict.

If, then for Sallust rhetoric inevitably involves the danger of misnaming virtues and vices and the undermining of cohesion, and the solutions it offers are temporary, rhetoric is the only way to restore the true names of things, and it *can* channel conflict – though its success will always be contingent; it will need to be practiced again and again. The community, unless pressed and compressed by foreign enmity, is marked by overt conflict that can get out of hand: between individuals, between classes. Even in the *face* of foreign enemies the conflict is latent, especially in the *Histories*. How deep was agreement in Rome if it could collapse so quickly? More to the point: How deep did agreement need to be to have a republican community in the first place?

Rather than look to permanent and deep agreement, Sallust's account highlights the impermanence – and importance – of consensus in light of and in response to conflict and antagonism. Indeed, the standard of judgment to which orators appeal is consensus; the standard of argument is probability, not certainty. The subject matter of rhetoric, especially deliberative rhetoric, is itself contingent and uncertain. As Remer notes:

The orator's audience must decide between two opposing but generally plausible opinions. The reasonableness of the two conflicting positions is only emphasized by the orator's ability to argue, like the skeptical philosopher, *in utramque partem*, on either side of a question, as well as against every opinion forwarded.[130]

Indeed, Cicero's perfect orator is precisely the one who can:

speak on both sides of an issue about all subjects and, having learned his precepts, in every case unfold two opposing speeches, or who argues, in the manner of Arcesilaus and Carneades, against every proposition that is put forward, and who adds to that method and that practice, our manner and experience, our practice of speaking – then he shall be the true, the perfect, the one and only orator.[131]

[129] Levene, "Sallust's Catiline and Cato the Censor," 191.
[130] Gary Remer, "Hobbes, the Rhetorical Tradition, and Toleration," *The Review of Politics* 54, no. 1 (1992): 5–33, 13.
[131] Cicero, *On the Ideal Orator*, 3.80.

This is precisely the practice of Sallust the historian, who breaks down seemingly stable dichotomies, providing distinct yet plausible views on different matters of policy. By constructing antithetical speeches, Sallust's Cato and Caesar each embody a part of him, just as each embodies an element of ancient Rome. Opposites must be balanced in a productive tension; neither Cato and his virtues, nor Caesar and his virtues – nor the warlike virtues or peaceful virtues of ancient Rome – are sufficient in themselves. They are all necessary and complementary, and rhetoric, like politics itself, strives to give space to complementary and conflicting elements. And the practice of arguing *in utramque partem* lent itself to just this purpose. Though the practice entails skepticism, it need not entail "total doubt and the suspension of judgment;"[132] what it did entail, though, for Academic skeptics such as Cicero, was the idea that through argument, the closest thing to truth in rhetoric would emerge: probability backed by consensus.

In the preface to the *War with Catiline*, Sallust writes that:

for a long time mortal men have discussed the question whether success in arms depends more on strength of body or excellence of mind; for before you begin, deliberation is necessary, when you have deliberated, prompt action. Thus each of these, being incomplete in itself, requires the other's aid.[133]

Body and mind are incomplete in themselves; action without deliberation is ineffective, and deliberation on its own achieves nothing. Cato and Caesar were, like Romulus and Numa, complementary and different, but not antithetical; each represented good qualities, qualities perhaps incomplete in themselves, but which could coexist in a complex field bound by antagonistic rhetoric.

Deliberation and the practice of rhetoric bring with them no certainty of success, no certainty of trust, and no guarantee of unanimity. Nor should they be expected to do so, given not just their strong connections to skepticism but also their difference from theories seeking unanimity, as Allen and Garsten point out.[134] Without deliberation and rhetoric, however, decisions cannot be made, and trustful communication and political community

---

[132] Gary Remer, "Humanism, Liberalism, & the Skeptical Case for Religious Toleration," *Polity* 25, no. 1 (1992): 21–43, 25.
[133] Sallust, *War with Catiline*, 1.5–7.
[134] On skepticism, see Victoria Kahn, *Rhetoric, Prudence, and Skepticism in the Renaissance* (Ithaca: Cornell University Press, 1985), 35–6, 42–4.

would be difficult, if not impossible, to sustain. Nor would antagonistic energies have safe internal outlets in lieu of open aggression. As Thucydides, Sallust's stylistic model, has Diodotus put it, "anyone who maintains that words cannot be a guide to action must be either a fool or one with some personal interest at stake; he is a fool, if he imagines that it is possible to deal with the uncertainties of the future by any other medium."[135] And as Sallust himself writes, in a passage we have encountered, it is necessary to combine mind and body, or deliberation and action, as each is "incomplete in itself."[136]

---

[135] Thucydides, *History of the Peloponnesian War*, 3.42.
[136] Sallust, *War with Catiline*, 1.7.

4

EXEMPLARITY AND GOODWILL IN LIVY'S
FROM THE FOUNDING OF ROME

I. INTRODUCTION

Sallust's Rome was marked by antagonism and centrifugal energies, constrained – though not eliminated – by collective fear. Conflict and competition between individuals and groups threatened to imperil the community, yet conflict and competition – rightly shaped and manifested – were also the source of the community's strength. The constraint provided by the fear of foreigners channeled and structured this competition; with the removal of this constraint, the energies that had been directed toward the common good began to be turned toward private concerns. Yet the antagonism of rhetoric, practiced by outstanding individuals, held the potential of checking this conflict by transforming it into political contestation and helping to create a space for the expression of tensions in the body politic. This check, however, was contingent and relied upon the practice of antagonistic rhetoric on the part of outstanding individuals.

I argue in this chapter that Livy, as opposed to Sallust, navigates the conflicts that emerge in republics by emphasizing consensus and accommodation. Consensus emerges in the context of conflict and competition, to be sure, but the driving force behind this consensus is goodwill: goodwill directed toward individuals that paves the way for broader-based consensus between individuals and groups. This goodwill is rooted in the friendly attraction to and admiration for virtue, and is akin to the *ethos-* and *pathos-*based relationships between speaker and audience. Rhetoric and its tools thus provide Livy with a foundation for building and maintaining consensus. This consensus, however, is contingent and depends on the continuous actions and reactions – that is, the display and observation of behavior and character – of Rome's citizens.

My reading of Livy's consensualism does not easily fit the sense of Livy that we get from his most famous reader, Machiavelli, through whose *Discourses* Livy is perhaps best known to political theorists. I begin by briefly exploring Machiavelli's reading to highlight the different approach that I take to Livy. Machiavelli's use of Livy is well documented – but this use, like Machiavelli's use of so many classical sources, is idiosyncratic; the relationship is not one of straightforward adoption.[1] We may note, for instance, Livy's description of the civil war in Ardea:

This is said to have had its cause and origin in the rivalry of factions [*ex certamine factionum*], which have been and will be fraught with destruction to more nations than foreign wars, or famine and pestilence, or whatsoever other scourges men attribute, as the most desperate national calamities, to the wrath of Heaven.[2]

The phenomenon compares poorly against not just war and famine, but even *morbus* – pestilence – recalling the vices (*vitia*) in need of remedies (*remedia*) in the *Preface* to Book 1, to which we will shortly turn.[3] Like Sallust, whose complicated – though generally favorable – account of agreement and harmony we encountered in Chapters 2 and 3, Livy's preference for agreement and harmony, and his hostility to conflict, seems clear. Indeed, part of the problem that Livy is concerned with is that the Roman people have lost a sense of "common purpose," replaced by factional conflicts due to the demise of a shared "civic identity."[4] Machiavelli does not agree with Livy's evaluation, as factional conflict, especially between the people and the great, is a *good* thing, productive of liberty and greatness; Machiavelli writes that conflicts "between the populace and the senate should, therefore, be looked upon as an inconvenience which it is necessary to put up with in order to arrive at the greatness of Rome."[5] If we saw in Sallust's writings an attitude toward conflict that seemed, anachronism aside, "Machiavellian" – that

---

[1] On Machiavelli's use of Livy, see J. Patrick Coby, *Machiavelli's Romans* (Lanham: Lexington Books, 1999).

[2] Livy, *From the Founding of the City*, trans. B.O. Foster (Cambridge: Harvard University Press, 1922), 4.9.2–3. Ogilvie suggests the passage is Thucydidean. R.M. Ogilvie, *A Commentary on Livy Books 1–5* (Oxford: Oxford University Press, 1965), 546.

[3] Livy, *From the Founding of the City*, *Praef.* 9.

[4] Hammer, *Roman Political Thought and the Modern Theoretical Imagination*, 91.

[5] Niccolo Machiavelli, *The Discourses on Livy*, ed. Bernard Crick (New York: Penguin, 1983), 123–4. On this point, see Coby, *Machiavelli's Romans*, 203. For a recent reading of Machiavelli's theory of participatory government that emphasis antagonism, see John P. McCormick, "Machiavelli against Republicanism: On the Cambridge School's

is, viewing social conflict as potentially beneficial within the confines of particular boundaries – we do not seem to find this in Livy.[6]

Livy, then, unlike his later admirer, does not seem favorably disposed toward social conflict; far from it – *concordia*, and in particular the *concordia ordinum*, is central to his narrative of the rise of Rome.[7] As Momigliano pointed out, Livy's use of *concordia* – as opposed to the Roman *praxis* of *concordia* – echoes Greek "political Homonoia," which "is a sentiment of friendliness among citizens of one or more cities."[8] This treatment of *concordia* recalls Cicero's political thought, in which he frequently links harmony – *concordia* – between Rome's different orders (Senate, knights, and people) to the well-being of the republic; the republic itself rested on agreement, for Cicero, and emerged in part through the eloquence of the orator-statesman.[9] In *On the Commonwealth*, Cicero describes *concordia* as the civil equivalent of musical harmony; it is "the tightest and best bond of safety in every republic; and … concord can never exist without justice."[10] For Cicero, the ideal of *concordia* functions to preserve and solidify relationships among those who live in the same community and are dissimilar; "different [*distinctis*] sounds" and "very different [*dissimillamarum*] voices" in music are in harmony with each other despite these differences, as are the different classes of the commonwealth.[11] These are differences of status, between highest, middle, and lowest classes (Senate, knights, and people) – corresponding to the three notes in a harmony that are also dissimilar (*dissimil-limorum*), yet are bound by consensus (*consensu*) in civil concord.

Cicero's account of the bond of *concordia*, uniting what is dissimilar through agreement, may be compared to Aristotelian political friendship, a discussion

'Guicciardinian' Moments," *Political Theory* 31, no. 5 (2003): 615–43; John P. McCormick, "Machiavellian Democracy: Controlling Elites with Ferocious Populism," *American Political Science Review* 95, no. 2 (2001): 297–313.

6 For a reading of Sallust and Machiavelli along these lines, see Fontana, "Sallust and the Politics of Machiavelli."

7 On the theme of *concordia* in Livy, see Robert Brown, "Livy's Sabine Women and the Ideal of Concordia," *Transactions of the American Philological Association* 125 (1995): 291–319.

8 Arnaldo Momigliano, "Camillus and Concord," *The Classical Quarterly* 36, no. 3/4 (1942): 111–20, 118–19.

9 See, e.g., Cicero, *On the Ideal Orator*, 1.30–4. Cf. Cicero, *On the Commonwealth*, 1.39a, 3.43.

10 Cicero, *On the Commonwealth*, 2.69a. The Latin consulted is Cicero, *De Republica*, trans. Clinton Walker Keyes, *Cicero: De Republica and De Legibus* (Cambridge: Harvard University Press, 2000).

11 Cicero, *On the Commonwealth*, 2.69a.

to which Allen serves as a useful guide. Allen argues – drawing on Aristotle – that "citizens who behave with propriety toward strangers avoid acting, on the one hand, like acquiescent people who accept everything … and, on the other, like domineering people."[12] *Concordia* – rooted in consensus and exemplary behavior, for Cicero – thus functions analogously to political friendship, maintaining relationships between those who are different: "Real brothers and real polities, too, with diverse and less than virtuous citizens, Aristotle admits, will be persistently troubled by problems of rivalrous self-interest."[13]

Concordia, for Cicero, and political friendship, for Aristotle, help to cement communities composed of those who are unequal and unlike. The rhetorical dimension of character and its observation, I argue, has a similar function for Livy; in effect, Livy rhetoricizes political behavior, conceiving of the relationship between leaders and led, the people and the great, and the few and the many, as a relationship of persuasion and accommodation that can, as in Cicero's thought, lead to harmony. Leaders and leadership are rhetorically constructed, as are elites' relations with non-elites; these leaders, acting and speaking before a non-elite audience that evaluates and responds to their character, are less the locus and outlet of antagonistic contestation than the impetus behind cooperation and consensus. Drawing on rhetorical treatments of the relationship between a speaker's character (*ethos*) and an audience's response (*pathos*), I argue that the perceived character of leaders – manifested especially in their actions – is evaluated by non-elite audiences with respect to its qualities and, in turn, arouses emotional responses from them.

Livy's republic is a hierarchical community, bound together by goodwill generated through the virtuous behavior of elites, which is in turn observed and evaluated by the many. Elites depend on the many for honor and recognition, and the many are the ultimate source of judgment and power; neither can exist without the other, however, and their relationship is rhetorically constructed, just as rhetoric and its elements treat the fissures in this relationship. This cooperative and accommodative rhetoric stands in contrast to Sallust's antagonistic conception of rhetoric and politics. Livy, as we shall see, is more Ciceronian than Sallustian, emphasizing consensus and goodwill. Livy's rhetorical construction of leadership serves to build trust and harmony in the body politic, fostering agreement and cooperation among its distinct members.

---

[12] Allen, *Talking to Strangers*, 121.
[13] Ibid., 125.

In making this argument, I turn first in Section II to a discussion of *ethos*, *pathos*, and goodwill in Aristotle's and Isocrates' writings, as well as several Roman works on rhetoric. I then turn to Livy in Section III, focusing first on his relationship to Sallust, and then on his emphasis on *mores* – that is, habits and customary behaviors. Turning to specific examples of behavior and the ideals underlying them in Section IV, I explore the development of consensus and goodwill in Livy's writings, highlighting the importance of accommodation. Drawing especially on Cicero's *On the Commonwealth, On Duties*, and *On Friendship*, I bring attention to the parallels between politics, rhetoric, and friendship with respect to the importance of displaying virtue and its recognition in Section V. Finally, I turn in Sections VI and VII to the relationship between fear and love, on the one hand, and discord and consensus, on the other, in Livy's depiction of the republic and the rhetorical construction of leadership. Guiding my analysis is the importance of vision and seeing in Livy's history, encountered, as we will see, in his understanding of the past as a kind of monument; this emphasis on seeing and vision, in turn, helps to make sense of the interactions between elites and the many in terms of display and recognition.

II. ETHOS, PATHOS, AND GOODWILL

In his *Rhetoric*, Aristotle argued that those who persuade use artless proofs ("witnesses, evidence given under torture, written contracts") and artful proofs emerging by a speaker.[14] The latter consists of three modes of persuasion:

The first kind depends on the personal character of the speaker; the second on putting the audience into a certain frame of mind; the third on the proof, or apparent proof, provided by the words of the speech itself.[15]

Of particular interest to the present topic are the first two modes of persuasion. The first, involving the character of the speaker (*ethos*) increases his persuasiveness, making him appear credible. If a speaker is able to speak such that he can "make us think him credible," he has succeeded, as we tend to believe those whom we judge good.[16] Such proof relies on what

[14] Aristotle, *Rhetoric*, 1355b37.
[15] Ibid., 1356a3–4.
[16] Ibid., 1356a5

the speaker himself says, and not how his character is perceived prior to speaking. *Pathos*, which has to do with "putting the audience into a certain frame of mind," involves arousing particular emotions in the audience. This mode of persuasion is important because "Our judgments when we are pleased and friendly are not the same as when we are pained and hostile."[17]

In Book 2, Aristotle argues that there are three causes in the orator himself that enable an orator to convince his audience: "good sense, excellence, and goodwill" – φρόνησις, αρετή, and εύνοια.[18] Speakers who seem to have all three qualities "will necessarily convince" their audiences, and the speaker makes himself appear "sensible and good" based on an understanding of the virtues. By contrast, εύνοια and φιλία (affection) are intimately related; understanding how to attract one's audience to oneself – toward a sense of friendship with oneself – relies upon an understanding of the emotions, and what produces them. As Garver puts it:

The quality of *eunoia* in the speaker is generated through producing emotions in the audience ... Stimulating the appropriate emotions in an audience is a necessary part of displaying the desired character in a speaker.[19]

The audience, however, is not merely passive; in this relationship, it has a crucial evaluative role through its observation of the orator.

Goodwill was also of great importance to Isocrates, and part of its importance derived from his status as a teacher of rhetoric, who "had to keep in mind the importance of *captatio benevolentiae*" – that is, winning benevolence.[20] But εύνοια also had a key political role for Isocrates, as Romilly argues that the centrality of εύνοια was linked not just to the dictates of rhetoric, but to the activity of persuasion, in turn linked to the value of opinion: "Isocrates defends the value of *doxa*, opinion, against empty wishes for an impossible *episteme*."[21] Εύνοια is related to όμόνοια – concord, or the Latin *concordia* – but it differs in a crucial way: "When one speaks of concord, one considers any group of people as a whole, whereas good will is generally

---

[17] Ibid., 1356a14–15.
[18] Ibid., 1378a8. The Greek consulted Aristotle, *The "Art" Of Rhetoric*, trans. John Henry Freese (Cambridge: Harvard University Press, 1947).
[19] Eugene Garver, *Aristotle's Rhetoric: An Art of Character* (Chicago: The University of Chicago Press, 1994), 110.
[20] Jacqueline de Romilly, "Eunoia in Isocrates or the Political Importance of Creating Good Will," *The Journal of Hellenic Studies* 78 (1958): 92–101, 95.
[21] Ibid., 95.

directed towards one special person or city."[22] Those who display virtues in dealing with others bring about goodwill; Isocrates contrasts Athens' turn to compulsion and meddling with justice: "as the result of keeping our city in the path of justice and of giving aid to the oppressed and of not coveting the possessions of others we were given the hegemony by the willing consent of the Hellenes."[23]

Isocrates states that "it is by the good qualities which we have in our souls that we acquire also the other advantages of which we stand in need," and that virtue is a surer path to success than coercion.[24] We see, in these passages, the link between rhetoric and politics: εύνοια, cultivated by a speaker (or actor) but granted by the audience (or observer), brings about the voluntary agreement of those affected by virtues, while ill-will would bring about the opposite.

In Roman oratory, the corresponding goal to bringing about εύνοια – and hence agreement – was to win *benevolentia* – goodwill – from one's audience. For the author of the *Rhetoric to Herennius*, the goal of the orator was "to have our hearer receptive, well-disposed, and attentive" – *docilem, benivolum, adtentum*.[25] Making one's audience well-disposed could be secured by four devices: "discussing our own person, the person of our adversaries, that of our hearers, and the facts themselves."[26] From our own person, we ought to emphasize, in pursuing *benevolentia*, "our services without arrogance and [reveal] also our past conduct toward the republic, or toward our parents, friends, or the audience" – so long as this is relevant to the case at hand.[27] Similarly, one might appeal to the audience's pity, emphasizing, for instance, our "misfortune" – the rhetorical device of *pathos*.[28]

We find a similar account in Cicero's *On the Ideal Orator*, though with even more of an emphasis on winning the audience over with our character; so Antonius argues in Book 2 that:

nothing in oratory ... is more important than for the orator to be favorably regarded [*faveat*] by the audience, and for the audience to be moved in

---

[22] Ibid., 98.

[23] Isocrates, *On the Peace*, tr. George Norlin, *Isocrates II* (London: William Heinemann, 1929), 30.

[24] Ibid., 32. Cf. Isocrates, *Areopagiticus*, tr. George Norlin, *Isocrates II* (New York: William Heinemann, 1929), 17.

[25] *Ad C. Herennium De Ratione Dicendi*, 1.4.7.

[26] Ibid., 1.4.8.

[27] Ibid., 1.5.8.

[28] Ibid., 1.5.8.

such a way as to be ruled by some strong emotional impulse rather than by reasoned judgment.[29]

This echoes an earlier comment of Antonius, when he noted the "three things which alone can carry conviction" – that is, "the winning over [*concilientur*], the instructing, and the stirring of men's minds."[30] Central to winning over one's audience is to be sure that "the character, the customs, the deeds, and the life, both of those who do the pleading and of those on whose behalf they plead ... be approved of."[31] One's goal, then, was to bring about the greatest goodwill – *conciliari quam maxime ad benevolentiam*. This might be achieved by giving forth certain signs – *signa* – of one's character:

generosity, mildness, dutifulness, gratitude, and of not being desirous or greedy. Actually all qualities typical of people who are decent and unassuming, not severe, not obstinate, not litigious, not harsh, really win goodwill [*valde benevolentiam conciliant*], and alienate the audience from those who do not possess them.[32]

The contrary qualities, by contrast, alienate our audience – *abalienant*.[33] Good character, perceived by audiences, attracts, just as perceived bad character repels.

In Cicero's later *Orator*, he argues that:

The eloquence of orators has always been controlled by the good sense of the audience, since all who desire to win approval have regard to the goodwill [*voluntatem*] of their auditors, and shape and adapt themselves completely according to this and to their opinion and approval.[34]

Similarly, Cicero discusses the topics appropriate to *ethos* and *pathos*. The prior is related to men's nature and character, their habits and all the intercourse of life; the other, which they call παθητικόν or "relating to the emotions," arouses and excites the emotions: in this part alone oratory reigns supreme. The former is courteous and agreeable, adapted to win goodwill [*ad benevolentiam conciliandam*

[29] Cicero, *On the Ideal Orator*, 2.178.
[30] Ibid., 2.121.
[31] Ibid., 2.182.
[32] Ibid. 2.182.
[33] Ibid., 2.182.
[34] Cicero, *Orator*, 24.

paratum]; the latter is violent, hot and impassioned, and by this cases are wrested from our opponents; when it rushes along in full career it is quite irresistible.[35]

It is crucial to note that even though Cicero's orator is ideal, he is not independent of his audience; as Antonius remarks in *On the Ideal Orator*, "We must avoid being thought ridiculous because we resort to histrionics over a trifle, or odious because we attempt to uproot what cannot even be moved."[36] The persuasiveness of the orator is not a one way street; the expert and the many could and did agree on the efficacy of the orator, for Cicero.

III. FROM RHETORIC TO ACTION

With this discussion of character, its perception, and the production of goodwill in mind, I turn to Livy and to what I have termed the rhetoricization of behavior. Central to the rhetoricization of behavior is Livy's focus on *mores* – morals – and their role in the construction of relationships between leaders and led and in structuring the political community as a whole. Thus, he tells us in his first *Preface* that he will ask *quae vita, qui mores fuerint* – what life, and what mores there were among the ancient Romans, *mores* which "first gave way ... then sank lower and lower," culminating in the present decay.[37] Particular virtues play significant roles in his narrative, with some books centering on single virtues: concord, discipline, chastity, good faith.[38]

   Concordia is of special importance to Livy. In his narrative, *concordia* leads to victory abroad; *discordia* leads to weakness. *Concordia* arises from virtue; *discordia* arises from vice. So important is *concordia* that Livy has the Senate suggest, after the virtuous Camillus' colleagues lay down their *imperium* to him:

that the state would never need a dictator if it might have such men in office, united in such loving concord [*tam concordibus iunctos animis*], equally ready to command and obey, and rather contributing to the common stock of glory than drawing upon it for their own behoof.[39]

---

[35] Ibid., 128.
[36] Cicero, *On the Ideal Orator*, 2.205.
[37] Livy, *From the Founding of the City*, Praef. 9.
[38] P. G. Walsh, *Livy: His Historical Aims and Methods* (Cambridge: Cambridge University Press, 1961), 66–78.
[39] Livy, *From the Founding of the City*, 6.6.18.

The passage is illustrative: The selfless behavior of Camillus' colleagues, and their observation and recognition of his singular merits – Camillus strove "to make the very high opinion which his fellow citizens so unanimously entertained of him an abiding one" – lead to harmonious agreement that would obviate the need for extraordinary powers and ensure the safety of the republic.[40]

Despite the importance of *concordia* to his narrative, however, Livy does not seem to put much stock in Sallust, in whose history we saw an emphasis on *concordia* coexisting with his conception of an antagonistic republic. Syme argues that:

The style of Sallust was repellent to Livy. Not less the man and his opinions – the turbulent politician expelled from the Senate but restored by Caesar and enriched by civil war; the comfortable author of a depressing history; the austere moralist of equivocal conduct.[41]

Syme notes Livy's slight to his predecessors in his *Preface* as evidence of a slight to his most immediate predecessor – those who believe "that in their style they will prove better than the rude attempts of the ancients."[42] Sallust, influenced by Thucydides, wrote in a pessimistic fashion; "Livy generally came to adopt an optimistic view of Roman history which he reinforced by writing in the style that Cicero had recommended."[43]

The departure is not just stylistic; it is also thematic. The "profound and overwhelming social dislocation" that so influenced Sallust seems not to have similarly affected Livy, who held out hope for a remedy to Rome's troubles in his preface.[44] Sallust's antagonistic conception of rhetoric, revolving around elite conflict and its channeling and enacting of social conflict writ large, stands in stark contrast to Livy's consensual and accommodating rhetoric. This distinction, in turn, reflects their understanding of Rome's history and its decline. For Sallust, as we saw, Rome's decline was deeply

---

[40] Ibid., 6.6.9.

[41] Ronald Syme, "Livy and Augustus," *Harvard Studies in Classical Philology* 64 (1959): 27–87, 54.

[42] Livy, *From the Founding of the City*, *Praef*. 2. Ogilvie, too, notes that Livy had Sallust in mind based on the "closeness of *Praef*. 9–11 to the language used by Sallust." Ogilvie, *A Commentary on Livy Books 1–5*, 23.

[43] Woodman, *Rhetoric in Classical Historiography*, 146.

[44] D.S. Levene, "Sallust's Jugurtha: An 'Historical Fragment,'" *The Journal of Roman Studies* 82 (1992): 53–70, 69. On the potential reversal of the decline, see Woodman, *Rhetoric in Classical Historiography*, 136–7.

conditioned by the absence of the *metus hostilis*, and in part by the problem of unchecked *ambitio*. The *metus hostilis*, though certainly a common theme in Livy's *From the Founding of the City*, is not mentioned as a cause of Rome's decline in the *Preface*. Sallust's decline (in the *War with Catiline* and the *War with Jugurtha*) is strikingly abrupt, hinging as it does on the removal of the *metus hostilis*; the process is, for Livy, more gradual than for Sallust – Ogilvie suggests that Livy "recognizes that whereas the opportunities for affluent living only became available in the second century, forces such as *ambitio* had always been at work from the very foundations of the city."[45]

If the fall of Carthage was the necessary cause of Rome's decline, decline was perhaps only a matter of time for Sallust; enemies are eliminated, even those as great as Carthage. Was Rome's decline inevitable for Livy? Luce suggests that "there is nothing in Livy that would lead to the conclusion that for him decline was ultimately necessary or inevitable" – instead, Rome's decline was "in origin and effect ... like a contagious disease."[46] Thus, the *remedia* of the *Preface*, the likening of faction to *morbus*. The loss of the *metus hostilis* is not the tipping point of decline; *ambitio* is likewise omitted as a cause. Livy singles out two different causes of decline: *avaritia luxuriaque* – avarice and luxury.[47] They came to Rome later than in all other states; Rome's richness "in good examples" and the fact that in it "humble means and thrift were so highly esteemed and so long held in honor" postponed its decline.[48] *Luxuria* shows "the power of wealth to distract Romans from their essential responsibilities," especially weakening *pietas* after the fall of Veii.[49] Yet when we meet with decline in Livy – for instance, the sack of Rome by the Gauls – we meet with rebirth and refoundation; thus the refoundation of Rome at the beginning of Book 6 and the model leaders who govern and refound Rome.

Models abound to illustrate the danger of *luxuria* and the virtue of those who transcend it; most famous, perhaps, is the figure of Cincinnatus, savior of the republic and dictator: He was "intent upon some rustic task," working "a field of some four acres," when summoned to be dictator, the "sole hope of the empire of the Roman People."[50] His example – moderation, frugality,

---

[45] Ogilvie, *A Commentary on Livy Books 1–5*, 24.
[46] Luce, *Livy: The Composition of His History*, 279.
[47] Livy, *From the Founding of the City*, *Praef.* 11.
[48] Ibid., 11.
[49] Gary B. Miles, *Livy: Reconstructing Early Rome* (Ithaca: Cornell University Press, 1995), 80.
[50] Livy, *From the Founding of the City*, 3.26.7–8.

patriotism – is worth "the attention of those who despise all human qualities in comparison with riches, and think there is no room for great honors
or for worth but amidst a profusion of wealth."[51] Wealth distracts – from
duty, from patriotism – and patriots look askance on it. Two other incidents
may be adduced: In Book 7, Livy contrasts the ease with which ten legions
had been enrolled in the distant past, noting that this would be difficult to
achieve in his own time, "so strictly has our growth been limited to the only
things for which we strive – wealth and luxury."[52] In the same book, we see
Valerius note the dangerous effects of "enervation resulting from excessive
luxury" in rallying his troops.[53]

Earlier in the narrative, when discussing conflict between the consuls and
the tribunes, Livy remarks that the "tendency which a state rewarded always
attained the greatest growth; it was thus that good men were produced, both
in peace and in war. In Rome the greatest reward was given to sedition,
which had, therefore, ever been held in honor by all and sundry."[54] What is
valued and rewarded guides behavior and pushes the republic in its direction.
Sedition and faction were sure to continue "so long as the fomenters of the
insurrection were honored in proportion to the success of their projects."[55]

IV. MORALS AND EXAMPLES IN LIVY'S *HISTORY*

We have seen in Chapter 1 that moral concerns were of great importance to
Roman historians in general, including Sallust, Livy, and Tacitus.[56] But Livy's
history is distinctive, in that it is exemplary in its structure and intended effect,
given his emphasis on vision and observation of *exempla*.[57] History's utility –
what makes it "wholesome and profitable" – is that it contains *exempla* that
can be seen – *intueri* – as if they were on a "conspicuous monument."[58]
Such a history, which portrays quasi-visual *exempla* of character and behavior,

---

[51] Ibid., 3.26.7.
[52] Ibid., 7.25.9.
[53] Ibid., 7.32.7.
[54] Ibid., 4.2.3.
[55] Ibid., 4.2.4.
[56] Chapter 1.
[57] See Chaplin, *Livy's Exemplary History*. On the importance of vision and observation in
Livy's depiction of Roman history, see chapter 3 of Hammer, *Roman Political Thought and
the Modern Theoretical Imagination*.
[58] Livy, *From the Founding of the City, Praef.* 10.

allows us, as readers, to "'see' the event in our mind's eye," enabling us to "feel the emotions and understand the thoughts and motives of the actors from inside."[59] *Exempla*, as we have seen in Chapter 1, were of great importance in Roman historiography. They also had an important "place in the education of young Romans, who learn by having pointed out to them the actions of others as worthy of avoidance or imitation."[60] Historical examples were similarly important to rhetorical training and effective oratory; Cicero, for instance, writes *in propria persona* in *On the Ideal Orator* that "one must know the whole past with its storehouses of examples and precedents" if one is to be a good orator.[61] History thus provided examples of behavior to imitate or avoid; in his first *Preface*, then, Livy writes that history provides lessons from which "you may choose for yourself and for your own state what to imitate, from these mark for avoidance what is shameful in the conception and shameful in the result."[62] The past thus provides useful lessons that can, in a sense, be seen, rich examples from the past that are superior to present luxury.

What concepts, though, are central to Livy's narrative, and to his depiction of the republic and its functions? Certainly, *concordia* is an exceptionally important concept for Livy, especially in the first ten books (the concern of this chapter). In this respect, he and Sallust are similar. Yet his *concordia* is not linked to the *metus hostilis* in the way Sallust's is, as we have noted. To be sure, it is not entirely independent; indeed, it is striking just how frequently we see the *metus hostilis* deployed in Livy. In his own voice he describes as "the strongest bond of harmony" – *maximum concordiae vinculum* – the "dread of invasion" – *externus timor* – this in reference to an invasion by the Volsci in Book 2.[63] We see that "domestic strife" typically ceases in the face of a foreign threat in, for instance, Book 2; we see this in Book 5 as well, during Rome's conflict with Veii – "domestic differences [*discordiae*] began to subside, as generally happens, in the face of a common danger."[64] Just as foreign threats foster harmony, discord emboldens foreign enemies, evident in the thinking of the Etruscans who joined Veii's fight with Rome, "not so much roused by goodwill [*gratia concitata*] towards the men of Veii as by

[59] Kraus and Woodman, *Latin Historians*, 55.
[60] Chaplin, *Livy's Exemplary History*, 13.
[61] Cicero, *On the Ideal Orator*, 1.18.
[62] Livy, *From the Founding of the City*, *Praef.* 10–11.
[63] Ibid., 2.39.7.
[64] Ibid., 2.42.3, 5.17.10.

hopes that civil discord might effect the downfall of the Roman state."[65] Indeed, Livy suggests that Etruria's leaders believed "there would be no end to the power of the Romans unless factional quarrels should set them to fighting amongst themselves"; such quarrels were "the only poison, the only decay" that could weaken great empires.[66]

We find similar thinking in Book 3, credited in this instance to the Aequi and Volsci, who believed that "the plebs were no longer amenable to authority" and were thus emboldened in their hostility toward Rome.[67] Foreign threats typically – though not always – fostered unity; disunity invited foreign threats. And when the Romans were harmonious, good things happened: In his hypothetical discussion of war between the Romans and Alexander, Livy writes that "A thousand battle-arrays more formidable than those of Alexander and the Macedonians have the Romans beaten off – and shall do – if only our present love of domestic peace endure and our concern to maintain concord."[68] Strength through harmony, and harmony as a mark of strength – the echoes of Sallust seem strong.

A common pattern in Livy's narrative, the first five books in particular, is thus the coalescence of quarreling plebs and patricians in the face of foreign enmity. The source of the quarrels, and the backdrop of this pattern, is a series of conflicts between patricians and plebs – the Conflict of the Orders.[69] The term refers to the struggles between the Senatorial elite and the people during the period from 494 BCE (the date of the first secession of the Roman plebs from the city) to 287 BCE (the date of the passage of the Hortensian Law).[70] In this period, the Roman polity gradually shed various institutions and practices rooted in monarchy and incorporated those institutions and practices that would come to characterize the republic. The term itself is something of a misnomer, as there were many conflicts, and

---

[65] Ibid. 2.44.7

[66] Ibid., 2.44.8.

[67] Ibid., 3.66.3

[68] Ibid., 9.19.17.

[69] For a fuller discussion of the Conflict of the Orders, see Kurt A. Raaflaub, "From Protection and Defense to Offence and Participation: Stages in the Conflict of the Orders," in *Social Struggles in Archaic Rome*, ed. Kurt A. Raaflaub (Berkeley: University of California Press, 1986): 198–243; Kurt A. Raaflaub, "The Conflict of the Orders in Archaic Rome: A Comprehensive and Comparative Approach," in *Social Struggles in Archaic Rome*, ed. Kurt A. Raaflaub (Berkeley: University of California Press, 1986): 1–51.

[70] This law "declared that the decrees of the plebs should stand on an absolute footing of equality ... with those of the whole community." Mommsen, *History of Rome*, vol. 1, 385.

these conflicts had multiple aims, depending on their particular context. Chief among the issues being contested was the kind, or kinds, of power the plebs would have vis-à-vis the patricians. The conflict produced a number of Roman institutions and practices – the tribunate, for example, as well as the abolition of debt bondage.

The conflict is set against, and often constrained by, the *metus hostilis*. Yet the loss of the *metus hostilis* is not singled out as a factor in Rome's decline in Livy's *Preface* – there, he focuses on luxury and avarice: *Mores* are more significant than *metus*. And when we turn to his narrative, we see that *concordia* arises from many sources beyond the *metus hostilis*. Specific figures – and in particular virtuous leaders – in Livy's narrative bring about *concordia*: Brutus in expanding the Senate to 300, for instance, "was wonderfully effective in promoting harmony [*concordia*] in the state and attaching the plebs to the Fathers."[71] Faced with the first plebeian secession, the Senate restored *concordia* by dispatching a certain Menenius Agrippa to persuade the plebs to return to the city; he deploys the image of the body politic, to "show how like was the internal dissension of the bodily members to the anger of the plebs against the Fathers."[72] The creation of the tribunate, by which the plebs received inviolable magistrates, helped to produce concord; when a Roman army met with disaster at Veii and the knights volunteered to serve on their own horses in battle, the plebs emulated them, with Senators saying "Rome was blest ... and invincible and eternal, by reason of this noble harmony."[73] And Camillus, Rome's latter day Romulus, brings about concord after implementing a political compromise, giving the plebs a consul and the nobles a praetor: "after their long quarrel the orders were reconciled at last."[74]

Certain behaviors are productive or destructive of concord, just as certain kinds of character were persuasive or unpersuasive when displayed by orators and evaluated by audiences. Let us start with the latter: Immoderation, whether it be on the part of the patricians, the plebeians, or individuals, is productive of discord; thus the speech of L. Papirius Mugillanus, the interrex, who asked both plebs and patricians that each "abate somewhat of his full rights and compromise harmoniously on a middle course."[75] Other

---

[71] Livy, *From the Founding of the City*, 2.1.11.
[72] Ibid., 2.32.12.
[73] Ibid., 2.33.1; 5.7.10.
[74] Ibid., 6.42.12.
[75] Ibid., 4.43.12.

vices, too, could undermine concord – cruelty, for instance. One of the Appii, at the head of Rome's army while at war with the Aequi and Volsci, turned to "a savage exercise of authority," producing disagreement and hostility such that "neither shame nor fear" restrained the army.[76] The Appii Claudii are something of a transhistorical archetype of arrogance and misbehavior; but in the interactions between this particular Appius Claudius and his army, one of his underlings makes an important remark.[77] When Appius was about to call an assembly, faced with an army that refused to fight, his subordinate "warned him upon no account to seek a test of his authority [*imperium*], when its effectiveness all depended upon the goodwill [*in consensu*] of those obeying it."[78]

This is a puzzling passage: *Imperium* seems to be a central feature of the doggedly disciplined Roman mind, "the most significant word in the vocabulary of Roman constitutional statecraft," according to Adcock.[79] It was rooted in the kingly power – *regium imperium*, as Cicero puts it in *On the Laws* 3.8.[80] The term does not seem to admit of negotiation – military in origin, it entails "the power to give commands"[81] Wirszubski remarks that "the essential feature of the Roman magistracy was that while the magistrate was elected by popular vote he was not obliged to act as a delegate of the electorate."[82] Thus, Brunt remarks that it is no wonder we find no equivalent to the *ius provocationis* or the tribunate in Athens: Athenian magistrates lacked *imperium*, and "Particular forms of liberty are valued most when they become necessary in practice to protect men from some kind of coercion inimical to their desires and interests."[83]

Yet here we find *imperium* limited by the need for *consensus*. In this regard, it seems closer to *auctoritas*, "granted not by statute but by the esteem of one's

---

[76] Ibid., 2.58.6–7.

[77] On the Appii Claudii, see Ann Vasaly, "Personality and Power: Livy's Depiction of the Appii Claudii in the First Pentad," *Transactions of the American Philological Association* 117, no. 1987 (1987): 203–26.

[78] Livy, *From the Founding of the City*, 2.59.4.

[79] F.E. Adcock, *Roman Political Ideas and Practice* (Ann Arbor: University of Michigan Press, 1964), 5.

[80] Cicero, *De Legibus*, ed. Clinton Walker Keyes, *Cicero: De Republica and De Legibus* (Cambridge: Harvard University Press, 2000), 3.8.

[81] Lintott, *The Constitution of the Roman Republic*, 96.

[82] Chaim Wirszubski, *Libertas as a Political Idea at Rome* (Cambridge: Cambridge University Press, 1950). 47

[83] Brunt, "*Libertas* in the Republic," 309.

fellow citizens," rooted on occasion in inheritance, but more commonly in "an individual's superior record of judgment and achievement" – that is, to his demonstrated virtues.[84] Essential to *auctoritas*, however, is "the voluntary approbation and adhesion of those over whom it is exercised."[85] To the extent that Appius' power is effective when based in consensus, itself rooted in "voluntary approbation," his power is limited and tied to the approval of those he leads. Should they disapprove of him, and voice this either by protest or foot-dragging, his power becomes merely formal.[86] He is, then, not entirely independent of them; he requires their goodwill towards him if his power is to be *effective*.

Clearly, Appius does not possess the approbation and adhesion of his troops, voluntary or involuntary; nor should we expect him to, given his treatment of them. Though he possesses *imperium* in the formal sense, his *auctoritas* is not recognized – nor would such an outcome be likely for him, or any of his *gens*, given their attitude toward and vicious treatment of the plebs, and the plebs' consequent dislike of the *gens Appii*. He stands in pointed contrast to his colleague, Quinctius, of whom Livy writes this: "there subsisted between consul and soldiers an emulation of goodwill [*beneficiis certatum*] and kindness"; their relations were characterized by "complete harmony between commander and army," and his own soldiers "declared that to them the senate had given a parent [*parentem*], to the other army a tyrant [*dominum*]."[87] Quinctius' *imperium* is made effective by the affection of his soldiers and their goodwill toward him. His behavior and virtues attract them; Appius' behavior repels them. Quinctius is in nature more gentle – *lenior* – than Appius.

Goodwill (*benevolentia*) and a cluster of terms related in usage – *voluntas*, *gratia*, *in consensus*, *beneficiis certatum* – were the backbone of consensus between individuals, groups, leaders, and the led. Goodwill, which emerges through interactions between individuals or between individuals and groups, gives rise to concord, evident in examples that occur at other points in Livy's narrative. They are similarly connected to models of good and bad

[84] Karl Galinsky, *Augustan Culture: An Interpretive Introduction* (Princeton: Princeton University Press, 1996), 14.

[85] J. Hellegouarc'h, *Le Vocabulaire Latin Des Relations Et Des Partis Politiques Sous La Republique* (Paris: Société d'Édition "Les Belles Lettres," 1972), 302.

[86] For a recent discussion of popular agitation in Livy's depiction of camp scenes, see Stefan G. Chrissanthos, "Freedom of Speech and the Roman Republican Army," in *Free Speech in Classical Antiquity*, ed. Ineke Sluiter and Ralph M. Rosen (Leiden: Brill, 2004): 341–68.

[87] Livy, *From the Founding of the City*, 2.60.1–3.

leadership and their collective recognition. We may, for instance, contrast the king Servius Tullius and his successor, L. Tarquinius. Tullius was successful in war, winning battles with the Veientes, and also in peace – instituting the census and the orders, a "most useful thing for a government destined to such wide dominion."[88] After such achievements, "Servius had … a definite prescriptive right to the supreme power" – *regnum possederat*.[89] Nevertheless, he perceived that he needed the goodwill of the commons, realizing that the young Tarquinius was a potential threat. Because the young Tarquinius suggested that Servius ruled the people unjustly – *iniussu populi regnare* – Tullius sought to conciliate himself to the plebs – *conciliata prius voluntate plebis*, language which recalls Cicero's emphasis on the need to win over [*conciliare*] one's audience and the importance of goodwill in *On the Ideal Orator* and *Orator*. His means for doing so was to redistribute land taken from the enemy – calling for popular approval of his rule after this boon, he "was declared king with such unanimity [*tantoque consensu*] as none of his predecessors had experienced."[90]

The young Tarquinius, urged onward by the equally ambitious Tullia (who had left her husband, Tarquin's brother Arruns, characterized by a "gentle disposition") plotted against Tullius; the outcome was Tarquin's violent ascent to the throne.[91] Not long after seizing the throne for himself, Tarquinius earned his *cognomen* Superbus – that is, arrogant. He denied Tullius a burial; he killed leading senators; "he assumed a body guard," having "no right [*ius*] to the throne but might [*vim*]."[92] Faced with a populace whose affection (*caritate*) he did not trust because he lacked goodwill, "he was compelled to safeguard his authority by fear."[93]

Absent goodwill and affection, lacking due to his vicious character and its display to and recognition by the people of Rome, then, he sought to impose his power by coercive means. Lacking love, he pursued fear, and in doing so, further eroded goodwill and his own security. To better accomplish this, he went so far as to try capital cases himself; trusting few, he "governed the nation without other advice than that of his own household."[94]

[88] Ibid., 1.42.5.
[89] Ibid., 1.46.1.
[90] Ibid., 1.46.1.
[91] Ibid., 1.46.4.
[92] Ibid., 1.49.3.
[93] Ibid., 1.49.4.
[94] Ibid., 1.49.7.

His reign is marked by his whim: "War, peace, treaties, and alliances were entered upon or broken off by the monarch himself, with whatever states he wished [*cum quibus voluit*], and without the decree of people or senate."[95] He is more a *dominus* than a leader of Romans; he rules Rome as if it were his household, and not as a king.[96]

V. THE BREAKDOWN OF CONSENSUS AND GOODWILL

We have moved from consensus and security to rule by whim and insecurity – the king, driven by his own desires, rules from his household as if the kingdom were his household. More importantly, fear replaces love, and Tarquinius' best allies are foreign; indeed, he seeks out foreign allies in the hope that "his strength abroad might contribute to his security at home."[97] The republic is not marked by harmony, but discord. Tarquinius is a step in Livy's narrative, the stimulus that drives an increasingly mature people away from the tutelage of kings and toward liberty. Tarquinius' plotting and success was "in order that loathing of kings might hasten the coming of liberty, and that the end of reigning might come in that reign which was the fruit of crime."[98]

The expulsion of the kings brought liberty to the Roman people – the "new liberty" of 2.1. Liberty is linked to the rule of law – "laws superior in authority [*imperia*] to men."[99] Yet the Roman people were unprepared for a free way of life – Brutus understands this, even after he leads the revolt which expels the Tarquinii – thus he has the people swear to "suffer no man to be king in Rome," so that they will not "later be turned from their purpose by the entreaties or the gifts of princes."[100] Brutus acted at the right moment: Had he acted earlier, it would have been from "a premature eagerness for liberty."[101] Livy asks:

For what would have happened if that rabble of shepherds and vagrants, having deserted their own peoples ... possessed themselves of liberty, or at

---

[95] Ibid., 1.49.7.
[96] On the idea of tyrants ruling like the head of a household, see Christopher Whidden, "Cyrus's Imperial Household: An Aristotelian Reading of Xenophon's Cyropaedia," *Polis* 25, no. 1 (2008): 31–62.
[97] Livy, *From the Founding of the City*, 1.49.8.
[98] Ibid., 1.46.3.
[99] Ibid., 2.1.1.
[100] Ibid., 2.1.9.
[101] Ibid., 2.1.3.

least impunity, had thrown off their fear of kings only to be stirred by the ruf-
fling storms of tribunician demagogues, breeding quarrels with the senators of
a city not their own, before even the pledges of wife and children and love of
the very place and soil (an affection of slow growth) had firmly united their
aspirations? The nation would have crumbled away with dissension before it
had matured.[102]

For liberty to flourish, the people needed to mature, to cultivate certain
mores; and with this maturity came the expulsion of the monarchs, which
brought liberty not because the consuls' power was diminished "compared
with that which the kings had exercised," but because their authority was
limited to a single year.[103]
    Even earlier in the narrative we see the effect that good leaders have on
those they lead in the person of Numa Pompilius. He stands in contrast
to the more warlike Romulus, and is a second founder – "he prepared to
give the new City, founded by force of arms, a new foundation in law, statutes, and observances."[104] Doing this required that he change the conditions
of Rome itself, in particular bringing it peace, since the Romans' "nature
grew wild and savage through war." His people needed to be "softened by
the disuse of arms." Yet despite bringing about foreign peace, Numa feared
that "relief from anxiety on the score of foreign perils [*metus hostium*]" could
bring about "extravagance and idleness" – *luxuriarent otio animi*. The Romans
had been held back by fear and discipline before, and so Numa deploys religion, seeking to bring about "the fear of Heaven" – *deorum metum*.[105] To do
so, he "pretended to have nocturnal meanings with the goddess Egeria."
Numa, in short, turns to artifice and deception to bring about his goals.
    Yet the effects of this were quite good, as it "tinged the hearts of all with
piety," and "the nation was governed by its regard for promises and oaths, rather
than by the dread of laws and penalties."[106] Fear takes a back seat to morals.
Numa's character, and his own apparent *pietas*, profoundly affected his own
subjects, just as Tarquinius' character had similar effects. Yet while Tarquinius'
character undermined his role and status, as well as the goodwill of the people,
"Numa's subjects were spontaneously imitating the character of their king, as

---

[102] Ibid., 2.1.4–5.
[103] Ibid., 2.1.6.
[104] Ibid., 1.19.1.
[105] Ibid., 1.19.2–4.
[106] Ibid., 1.21.1.

their unique exemplar" – *unici exempli mores formarent.*[107] His observed character produces admiration and cements the bonds of the community.

We have seen, now, the relationship between character and goodwill in oratory and have begun to see similar patterns in Livy's *From the Founding of the City.* There is a fascinating parallel between Cicero's rhetorical writings and Livy, in this regard, and Cicero's *On the Commonwealth* and *On Friendship.* Scipio, in Book 2, outlines his conception of the statesman, whom he exhorts thus: "that he never cease educating and observing [*instituendo contemplandoque*] himself, that he summon others to imitate him, that through the brilliance of his mind and life he offer himself as a mirror [*speculum*] to his fellow citizens."[108] The statesman has a crucial role in maintaining concord within the community, aspiring to political harmony "in the concord of very different people." Concord is "the tightest and the best bond of safety in every republic; and that concord can never exist without justice."[109] The leader whose example draws his fellow citizens to him is instrumental in maintaining concord, and ultimately the agreement that is central to the commonwealth itself: "the commonwealth is the concern of a people, but a people is not any group of men assembled in any way, but an assemblage of some size associated with one another through agreement on law and community of interest."[110]

The ideal statesman – the *rector rei publicae* – "understands as well as utilizes the means by which the state's best interests are secured and advanced."[111] In Book 5 of *On the Commonwealth,* Cicero – in the context of discussing the importance of the natural sense of shame (*verecundia*) in preventing individuals from engaging in crime – describes the *rector rei publicae* thus:

The leader of commonwealths strengthens this sense of shame by his opinions, and he brings it to perfection by institutions and education, so that shame does as much as fear to keep citizens from crime.[112]

Part of this education is the example of the *rector* himself, the mirror of his people – a visual metaphor akin to Livy's understanding of his own writing

---

[107] Ibid.,1.21.2.
[108] Cicero, *On the Commonwealth,* 2.69a.
[109] Ibid., 2.69a.
[110] Ibid., 1.39a.
[111] Cicero, *On the Ideal Orator,* 1.211. On the *rector rei publicae* formulation, see, e.g., Cicero, *De Oratore,* 1.211.
[112] Cicero, *On the Commonwealth,* 5. 6. Cf. Cicero, *De Republica,* 5.6.

as a monument – who draws them toward him by his virtuous behavior. The ideal statesman is thus persuasive, and attractive, alluring others through his character. Much like Cicero's ideal orator, both possess a character that inspires and attracts.[113]

Similar language of virtue and attraction is to be found in Cicero's *On Friendship*. In addition to the attraction to virtue in politics and oratory, Cicero argues that friendship, rooted in love, establishes goodwill (*benevolentiam*).[114] As opposed to those who view friendship as rooted either in weakness or want, Cicero views friendship as originating in "nature," in particular in "an inclination of the soul joined with a feeling of love [*sensu amandi*]."[115] Love, in turn, is a kind of sense (*sensus*) that emerges "when once we have met someone whose habits and character are congenial with our own," insofar as we ourselves are virtuous. The reason for this is clear: "there is nothing more lovable than virtue, nothing that more allures us to affection" – *Nihil est enim virtute amabilius, nihil quod magis alliciat ad diligendum.*[116] Our natural attraction to virtue is so great that we can even "feel a sort of affection … for those whom we have never seen" – *quos numquam vidimus* – though vision is of great importance.[117] Such is the "force of integrity" – *vis probitatis* – that it can move us to love even aspects of our enemies.[118] Friendship – and hence *benevolentia* – is thus rooted in our perception of and natural attraction to virtue.

Good leaders, like friends and orators, possess an exemplary character, one that inspires those observing to emulate and honor it. We may turn back again to Livy: Valerius, in Book 7, urges Rome's soldiers that "it is my deeds [*facta*] and not my words [*dicta*] I would have you follow, and look to me not only for instruction but for example [*exemplum*]."[119] This in dealing with an army that was dispirited "by the enervation resulting from excessive luxury [*luxu*] and by their own effeminacy [*mollitia*]."[120] Valerius' good

---

[113] Elaine Fantham, *The Roman World of Cicero's De Oratore* (Oxford: Oxford University Press, 2004), 311–19. On the idea of the orator as *rector*, see Gary Remer, "The Classical Orator as Political Representative: Cicero and the Modern Concept of Representation," *Journal of Politics* 72, no. 4 (2010): 1063–82.

[114] Cicero, *De Amicitia*, trans. William Armistead Falconer, *Cicero: De Senectute, De Amicitia, De Divinatione* (London: William Heinemann, 1923), 26.

[115] Ibid., 27.

[116] Ibid., 27–8.

[117] Ibid., 28.

[118] Ibid., 29.

[119] Livy, *From the Founding of the City*, 7.32.12.

[120] Ibid., 7.32.7.

character is indeed instructive, and his effect on his army is palpable; "There was never a commander who more endeared [*familiarior*] himself to his men by cheerfully sharing all their duties with the meanest of the soldiers."[121] His display of virtue brings about the spontaneous adherence of his subordinates. Most popular of all, says Livy, is that "he was the same in office that he had been while a candidate."[122]

He may be contrasted with yet another Appius Claudius, one of the *decemviri* and their "guiding hand"; initially, "he came out all at once as the people's friend, and caught at every breath of popularity."[123] Yet he, after a fine beginning, transforms on his second term as *decemvir*, and "threw off the mask he had been wearing, and began from that moment to live as his true nature prompted him"; he even affects his colleagues, whom he molds "after his own character."[124] A false friend, in a sense, he corrupts them through his inconstancy, like Cicero's flatterer in *On Friendship* 93. Like Tarquinius Superbus and his rape of Lucretia, the *decemviri* meet their downfall as a result of runaway lust – in this instance, the attempted abduction of Verginia, whose *pudor* leads Tarquin to "cruel and tyrannical violence."[125] His lust, and the lust of the other *decemviri*, leads to a secession; in exchange for their return to the city, the tribunes are reinstated, and the *decemviri* lose power.

VI. FEAR, LOVE, AND CONSENSUS

What we see in the preceding examples – Appius and Quinctius, Servius and Tarquinius – is that vicious behavior repels and corrodes goodwill – *benevolentia* – while virtuous behavior attracts and creates it. Those who exercise authority effectively do not simply possess authority in the formal sense, but behave in an authoritative fashion and are seen and recognized as such. In doing so, they arouse the goodwill of their subordinates. Authority must be recognized voluntarily to be effective – this involves observation and recognition of the outstanding qualities of those who possess authority, and that they actually *have* the virtues. Good leaders are exemplary leaders, and they draw individuals toward them in a way that

---

[121] Ibid., 7.33.1.
[122] Ibid., 7.33.4.
[123] Ibid., 3.33.7.
[124] Ibid., 3.36.1.
[125] Ibid., 3.44.4.

intimidation and fear cannot. Why is this so? The answer, I suggest, has to do with the emotions aroused through observation of character and behavior.

To pursue this suggestion, let us turn first to another source on Tarquinius: Cicero's *On the Commonwealth*. Cicero describes Tarquinius Superbus as wanting "to be feared" because his reign was based on a crime, "relying on his victories and his wealth."[126] From this single person's action, "the form of the commonwealth was altered from a good one to the worst" – from monarchy to tyranny.[127] Cicero reflects, in this discussion, a broader pattern in ancient thought: Relying on fear, as opposed to goodwill, was a mark of bad rulership. Aristotle, for instance, held that "the way most tyrants exercise their rule" involved pursuing three goals: "that the ruled not trust one another; that they be powerless; that they think small." Coercion and fear play an important role in this activity, as does preventing the formation of trust among the tyrant's subjects.[128] Absent goodwill from his subjects, the tyrant turns to coercion; turning to coercion further erodes goodwill.

A ruler whose power was based on fear lacks the goodwill, and hence consensus, of those he governs. In this regard, Schofield has shown the importance of consensus and consent in Cicero's account of the *res publica*. Schofield argues that "One criterion of the non-existence of *res publica* in a regime or set-up is the dissolution of the mutuality and moral consensus which bind society together."[129] Cicero's commonwealth is rooted in consensus – a "shared sense of justice reflected in the moral life and institutional arrangements of a society."[130] The *res publica* was not simply a matter, then, of institutional arrangements; rather, "the *res publica* was defined in moral terms."[131] As Seneca noted, Brutus erred in thinking that, by killing Caesar, "the state could be recalled to its former constitution when its ancient ways had been abandoned."[132] Institutions are insufficient without morals, and the republic itself was a *moral* community.

Cicero devotes further attention to the topic in *On Duties*, arguing "there is nothing at all more suited to protecting and retaining influence than to

---

[126] Cicero, *On the Commonwealth*, 2.45.

[127] Ibid., 2.47.

[128] Aristotle, *Politics*, ed. C.D.C. Reeve (Indianapolis: Hackett, 1998), 1313a35, 1314a27.

[129] Malcolm Schofield, "Cicero's Definition of *Res Publica*," in *Cicero the Philosopher: Twelve Papers*, ed. J.G.F. Powell (Oxford: Clarendon Press, 1995): 63–83, 71.

[130] Ibid., 72.

[131] Galinsky, *Augustan Culture: An Interpretive Introduction*, 58.

[132] Seneca, *On Favors*, ed. John M. Cooper and J.F. Procope, *Seneca: Moral and Political Essays* (Cambridge: Cambridge University Press, 1995), 2.20.2.

be loved, and nothing less suited than to be feared."[133] The assassination of Caesar, who ruled by arms – that is, without a foundation of affectionate agreement – provides an example of his reasoning: "no amount of influence can withstand the hatred of a large number of men ... if it was unrecognized before, is certainly recognized now."[134] Cicero concludes thus: "Fear is a poor guardian over any length of time; but goodwill [benivolentia] keeps faithful guard for ever." He makes much the same point in On Friendship, where he argues that tyrants cannot have friends since their relationships lack "goodwill" – benevolentiae – because tyrants are the objects of fear, and perceive that their subjects are frightened of them.[135]

In On Duties, goodwill may be produced primarily "by kind services [beneficiis];" it may also be produced by "the willingness to provide kind service [voluntate benefica]" – even if one cannot do so.[136] One's name and reputation attracts the love [amor] of people if he is held to have "the very reputation and rumor of liberality, of beneficence, of justice, of keeping faith, and of all the virtues that are associated with gentleness and easiness of conduct."[137] Indeed, Cicero goes as far as to suggest that "the very thing we call honorable and seemly pleases us [nobis placet] in itself, and moves the hearts of all by its nature and appearance [specie sua]" – this because virtue and decorum both please and touch those who perceive it.[138] As we have seen, Cicero makes a similar argument in On Friendship, where virtue and its perception are also held to produce goodwill.

What is striking in these passages is the clear overlap between the goals of oratory – displaying goodwill and cultivating the desired emotions through one's appearance – and practical ethics – acting rightly such that we attract the love of others, whether in friendship or in politics. Each, in turn, involves a mutual process of display and observation; behavior must be observed and recognized by an audience. Just as the audience of an orator is more likely to be persuaded by an individual whose character they observe and admire, and just as the led are more likely to follow and recognize the authority of those whom they recognize as virtuous, we are far more likely to trust

---

[133] Cicero, On Duties, 2.23. The Latin consulted is Cicero, De Officiis, trans. Walter Miller (Cambridge: Harvard University Press, 1997).
[134] Cicero, On Duties, 2.23.
[135] Cicero, De Amicitia 52–3.
[136] Cicero, On Duties, 2.32.
[137] Ibid., 2.32.
[138] Ibid., 2.32.

those that we love than those that we hate. Whether a speaker or a leader, one must move beyond the mere facts of the moment and engage the emotions of those who observe them. We see this similarity, in particular, in the discussion of *ethos* and *pathos* and their utility in persuasion. Both are means by which the orator can persuade his audience, yet in relying on his audience's assent, they limit the orator's behavior. Rather than present us with a speaker who simply manipulates his audience, or panders to their whims, we meet with a situation of negotiation and accommodation. Audiences judge orators, just as members of political communities judge leaders and individuals judge the character of their friends. Just as leaders must look to the beliefs of the led, the orator must look to the actual usage of the community in engaging in persuasion.

An orator – like a leader – needed to cultivate a certain persona, then, one that was pleasing; and in doing so, the orator would arouse certain emotions. The same was true of moral actors, though with the caveat that what was pleasing and what aroused the desired emotions in the observer was virtue itself. Both the orator and the moral actor derive benefits from this persona and these emotions: The prior persuades, the latter attains glory. The catch in all of this is that one may seem good – to display a good character and arouse the desired emotions – while not being a particularly good person. This was certainly a danger for Cicero. We have already encountered the example of the persuasive individual who lacks the virtues of "integrity and the highest measure of good sense," and whose eloquence is like putting "weapons in to the hands of madmen."[139] Or we may think of *On Duties*, where Cicero famously remarks:

There are two ways in which injustice may be done, either through force or through deceit; and deceit seems to belong to a little fox, force to a lion. Both of them seem most alien to a human being; but deceit deserves a greater hatred. And out of all injustice, nothing deserves punishment more than that of men who, just at the time they are most betraying trust, act in such a way that they might appear to be good men.[140]

In both speech and action, then, there was the potential for deception along these lines in Cicero's mind; yet he also held out hope that "pretense

---

[139] Cicero, *On the Ideal Orator*, 3.55.
[140] Cicero, *On Duties*, 1.41.

can never endure," citing the examples of Tiberius and Caius Gracchus as evidence.[141] In the end, Cicero has at least some faith in popular judgment; as he puts it in *On Friendship*, "A public assembly, though composed of very ignorant men, can, nevertheless, usually sees the difference between a demagogue – that is a smooth-tongued, shallow citizen – and one who has stability, sincerity, and weight."[142] Indeed, it is precisely the inconstancy of the flatterer that gives him away: The flatterer "changes not only to suit another's humor and desires, but even his expression and his nod."[143] Flatterers' inner character, in effect, is observable through their external behavior.

Livy is similarly concerned with penetrating behind the façade and examining the character of leaders. Appearances, after all, can deceive – we saw this with Appius Claudius' first term as a decemvir. We may also turn to the example of M. Manlius Capitolinus, contemporary of Camillus, and envious of Camillus' success; "impetuous and passionate," Capitolinus "was the first of all the patricians to turn demagogue [*primus omnium ex patribus popularis*] and to cast in his lot with the plebeian magistrates."[144] He behaves in the way we might expect – attacking the system of credit, advocating land laws – evidence, perhaps, that "much of Livy's language and setting is colored by the struggles of the post-Gracchan era."[145] The potential anachronism aside, the episode of Capitolinus allows Livy to make an important point: Manlius "chose rather to be reputed great than virtuous."[146] Capitolinus echoes the false virtues of the Gracchi, and their deceptive qualities. He, though seeming to stand in favor of liberty (*pro libertate*) against the domination (*pro dominatione*) of the few, was actually seeking "kingly power."[147] In the end, Capitolinus is exposed, convicted, and thrown from the Tarpeian rock; "Such was the end of a man who, had he not been born in a free state, would have left a memorable name."[148] His counterpoint – Camillus – preferred virtue and was given glory because of his qualities.

[141] Ibid., 2.43.
[142] Cicero, *De Amicitia*, 95.
[143] Ibid., 93.
[144] Livy, *From the Founding of the City*, 6.11.6–7.
[145] J. Briscoe, "The First Decade," in *Livy*, ed. T.A. Dorey (London: Routledge and Kegan Paul, 1971): 1–20, 9.
[146] Livy, *From the Founding of the City*, 6.11.7.
[147] Ibid., 6.18.16.
[148] Ibid., 6.20.14.

VII. CONCLUSION

Maintaining Rome's moral community – the civic ties between its different members – and the goodwill-rooted consensus in which the republic itself was rooted, relied upon the successful negotiation of power's exercise by leaders. The consensus of the community, established in time and through action and reaction, contingent as it may have been, was not just a key limiting factor on power but also served to maintain and promote community through observation. Leaders needed to be virtuous, and to cultivate the goodwill of those they led. They did not simply need to *seem* virtuous; indeed, the desire to be virtuous rather than to seem virtuous might, in the short run, result in one not being terribly popular.

Like Cicero, Livy is concerned not just with the appearance of virtue and popularity, but true virtue and popularity. The reason why, I suggest, has to do with his conception of the republic's functioning and rhetoric. The republic was not just a set of institutions; it was a moral community, composed of different and distinct elements, bound and animated by its *mores*. Virtuous action and right rhetoric produce goodwill – and trust – through observation and recognition, and foster the healthy functioning of the republic. Observers respond to examples: When the example is bad, they are repelled, and trust and goodwill are undermined; when the example is good, they are attracted, and trust and goodwill are fostered. In both instances, however, exemplary individuals are not independent, but interdependent with the broader community.

To illustrate this interdependence, we may return to a passage in Book 2 noted earlier in brief: During the first plebeian secession, the Senate sent Menenius Agrippa to speak with the plebs as ambassador (*oratorem*), "an eloquent man and dear to the plebeians [*plebi carum*] as being one of themselves by birth."[149] Agrippa tells a story to the plebs about a time in which "man's members did not all agree amongst themselves," but instead had their own aims and desires and "thought it unfair that they should have the worry and the trouble of providing everything for the belly, while the belly remained quietly in their midst with nothing to do but to enjoy the good things which they bestowed upon it."[150] The other parts of the body decided to starve the belly, and in doing so "the members themselves and

[149] Ibid., 2.32.8.
[150] Ibid., 2.32.9.

the whole body were reduced to the utmost weakness."[151] The implication
of the story is clear: The sedition (*seditio*) of the parts of the body was like
"the anger of the plebs against the Fathers;" the parts cannot survive without the whole, and each part has a particular function.[152]

It is the appearance of the parts not doing what they should do that
promotes discord; that is, discord emerges as a result of discontent and
dissatisfaction rooted in the perceived non-performance of duties. When
the seceded plebs saw themselves, in a sense, as part of an interdependent
organism, they relented. After this speech, moves were made "towards harmony" – *de concordia coeptum*.[153] Harmony among the political community thus depends on each part fulfilling its proper role, but this harmony
among the parts of the community relies upon *consensus* and thus goodwill.
Goodwill produces and reinforces trust; whereas Sallust's moral order was
conditioned by the presence of collective fear, the moral order of Livy's
republic was a kind of equilibrium reached between exemplary virtuous
leaders and observing citizens.

Livy's republic is not a republic of equals; it is a republic of unequals. As
such, it is the locus for great potential conflict between many and few, leaders and led. Yet maintaining harmony between unequals requires not simply
that those of lesser status obey their superiors, but that those of superior
status draw their inferiors to them. They exist in a relationship of interdependence, not independence; elites depend on non-elites for recognition and honor, while non-elites depend on elites for leadership and moral
example. The health of the political community, and the maintenance and
enjoyment of liberty, thus depends on how citizens deal with each other.
As Pettit puts it, "the enjoyment of non-domination in relation to another
agent … goes with being able to look the other in the eye, confident in the
shared knowledge that it is not by their leave that you pursue your innocent, non-interfering choices, as of publicly recognized right. You do not
have to live either in fear of that other, then, or in deference to them."[154]

Livy's elites must engage in persuasion, whether through their words or
through their characters, displayed in words and actions. Authority is thus
mutually constructed; it entails both the possession and projection of an

---

[151] Ibid., 2.32.10.
[152] Ibid., 2.32.12.
[153] Ibid., 2.33.1.
[154] Pettit, *Republicanism*, 71.

authoritative persona, as well as the recognition of this persona by the many. Concord emerges through action and perception, and the republic is bound together in a community based on shared values and their recognition. Sustainable republican politics entailed harmonious relationship emerging through and from conflict; to return to a passage we noted earlier, Allen writes that "citizens who behave with propriety toward strangers avoid acting, on the one hand, like acquiescent people who accept everything ... and, on the other, like domineering people."[155] Those judging the actions and characters of others could well err, and this process does not guarantee success or stability; nor does it guarantee that actually virtuous leaders will always be recognized as such, nor that actually vicious leaders will always be recognized as such. Despite the dangers, consensus and the judgment of the community offer hope for a harmonious mix of the distinct members of political communities. As Allen argues in discussing the role of rhetoric in contemporary democratic societies, the rhetorical construction of leaders, then, provides a resource for treating and ameliorating the tensions and fissures that emerge within the political community in Livy's conception of Rome's past.

The relationship between leaders and led, like that of orator and audience, or between friends, is one of negotiation and accommodation based on the observation and recognition of character and behavior. Again, history is akin to a monument, for Livy, that may be viewed and that provides its readers with a wealth of examples. Examples – good or bad – need to be recognized as such through a mutual process of performance and observation. Just as the orator can neither say nor do just anything because his audience constrains him, so, too, are leaders constrained through their followers' perception and recognition of their qualities. *Concordia* – and its origins in *benevolentia* – in Livy's *From the Founding of the City* thus serve to anchor relationships between those who are different and unequal. Rhetoric – and the rhetoricization of leadership – serves, then, to foster the cohesion and cooperation of republican political communities.

---

[155] Allen, *Talking to Strangers*, 121.

5

TACITUS ON GREAT MEN, BAD
RULERS, AND PRUDENCE

I. INTRODUCTION

We have seen in discussing Sallust and Livy that each sought to navigate the tensions and conflicts that emerged in the political community in different ways. Sallust's Rome, characterized by competition and antagonism, had been constrained by fear. With fear removed, the competitive and antagonistic energies of Rome threatened to become destructive, but the process and practice of antagonistic rhetoric offered hope for these energies' treatment and expression, however contingent and temporary this treatment and expression may have been. In Livy, by contrast, we saw the importance of consensualism and harmony, created through the display and observation of action and character, with goodwill functioning to bind the political community together. The rhetorical construction of leadership was central to achieving a vital and healthy republic, negotiating conflicts that emerged partly as a result of difference and inequality.

We are now moving, however, to a very different context, one in which the republic as a system of participatory government was not simply a memory, as it was for both Sallust and Livy, but a *distant* memory. This entails, as we shall see, not just changes in how the relationship of rhetoric to politics and power can be theorized, but also changes in what free action and speech might mean. We might expect such changes to have attended the displacement of participatory government by monarchical government, given both what we have seen of contemporary discussions of republican liberty and its connection to participatory government, on the one hand, as well as the broader link between rhetoric, persuasion, and participation, on the other.

Indeed, freedom and the practice of a certain kind of rhetoric were tightly connected, a connection evident in Aristotle's *Rhetoric*. Aristotle writes that "it is the mark of a free man not to live at another's beck and call."[1] The immediate context is Aristotle's discussion of the ignobility of practicing a "sordid craft," but the broader point is important. To be free is to be independent of the wills of others. This is not simply a matter of being able to act without being subject to the whims of another, but being able to *speak* freely and independently. For Cicero, to be unable to speak freely might mean being unfree altogether: In his speech *For Sulla*, and in response to the charge that it was tyrannical for him to "pick and choose whom ... to defend and attack," Cicero remarks, "it is servitude [*servitus*] not to do so."[2] As Brunt notes, "Freedom of speech for a senator meant that he could speak what he felt without being subject to fear or pressure."[3] Being unfree, whether in speaking or in acting, meant in both instances being subject not to the interference of the laws, but rather the arbitrary interference of other men.

Speaking freely becomes a problem – if not an impossibility – with the emergence of individuals who were more powerful than any other individuals. That is to say, great distinctions in power constrained speech: As Cicero argues in *On Friendship*, in thinking about what it means to be a friend, we must distinguish between comity (*comitas*) and flattery (*assentatio*), as the latter is unworthy "of a free man [*libero*]," and to be expected in the presence of a "tyrant."[4] Cicero thus connects servile speech – flattery – to political inequality. In a similar vein, we might note with a later writer in the republican tradition, Trenchard, that "It is one of the great Evils of Servitude, that let the Tyranny be ever so severe, 'tis always flattered; and the more severe 'tis, the more 'tis flattered." Fear and servitude lead to flattery, in that they "naturally produce, as well as have recourse to Flattery, as the best means of Self-Preservation." By contrast, flattering and obsequious speech is unnecessary in conditions of freedom, which "scorns" flattery.[5] Such speech

---

[1] Aristotle, *Rhetoric*, 1367a31–31.
[2] Cicero, *Pro Sulla*, trans. C. MacDonald, *In Catilinam I–IV, Pro Murena, Pro Sulla, Pro Flacco* (Cambridge: Harvard University Press, 1989), 48
[3] Brunt, "*Libertas* in the Republic," 314. The extent to which this freedom extended beyond the senatorial order is a matter of scholarly discussion; for a recent expansive view, however, see Chrissanthos, "Freedom of Speech and the Roman Republican Army."
[4] Cicero, *De Amicitia*, 89.
[5] John Trenchard, *Cato's Letters; or, Essays on Liberty, Civil and Religious, and Other Important Subjects*, 4 vols. (New York: Russell and Russell, 1969), vol. 1, 188.

need not be a product of tyranny, however; extreme distinctions in power, and conditions of dependence, breed flattery and distorted speech. As Pettit argues, those who are unfree, in the sense of not being guaranteed the good of non-domination, "find themselves in a position where they are demeaned by their vulnerability, being unable to look the other in the eye, and where they may even be forced to fawn or toady or flatter in the attempt to ingratiate themselves."[6]

Those who are subject to arbitrary interference – that is to say, domination – must find ways to preclude it, ways that are not particularly dignified:

The self-censorship or self-inhibition that the person practices need not involve actively thwarting desire; it will occur just so far as there are any options, otherwise desired or undesired, that a wish to keep the dominating party sweet would stop them taking.[7]

The choice of words – keeping the dominator sweet – is instructive. The individual subject to arbitrary interference must find ways to ingratiate herself, to please the one who dominates her. Speech, rather than being the vehicle by which power is articulated and limited, maintains a relationship to power that is "oblique," and, in a monarchical system, the importance of pleasing one's audience is magnified by the constriction of one's audience in scope and number through the institution of monarchy.[8] The kinds of speech, and the kinds of behaviors, that would have served one well in the rough and tumble politics of the republic would seem ill-suited to the principate.

Tacitus, subject of this chapter and the following, seems acutely aware of the tenuous place of speech in the principate. Indeed, not only does he write a work – the *Dialogue on Orators* – in which he seems to pronounce the death of oratory; he seems in his own life to have turned away from the practice of oratory. What are we to make of Tacitus' apparent turn from oratory, and the seeming death of eloquence? What are the implications of monarchy for theorizing about rhetoric and republicanism? I explore these questions over the next two chapters. In this chapter I discuss the interplay between political action and political actors' expectations in the face of the principate

[6] Pettit, *Republicanism*, 5.
[7] Pettit, *A Theory of Freedom*, 137.
[8] Catherine Steel, *Roman Oratory* (Cambridge: Cambridge University Press, 2006), 21.

through a reading of Tacitus' *Dialogue on Orators* and *Agricola*. I do so in part by comparing them with Cicero's *On the Ideal Orator*, and in part by focusing on the ambiguity of peace in Tacitus' writings, an ambiguity that highlights the ambiguity of Tacitus's present and the importance of prudence. Rather than view Tacitus as a wistful republican eager to return to the glory days of Cicero, or as a realist who views eloquence and liberty as dead and favors quietism, I suggest that Tacitus is highly attuned to the ambiguities and tensions that exist for Romans seeking to speak and act with integrity in the face of the ambiguities of the principate. Tacitus is centrally occupied with finding some middle ground between withdrawal (or foolish opposition) and cooptation, and is thus concerned with the practice and cultivation of prudence, along with delineating the character of those who are – and are not – prudent.

In this chapter, I begin in Section II by exploring Cicero's account of the political role of the orator-statesman in *On the Ideal Orator*, focusing on the active, public, and assertive nature of the orator's activity. I then turn in Section III to theorizing the role of oratory given the concentration of power the principate brought about, as well as the optimism that attended the death of Domitian. Building on this discussion, I turn in Section IV to Tacitus' *Dialogue on Orators*, focusing on the political account of the decline of oratory – taken up by Maternus – and the apparent choice he offers between withdrawal and collaboration. Following my discussion of the *Dialogue*, I briefly explore in Section V the so-called quarrel between philosophers and rhetoricians, with an eye toward Plato's *Gorgias* and its echoes in the *Dialogue*. This leads to my discussion of Tacitus' *Agricola* in Section VI, which I read as focusing on the importance of prudence in navigating the apparent choice between collaboration, opposition, and withdrawal. I turn next in Section VII to the ambiguity of peace in the *Dialogue* and *Agricola*, and conclude by reconnecting the ambiguity of peace and the importance of prudence in Tacitus' writings with Cicero's thought.

II. CICERO'S *ON THE IDEAL ORATOR* AND THE ORATOR'S POLITICAL ROLE

Let us first turn to Cicero's account of the orator's political role in *On the Ideal Orator*. In this work, Cicero develops a conception of the ideal orator-statesman and his relationship to peaceful and free government.[9] Cicero, as we have seen, was well aware of the dangers of rhetoric and the risks that unprincipled orators might pose to civil life. Yet despite these dangers, Cicero provides an account of eloquence's role in the maintenance of a peaceful, quiet, and well-constituted society. This role centers in part on oratory's admirable directive power in public life: "being able, through speech, to have a hold on human minds, to win over their inclinations, to drive them at will in one direction, and to draw them at will from another."[10] The directive power of oratory is precisely what Crassus views as having "ever reigned supreme in every free nation and especially in quiet and peaceful communities [*pacatis tranquillisque civitatibus*]." Oratory thus accompanies and guides peaceful communities; though peaceful and quiet, this is a peace that was produced and maintained through an active and discursive politics, and these communities were not without political and social conflicts that necessitated the activity of the orator. Thus, the orator's speech can influence "popular upheavals, the scruples of jurors, or the authority of the Senate," serving as a stabilizing and guiding influence. It is the faculty of eloquence that enables one to help those in need, as well as to protect oneself and "challenge the wicked or take revenge when provoked," thus assisting in the maintenance of the community's moral health and the administration of justice.[11]

Crassus continues by asking:

what other power could have been strong enough either to gather scattered humanity into one place, or to lead it out of its brutish existence in the wilderness up to our present condition of civilization, as men and as citizens, or, after the establishment of social communities, to give shape to laws, tribunals, and civic rights?

Given the immense power of oratory, both in the formation and maintenance of communities, Crassus concludes by suggesting that the "perfect orator" provides "for the safety [*salutem*] of countless individuals and of the State at large," in addition to contributing to his own "dignity," through his wisdom and his statesmanship.[12]

---

[9] For an extended treatment, see Fantham, *The Roman World of Cicero's De Oratore*, 311–19.
[10] Cicero, *On the Ideal Orator*, 1.30. Cf. Cicero, *Brutus*, 183–189.
[11] Cicero, *On the Ideal Orator*, 1.31–2.
[12] Ibid., 1.33–4.

Crassus makes similar arguments in Book 3 regarding the ideal orator, but he also develops a new topic: the "rupture ... between the tongue and the brain." Thought and speech had been united prior to this rupture, evident, for instance, in the words of Phoenix in the *Iliad*, as well as the activities of individuals like Lycurgus, Solon, Cato, and Scipio, wise individuals who were intensely involved in practical politics.[13] There were others, such as Pythagoras and Anaxagoras, who turned "to the study of the universe," more tranquil than the inquiry joined with political affairs; the knowledge pursued by such individuals was more "pure," and hence "more pleasant"; and so "the most gifted people" turned to these rather than political pursuits. Whether they had been forced from politics "by the stormy circumstances of the time," or they had chosen other fields of inquiry, these individuals represented the rupture of the unity of speech and action.[14]

Despite these tensions, some still succeeded – Crassus names Pericles, Themistocles, and Theramenes – in political life, while others – such as Gorgias, Thrasymachus, and Isocrates – "were not themselves involved in the state, but were still teachers of this same wisdom." In this context, "others appeared who on their part were amply endowed with learning and natural ability, but shirked politics and its practices on deliberate principle," targeting in particular "this practice of speaking." The most important of these critics was Socrates, who "easily ranked above all the others, wherever he directed his attention – not only because of his intelligence, acumen, charm, and refinement, but also because of his eloquence, variety, and fullness." That is, Socrates was (ironically) a truly eloquent individual. Socrates divided the "shared title" of speaker and doer into "the knowledge of forming wise opinions and of speaking with distinction," despite the fact that they are "tightly linked."[15]

For Cicero, then, not only does oratory play a central role in the foundation and maintenance of free states, but this conception of oratory centers on the union between wisdom and eloquence, words and actions. Indeed, part of what is distinctive about Cicero's approach in *On the Ideal Orator* is that he borrows from both philosophy – with its claims to knowledge – and rhetoric – with its claims to eloquence – to develop a synthetic view of

---

[13] Cf. Homer, *The Iliad*, trans. Richard Lattimore (Chicago: University of Chicago Press, 1951), 9.443.

[14] Cicero, *On the Ideal Orator*, 3.56–8.

[15] Ibid., 3.59–61.

the relationship between the two. As Wisse argues, part of the reason why Cicero rejected the conventional rules of rhetoric was because they were "too inflexible," and what was required instead was that, "ideally speaking, the orator's knowledge should actually be universal."[16]

In addition to the philosophical knowledge and virtues that the consummate orator requires, however, Crassus adds one more crucial component to his conception of the ideal orator in Book 3: "without the vigor that is acquired in the forum, an orator cannot be sufficiently forceful and impressive."[17] Oratory is not merely a matter of knowledge and ability, then, but a matter of practice. Its practice, in turn, requires specific political and institutional venues featuring dispersed power and judgment and public competition between speakers, venues and practices, which, as we saw in Chapter 1, Cicero believed to be imperiled by the turmoil of the late republic.[18]

Without the appropriate arena, popular and antagonistic oratory – and political action – becomes incoherently focused, and in monarchical conditions the opinions and desires of one come to have greater influence than the opinions and desires of the many. The nature of politically effective speech itself may be expected to change, as Javitch points out in discussing Cicero in light of Castiglione's *Book of the Courtier*: "the political pressures of despotism shape and require an artful behavior quite foreign to Cicero's ideal of the civilized man."[19] Indeed, Cicero likens his orator to one engaging in a kind of combat, with eloquence serving as his arms, remarking of those who read the rules of rhetoric: "they should ask themselves what it is that they want, whether they are going to take up arms for sport or for battle" – *ad pugnandum arma sint sumpturi*.[20] Just as combat by arms was an avenue to glory, it is also worth noting that, for Cicero, eloquence was a path to glory:

For what is superior to eloquence, whether the admiration of one's hearers, or the hope of those in need, or the gratitude of those whom one has defended, is

---

[16] Jakob Wisse, "*De Oratore*: Rhetoric, Philosophy, and the Making of the Ideal Orator," in *Brill's Companion to Cicero: Oratory and Rhetoric*, ed. James M. May (Leiden: Brill, 2002), 375–400, 377–8.

[17] Cicero, *On the Ideal Orator*, 3.80.

[18] See Cicero, *On Duties*, 2.67; Cicero, *Brutus*, 6–7.

[19] Daniel Javitch, *Poetry and Courtliness in Renaissance England* (Princeton: Princeton University Press, 1978), 46.

[20] Cicero, *On the Ideal Orator*, 2.84. See also 3.85 on the image of eloquence as a kind of weapon.

in question? Therefore our ancestors gave to eloquence the foremost standing among civil professions.[21]

Eloquence was thus an essential component of ambitious and competitive Romans' activity in the public eye in the antagonistic context of the republic.

III. A CHANGED CONTEXT

We might expect the active, open and plain-speaking orator that Cicero idealizes to be out of place in a political system in which power is concentrated rather than widely dispersed. We can begin to glimpse the changes in the way in which the orator's political role could be conceived in a remarkable (and tormented) letter Cicero sent to Gn. Plancius in January of 45 BCE. Referring to two letters he received from Plancius, in which the latter congratulated him for having obtained his former dignity (*meam pristinam dignitatem obtinere*), Cicero is introspective:

Well, if "standing" [*dignitas*] means to feel as a loyal citizen and to have one's sentiments approved by honest men, then I do maintain my standing. But if it consists in the power to implement [*re efficere*] one's feelings, or even to speak freely in their defense [*libera oratione defendere*], not a vestige of standing is left to us.[22]

Here as elsewhere, Cicero is aware of his own diminished power and scope for political action under the rule of Julius Caesar, a development he laments: *Otium* is a nice word for expressing ineffectuality due to political marginalization. He is safe, but his dignity is a far cry from what it had been, just as his *otium* pails in comparison to the *otium* of Scipio Africanus.[23] What matters is not simply recognition and respect, but the power to act and to speak effectively, and it is instructive that Cicero's sense of loss focuses on the loss of political efficacy and free speech. To be free, as we have seen in discussing Pettit, is in part to be able to control one's own fate.

If Cicero faced such challenges in his own lifetime, we may expect a more tenuous situation with the final collapse of the republic and the establishment of the principate. By the time of Tacitus, the republic (in the sense

---

[21] Cicero, *On Duties*, 2.66.
[22] Cicero, *Letters to Friends*, 4.14.
[23] Cf. Cicero, *On Duties*, 3.1–6. Rawson notes that *otium* was "the time not spent on *negotia*, the care of one's property, clients and political advancement." Rawson, *Intellectual Life in the Late Roman Republic*, 19.

of a participatory political community) was long gone. The principate's first dynasty – the Julio-Claudians – had passed. So too had its second – the Flavians – a dynasty that had ended badly with Domitian. Domitian's assassination in 96 CE was welcomed by much of Rome's elite, bringing with it both respite and hope: respite from Domitian's paranoid and dangerous rule (especially in its final stages) and hope for a different and better future.[24] Domitian was particularly reviled, it seems, for his apparent harshness toward those whose speech and writings displeased him.[25] This was especially true of those martyred under Domitian: Helvidius Priscus, Junius Arulenus Rusticus, and Herennius Senecio.[26] Suetonius reports that Domitian had Hermogenes of Tarsus killed "because of some allusions in his History"; he had executed Junius Rusticus:

because he had published eulogies of Paetus Thrasea and Helvidius Pricus and called them the most upright of men; on the occasion of this charge he banished all the philosophers from the city and from Italy. He also executed the younger Helvidius, alleging that in a farce composed for the stage he had under the characters of Paris and Oenone censured Domitian's divorce from his wife.[27]

Not all *principes* had been so prickly; Julius Caesar, for instance, responded to Cicero's eulogy of Cato with his own *Anticatones*.[28] Such a response would not be likely under Domitian, whom a recent biographer suggests was a deeply paranoid individual, summing up his character thus: "unwilling to face criticism, inclined to be fiercely solitary, and heartily disliked."[29] The

---

[24] A story in Suetonius captures this paranoia: Toward the end of his reign, Suetonius reports Domitian to have lined the walls in the area in which he took his daily walks with "phengite stone," which had a mirror-like surface, "to be able to see in its brilliant surface the reflection of all that went on behind his back." Suetonius, *Domitian*, trans. J.C. Rolfe, Vol. II, *Suetonius* (Cambridge: Harvard University Press, 1992), 14.4.

[25] On Domitian's perceived hostility to the arts (in comparison with Trajan), cf. Pliny, *Panegyricus*, trans. Betty Radice, *Pliny; Letters and Panegyricus* (Cambridge: Harvard University Press, 1969), 47.1. To be sure, Domitian was not entirely hostile to eloquence; we might point to Martial, Statius, and Quintilian in this regard. Alex Hardie, *Statius and the Silvae: Poets, Patrons and Epideixis in the Graeco-Roman World* (Liverpool: Francis Cairns, 1983), 45–7.

[26] Suetonius, *Domitian*, 10.3–4. Syme writes, "Official patronage need not always be harmful to poetry, to education, to erudition. Oratory or history is another matter. An uneasy or suspicious emperor inhibited free comment about present conditions, and soon about the past even, with espionage, delation, and the burning of books." Syme, *Tacitus*, vol. 1, 90.

[27] Suetonius, *Domitian*, 10.1, 10.3–4.

[28] On the *Anticatones*, see Furhmann, *Cicero and the Roman Republic*, 147.

[29] Pat Southern, *Domitian: Tragic Tyrant* (Bloomington: Indiana University Press, 1997), 120.

character of the prince, and understanding how to act given this character, thus becomes paramount in establishing the bounds of possible and permissible behavior.

With a new emperor (Nerva, 96–98 CE) and his successor (Trajan, 98–117 CE) blossomed new hope. A further source of optimism was Trajan's highly symbolic punishment of the *delatores*.[30] This hope and optimism were powerfully expressed in Pliny's *Panegyricus*, which notes the return of liberty no less than five times, and which couples its praise of Trajan with criticism of his predecessor Domitian. What would it mean, though, for liberty to be restored? In the context of the principate, surely this is not quite liberty as non-domination, unless we (with exceeding charity) conceived of the emperor as a benevolent autocrat constrained by the rule of law – the work is addressed to a *dominus*, after all, and it was his will that mattered most. We may, however, glimpse this liberty by examining what Pliny praises about Trajan, and what he condemns in Domitian. Part of this praise centers on Trajan's attitude toward letters, an especially relevant point given Domitian's alleged hostility to literature:

Under you the liberal arts are restored, to breathe and live in their own country – the learning which the barbarity of the past punished with exile, when an emperor acquainted with all the vices sought to banish everything hostile to vice, motivated less by hatred for learning as by fear for its authority.[31]

Domitian, hostile to and fearful of virtue, had banished what he viewed as a threat to his own status. Pliny, for one, not only shows us in his practice that oratory might be witnessing a rebirth with the death of Domitian; he tells us as much in his letters, suggesting that there was evidence of brilliant oratory in this time. Pliny describes having heard "two young men of outstanding ability and promise plead opposite each other."[32] The two would prove to be ornaments "not only to the present age but to literature itself."[33]

---

[30] See Pliny, *Panegyricus*, 58.3; cf. 66.2, 66.4, 78.3. Pliny, *Letters*, trans. Betty Radice.
[31] Pliny, *Panegyricus*, 47.1.
[32] Pliny, *Letters*, 6.11.1. *Pliny: Letters and Panegyricus* (1969). On the *delatores*, see Steven Rutledge, *Imperial Inquisitions: Prosecutors and Informants from Tiberius to Domitian* (New York: Routledge, 2001).
[33] Ibid., 6.11.1. To be sure, Pliny's views were not naive; as Brink notes, "Early in the first decade of the new century, perhaps after four to five years, perhaps sooner, Pliny felt moved to complain of the decline of oratory." C.O. Brink, "Can Tacitus' *Dialogus* Be Dated? Evidence and Historical Conclusions," *Harvard Studies in Classical Philology* 96 (1994): 251–280, 278.

Quintilian, the first-century rhetorician, author, and Pliny's rhetorical teacher, was also optimistic about the future of oratory along Ciceronian lines. For while "Cicero himself has failed to find his orator in actual life," Quintilian believed that perhaps "something more perfect may be found than has yet existed."[34] Quintilian also suggests that "the consummate advocates of the present day are serious rivals of the ancients."[35] Quintilian's *Institutes*, spanning twelve volumes, cover many topics: the nature of rhetoric and its educational requirements, the system of rhetoric and also the moral and political functions of oratory. For Quintilian, the practice of oratory was part of the responsibilities of a noble Roman, among which was the need to choose cases carefully from a moral perspective:

A good man will undoubtedly prefer defense to prosecution, but he will not have such a rooted objection to the task of accuser as to disregard his duty towards the state or towards individuals and refuse to call any man to render an account of his way of life.

Without advocates to support it through prosecution and defense, the law would be "powerless."[36] In both Quintilian and Pliny, then, we are provided testimony of oratory's importance and prowess; together, they provide us with a portrait of oratory and orators and their role in imperial political life that echoes what we have seen in Cicero.

My concern is not with the historical accuracy of these accounts, per se, and it is worth noting that opinion is divided on the discontinuity of oratory from the republic to the principate;[37] from a theoretical perspective, however, we should, given the link between rhetoric and liberty which we have encountered in Cicero's thought and between freedom and frank speech in republicanism, be suspicious. No longer was oratory a matter of competitive – even combative – speech to or before plural bodies; rather, the orator's activity was conducted with the "emperor as the figure of intercession between speaker and *populus*."[38] Against this backdrop of renewed interest and effort,

---

[34] Quintilian, *Institutio Oratoria*, 12.1.21.
[35] Ibid., 10.1.122.
[36] Ibid., 12.7.1.
[37] For a view emphasizing continuity, see Steven Rutledge, "Oratory and Politics in the Empire," in *A Companion to Roman Rhetoric*, ed. William J. Dominik and Jon Hall (Oxford: Blackwell, 2007): 109–21. For a view emphasizing discontinuity, see Steel, *Roman Oratory*, 21.
[38] Connolly, *The State of Speech*, 11.

Tacitus' attitude – his apparent turn from oratory to history – is striking, for he chooses to abandon oratory at precisely the moment when its future seemed promising given the optimism that attended Domitian's death. This optimism was evident not just in Pliny and Quintilian's writings, but in Tacitus' own *Agricola* ("this happy age," as Tacitus describes the era), and yet he writes a dialogue which seems to justify his own apparent decision to abandon oratory through the words of the poet Maternus, and to proclaim the death of oratory itself.[39]

Such a move on Tacitus' part is both understandable and puzzling. On the one hand, the institutional settings and purposes of oratory had greatly changed since the period of the late republic and Cicero; it is hard to imagine that oratory could be what it was under the watchful eye of a single and powerful ruler, especially given Cicero's emphasis on winning the approval of the crowd, his own awareness of the danger Caesar's great power posed to oratory, and the idea of orators engaging in a kind of combat. On the other hand, were the circumstances of oratory so bleak, Tacitus' optimism in the *Agricola* seems puzzling.

IV. GAIN-GETTING RHETORIC GREEDY FOR HUMAN BLOOD: POLITICS AND POETRY IN A *DIALOGUE ON ORATORS*

Given Tacitus' activity as an orator,[40] we may be more surprised with Tacitus' apparent turn from oratory when we turn to his own description of the post-Domitian era: Nerva had "united things long incompatible, the principate and liberty"; meanwhile, under Trajan there was "the rare good fortune of an age in which we may feel what we wish and may say what we feel."[41] This seems

---

[39] Tacitus, *Agricola*, trans. M. Hutton and W. Peterson, *Tacitus: Dialogus, Agricola, Germanicus* (Cambridge: Harvard University Press, 1963), 3.1. On Tacitus' apparent decision to turn "his back on the eloquence of the Senate and lawcourts," see Ronald Syme, *Tacitus*, vol. 1, 116. For a skeptical view of identifying Maternus and Tacitus on biographical grounds, see C.O. Brink, "Can Tacitus' *Dialogus* Be Dated? Evidence and Historical Conclusions," 271–2.

[40] Tacitus, as noted, was himself a renowned orator; he and Pliny had cooperated in prosecuting Marius Priscus, a trial whose topic paralleled the trials of the late republic: "indictment of a proconsul ... a province pillaged and the killing of Roman citizens." Syme, *Tacitus*, vol. 1, 102.

[41] Tacitus, *Agricola*, 3.1; Tacitus, *The Histories*, trans. Clifford H. Moore (Cambridge: Harvard University Press, 1925), 1.1

different, and more desirable from the perspective of the elite Roman than the rule of Domitian, given what we saw in Cicero's letter to Plancius. The conditions seemed highly promising for oratory, yet Tacitus seems to have turned from oratory to history, thus affirming the irrelevance and uselessness of the prior through the words of Maternus in his *Dialogue on Orators*.

Tacitus' position is striking, but not original; as Fantham notes, by the time of Quintilian, "The decline of eloquence had long been a hackneyed complaint. Sixty years earlier the elder Seneca had accepted decline as a fact, and associated it, as did Velleius, with the law of organic decay."[42] The comic writer Petronius, for instance, has his hero Encolpius blame the rhetoricians for "the decay of eloquence," the result of their "cult of euphony" making speech into "a pointless game."[43] No less than Cicero himself had mentioned a decline of oratory in the *Tusculan Disputations*, the product of an earlier and freer period: Cicero describes oratory as having "reached its zenith, with the result that now, as is the law of nature in almost everything ... [it] is beginning its decline and seems destined in a short while to come to nothing."[44]

If Tacitus' originality is not evident, even more striking, for our purposes, is that he does not actually endorse the view that oratory has declined; as Goldberg notes "there is little basis for the frequent claim that in [the *Dialogue*], 'Tacitus clearly asserted the decline, even the death, of oratory.'"[45] Tacitus distances himself from the speeches that *all* of the characters give: After all, he claims to reproduce "a conversation between certain persons," making his own abilities less the issue than simply being able to remember well.[46] His very framing of the debate is equivocal, as he notes that "the opposite point of view" (from Fabius Justus' belief in oratory's decline, that is) was expressed, praising the present over the past.[47]

---

[42] Elaine Fantham, "Imitation and Decline: Rhetorical Theory and Practice in the First Century after Christ," *Classical Philology* 73, no. 2 (1978): 102–16, 112.

[43] Petronius, *Satyrica*, trans. R. Bracht Branham and Daniel Kinney (Berkeley: University of California Press, 1996), 3.

[44] Cicero, *Tusculan Disputations*, trans. J.E. King (Cambridge: Harvard University Press, 1966), 2.5. The decline is linked to politics; and with this decline, philosophy is of greater importance.

[45] Sander M Goldberg, "Appreciating Aper: The Defense of Modernity in Tacitus' *Dialogus De Oratoribus*," *Classical Quarterly* 49, no. 1 (1999): 224–37, 224. Goldberg is here citing Gordon Williams, *Change and Decline: Roman Literature in the Early Empire* (Berkeley: University of California Press, 1978), 49. See Brink, "Can Tacitus' *Dialogus* Be Dated? Evidence and Historical Conclusions," 276–7.

[46] Tacitus, *A Dialogue on Oratory*, 1.2.

[47] Ibid., 1.4.

It is worth keeping these points in mind as we move forward, as I will argue later that Maternus – with whom a declinist reading of the *Dialogue* identifies Tacitus – does not serve as a viable example of prudence. With respect to the dialogue itself, however, Tacitus writes the work in response to a question from Fabius Justus: namely, why the present is so lacking in oratory. The piece is set in the reign of Vespasian, when Tacitus was young; the immediate context is that the poet Curiatius Maternus has written and recited a play, *Cato*, which offended powerful individuals in Rome, as we might expect, given that Cato had not only served a leadership role in the fight against Caesar, but had famously chosen suicide to life under a single ruler, no matter how merciful that ruler might be.[48] Marcus Aper, Julius Secundus, the young Tacitus (a silent observer), and Messalla visit Maternus to persuade him not to continue his practice, or at the very least to moderate the more offending aspects of his play; understandably, they fear for their friend.

Undaunted, Maternus announces that he will write yet another play, the *Thyestes*, sure to be at least equally inflammatory. Faced with the intransigence of the poet Maternus, Marcus Aper makes what seems to be a highly Ciceronian argument in favor of oratory and against Maternus' art of poetry. His criticisms of Maternus echo the criticisms Cicero made of those who turned from the practical life to the life of contemplation in Book 3 of *On the Ideal Orator*. Maternus has turned from a practice (eloquence, which is to say oratory) that brings great benefit, satisfaction, and fame to its practitioners. Its benefit lies in the fact that oratory is an art providing one with weapons to protect friends and strangers, "to strike fear and terror into the hearts of malignant foes," all the while being protected "behind a rampart of inalienable authority and power;" the military analogies echo Cicero's imagery.[49] Eloquence is of great "practical advantage" (*utilitate*), bringing with it respect and friendship, as well as great power: "Think of the growing crowd streaming round about the speaker, and taking on any mood in which he may care to wrap himself, as with a cloak."[50] The account – emphasizing attack and defense, authority, utility, and fame – is reminiscent of Cicero's valorization of eloquence in *On the Ideal Orator*.

But Aper goes somewhat beyond Cicero in *On the Ideal Orator*. He notes that Maternus' desire for "peace and quiet" (*quietis et securitatis*) is empty,

---

[48] On date and context, see Syme, *Tacitus*, vol. 1, 104–5.
[49] Tacitus, *A Dialogue on Oratory*, 5.5.
[50] Ibid., 5.7, 6.4.

since he chose as a topic for his play one which was sure to arouse enmity.[51] He is too bold for his times, despite his protestations; he is too political, and insufficiently prudent, it seems. Unlike an orator who, if she happens to offend in the course of a speech may "win commendation for loyalty and indulgence for outspokenness [*libertas*]," Maternus' writings:

cannot be held excused by the obligation to render a friendly service, or by loyalty to a client, or by the excitement of an unpremeditated utterance, made off-hand; no, it looks as if of set purpose you had selected a notorious personality, whose words would have great weight.[52]

Poetry leaves, by this account, no excuse for the poet analogous to the excuse of the orator when she gives offense. This makes Maternus' desire for quiet and security empty given the clear political messages of his plays.

Maternus, in his response, places his hopes for security in his *innocentia* rather than *eloquentia*: "Everyone finds in uprightness a readier protection than in eloquence for his personal standing and peace of mind; and I am not afraid of ever having to address the senate except in the interests of someone else who is in jeopardy." Poetry, argues Maternus, is *eloquentiae primordia* – primordial eloquence – "streaming into hearts that were as yet pure and free from any stain of guilt." Poetry precedes oratorical eloquence, then, and finds its origins in an earlier mode of life, free from corruption. By contrast, "gain-getting rhetoric … greedy for human blood, is a modern invention, the product of a depraved condition of society [*ex malis moribus natus*]."[53] Maternus, in this passage and elsewhere, fixates on the questionable morality of oratory, as does Scaevola in his critique of oratory in *On the Ideal Orators*.[54] As opposed to orators, poets sang "the praises of those that did well rather than defend the evil-doer." Maternus wishes to have nothing to do "with the mad racket and the hazards of the forum."[55] Rather, like those Cicero chides for abandoning the tumults and dangers of the public life, he prefers the peace and quiet of the poetic life.

Aper and Messalla then speak concerning the relative merits of ancient and modern oratory and the causes of the difference, Aper belittling those

---

[51] Ibid., 10.7.
[52] Ibid., 10.8, 10.6.
[53] Ibid., 11.3, 12.2.
[54] Cf. Cicero, *On the Ideal Orator*, 1.37–9.
[55] Tacitus, *A Dialogue on Oratory*, 12.3, 13.5.

who idolize the ancients (and the very distinction between ancients and moderns), Messalla focusing on the training of the orator. There follows a lacuna in the text, after which Maternus is speaking; he has taken up the theme of why modern oratory pales in comparison to ancient oratory. For him, the explanation is primarily social and political, and not educational, as it was in the earlier speech of Messalla. He likens great eloquence to fire: "it needs fuel to feed it, movement to fan it, and it brightens as it burns."[56] Today's orators, he argues, have "all the influence that it would be proper to allow them under settled, peaceable, and prosperous political conditions [*composita et quieta et beata re publica*]."[57] In the unsettled past, eloquence was the source of many evils, Maternus suggests, such as "schisms [*factiones*] between the aristocracy and never-ending struggles [*certamina*] between the senate and the commons."[58] Indeed, this tension and disunity, the result of eloquence, destroyed the commonwealth itself (*distrahebant rem publicam*).[59] Maternus argues that ancient Roman orators, as well as the Roman people of former times, were "without the strong hand of a single ruler."[60] In such times an orator knew as much as she was able to persuade the ignorant populace (*orator saperet quantum erranti populo persuadere poterat*).[61]

Nevertheless, the very chaos and danger of this period "provided a sphere for the oratory of those days and heaped on it what one saw were vast rewards." What were these rewards? The power of the orator here echoes Cicero's account: attaining and advancing in office, as well as authority and fame. Those who were the most effective speakers had the greatest power, "even when out of office"; the orators "could bend both the senate and the people to their will," as could Cicero's ideal orator. Eloquence brought both success and security: "without eloquence it was impossible for anyone either to attain to a position of distinction and prominence in the community, or to maintain it."[62] That is to say, it was precisely because of eloquence that Rome's elites earned and claimed to merit their station, as Cicero argued in *On the Ideal Orator*. Eloquence "was a sheer necessity"; to be held learned (*disertum*) was beautiful

---

[56] Ibid., 36.1.

[57] Ibid., 36.2.

[58] The language is reminiscent of Scaevola's description of the Gracchi in *On the Ideal Orator*, 1.38.

[59] Tacitus, *A Dialogue on Oratory*, 36.3–4

[60] Ibid., 36.2.

[61] Ibid., 36.2. Maternus echoes Plato, who has Socrates suggest that orators appear to know in front of the ignorant. Plato, *Gorgias*, 459c.

[62] Tacitus, *A Dialogue on Oratory*, 36.4–6.

and glorious (*pulchrum et gloriosum*), whereas to be mute and ineloquent (*mutum et elinquem*) was to be unseemly (*deforme*).[63] Yet even the grand materials with which orators were furnished were wicked (*mala*): "electioneering practices, the robbery of a province, and the murder of fellow-citizens."[64]

Maternus argues that it is better "that such horrors should not occur at all, and we must regard that as the most enviable political condition in which we are not liable to anything of the kind."[65] That is to say, the peaceful and quiet tranquility of the imperial present seems preferable to the turbulence of the past, just as Maternus' preferred pre-oratorical and peaceful poetry is a better mode of eloquence, unaccompanied by corruption or tumult. Likening eloquence to warfare, Maternus suggests that just as war produces better soldiers than peace, political turmoil produces better orators than does its opposite. Yet in both cases, he does not doubt that "the blessings of peace [*pace*] bring more profit and greater happiness than the horrors of war [*bello*]."[66] Just as times of peace produce few good soldiers, times of civil tranquility produce few good orators, despite Cicero's claims that peace and eloquence go together. Moreover, the tranquil present, lacking the tumults and conflicts of the past, leaves oratory without a great theme; thus, it is a sheer impossibility for anyone to produce a great and glorious oration," notwithstanding the hopes of Quintilian and Pliny.[67] Oratory, for Maternus (and as opposed to Cicero) is "an art which comes to the front more readily in times of trouble and unrest" (*turbidis et inquietis temporibus*).[68] The reign of Augustus brought "peace" (*quies*) and "inactivity [*otium*] on the part of the commons and of peaceableness [*tranquillitas*] on the part of the senate," and it was because of this peace that "a hush had fallen upon eloquence, as indeed it had upon the world at large."[69] The peace resulting from the rule of one meant the quieting of the past's noise and tumults.

Maternus also shows that oratory is linked to the political institutions that characterized the republic: the orator:

must have what I may call his stage. This the orators of former times could command day after day, when the forum was packed by an audience at the same time numerous and distinguished, when persons who had to face the hazard of

[63] Ibid., 36.8.
[64] Ibid., 37.4.
[65] Ibid., 37.5.
[66] Ibid., 37.7.
[67] Ibid., 37.5.
[68] Ibid., 37.6.
[69] Ibid., 38.2.

a public trial could depend on being supported by shoals of fellow-tribesmen, and by deputations also from the country towns.[70]

Maternus' language here echoes Cicero's *On the Ideal Orator* (3.80) yet again, but the very condition of being a complete orator, which Cicero held central to the practice of eloquence, Maternus here notes to be absent from the present. This renders the antagonistic and popular mode of oratory Cicero described obsolete, notwithstanding the aspirations of latter-day Ciceronians. Maternus describes the "incessant public meetings … the privilege so freely accorded of inveighing against persons of position and influence" – even Scipio, Sulla, and Pompey were not left alone; this shows that people "made public meetings also the opportunity of launching characteristically spiteful tirades against the leading men of the state."[71]

Maternus' description of eloquence is striking: As opposed to Cicero's account of eloquence, it is "not a quiet and peaceable art, or one that finds satisfaction in moral worth and good behavior;" rather, "a foster-child of license, which foolish men called liberty, an associate of sedition, a goad for the unbridled populace" – *eloquentia alumna licentiae, quam stulti libertatem vocabant* – language which recalls and subverts Cicero's language in *Brutus* 45. For Maternus, "It is a plant that does not grow under a well-regulated constitution" – *bene constitutis civitatibus non oritur.*[72] Insofar as the present is well regulated, then, oratory was of little value.

When the people are inclined to obedience and possess good character, oratory is simply not useful, lacking both purpose and material; he points to Crete and Sparta, examples of well-ordered constitutions (*bene constitutis civitatibus*) to demonstrate his point.[73] Of these regimes, says Maternus, their discipline and laws are held most severe (*quarum civitatum severissima diciplina et severissimae leges traduntur*). Nor do we find oratory in regimes with settled rule – regimes such as Macedonia and Persia. By contrast, it was useful in Athens, in which "all power was in the hands of the populace – that is to say, the untutored democracy, in fact the mob"; so too was the case in Rome of old:

so long as the constitution was unsettled, so long as the country kept wearing itself out with factions and dissensions and disagreements, so long as there was no peace [*pax*] in the forum, no harmony in the senate, no restraint in the courts

---

[70] Ibid., 39.4.
[71] Ibid., 40.1.
[72] Ibid., 40.2.
[73] Ibid., 40.3. On his invocation of Sparta and Crete, see Saxonhouse, "Tacitus' *Dialogue on Oratory*: Political Activity under a Tyrant," 66.

of law, no respect for authority, no sense of propriety on the part of the officers of state, the growth of eloquence was doubtless sturdier, just as untilled soil produces certain vegetation in greater luxuriance.[74]

The Gracchi may have benefited the country by their oratory, but "the country suffered from their laws"; Cicero paid "by the death he died for his renown in oratory."[75] As opposed to Cicero, who argues that oratory accompanies the settled, peaceful, and well-constituted regime, Maternus thus links it to turmoil and discord.

Yet the present has its orators, and their very activity, limited as it was, "goes to show that our civil condition is still far from being ideally perfect."[76] That is, orators still have a function because the state is not perfect — a remarkable contradiction given Maternus' apparent claim that oratory has ceased to be. Maternus avers that "it were better to have no grievances than to need to seek redress," and could a morally pure community be found, "orators would be just as superfluous among saints as are doctors among those that need no physician."[77] Among good morals and those ready to obey their rulers (*inter bonos mores et in obsequium regentis paratos*), oratory is thus as useless as is medicine among the healthy.[78] Were his companions to be transported back in time to the period of the great orators, however, Maternus suggests that they "would have attained to their brilliant reputation for eloquence just as surely as they would show your restraint and self-control."[79] He concludes by suggesting that since "it is impossible for anybody to enjoy at one and the same time great renown [*magnam famam*] and great repose [*magnam quietem*]," we should make the most of our own time "without disparaging any other age."[80] Maternus chooses the *in*active way of life, trusting in his innocence as the best protection.

V. CICERO, MATERNUS, AND THE QUARREL BETWEEN RHETORIC AND PHILOSOPHY

There is a good deal of irony in Maternus' speech: For one who seems so well to understand the differences between the principate and republic on the

---

[74] Tacitus, *A Dialogue on Oratory*, 40.3–4.
[75] Ibid., 40.4.
[76] Ibid., 41.1.
[77] Ibid., 41.2–3.
[78] Ibid., 41.3.
[79] Ibid., 41.5.
[80] Ibid., 41.5.

place of oratory, he seems woefully naïve when it comes to his own affairs. He hopes for personal security and peace through his blamelessness, yet he writes a play that he knows will offend, and rather than alter his behavior to avoid future danger, he promises to up the ante with his *Thyestes*. His desire for security, which he links to his belief in his own innocence, is empty, not simply because of the times in which he lives, but rather because of the *imprudent* actions he has chosen. He does not keep quiet, though he knows the danger of being outspoken, and in fact cites the dangers of an active life as a reason for *not* being political; the vocal outsider and critic, lacking a familiarity with and respect for conventional eloquence – he is more than reminiscent of Socrates, and especially the Socrates of the *Gorgias*.

This is not the only similarity; the *Dialogue*, as we have seen, echoes and subverts Cicero's *On the Ideal Orator*. In doing so, it emphasizes a Platonic theme that Cicero emphasized much less in defending oratory: the *moral* objection to oratory. In Plato's *Gorgias*, Socrates famously draws a distinction between two ways of life – the philosophical way of life (his own) and the political way of life – what he terms the "manly activities."[81] The distinction rests, in part, on the dichotomy Socrates develops between a mode of speaking that looks to truth (philosophy) and a mode of speaking that looks to opinion (rhetoric). It also relies on a dichotomy that he draws between the ends of speaking. True oratory, for Socrates, attacks injustice; useless oratory – that is, conventional oratory – "is of no use to us at all" precisely because it is used to defend injustice.[82] True and *useful* oratory, like medicine, looks to the health of its objects; Tacitus echoes this passage, as we have seen, in suggesting that oratory would be as useful among the just as medicine is among the healthy.[83]

That they are different and opposed ways of life is not simply a function of the mode and ends of speech, however; they differ in their attitudes toward self-protection. For Callicles, the most important component of self-protection is defending oneself from suffering injustice, whereas for Socrates – as with Maternus – it is defending oneself from *committing* injustice. Socrates suggests that if one's priority is simply to protect oneself from harm, then one might either be a tyrant oneself (which is to have total ability to do as one likes), or else be a partisan of the regime. To be a partisan is

---

[81] Plato, *Gorgias*, 500c.
[82] Ibid., 480b.
[83] Cf. Tacitus, *A Dialogue on Oratory*, 41.3.

to be a friend, and to be a friend is to be like one's friend. What this means, for Socrates, is that one would either need to imitate the tyrant or whatever regime happened to be in power. And precisely because the regime being imitated is unjust, the one doing the imitating will have committed injustice. Rather than simply focus on "preserving and being preserved," though, the goal in life should be to live well, and what this means, for Socrates, is not simply trying to be a friend to the regime.[84] Instead, true self-protection is to say and do nothing unjust, and especially to avoid what he terms "flattering oratory."[85]

This dilemma is akin to what Arendt describes as the conflict "between truthteller and citizens."[86] Socrates would have been safe so long as he "did not interfere with the course of the world," but when Socrates "forced his fellow-citizens to take him seriously by trying to set them free from falsehood and illusion," he was no longer safe.[87] We might take Arendt's point and modify it slightly: The kinds of compromises that one needs to make to take part in politics as Maternus conceives it – the flattery, in particular – make it difficult to live with integrity. Better, then, to simply avoid politics entirely, as Socrates remarks in the *Apology*, and as Maternus suggests in the *Dialogue*.[88] Thus, Socrates draws the lines between the active, manly life and his own philosophical way of life quite sharply, with a distinction that Maternus echoes: The best defense is not eloquence, but innocence. To take part is to compromise one's integrity. For Socrates, the favored task was philosophy; for Maternus, the favored task was poetry. For both, the task to be avoided was oratory, and the way of life to be avoided was the noisy life in the public eye.

Despite the apparent Socratic character of Maternus, however, Tacitus does not explicitly endorse any position in the text. Moreover, Maternus' *speeches* are not, as we have noted, consistent. In the first speech, blood-stained eloquence abounds; in the second speech, oratory has all but vanished. The first speech features a corrupt, dangerous, and immoral present; the second speech features a peaceful, quiet, and auspicious present. If Maternus

---

[84] Plato, *Gorgias*, 512e.
[85] Ibid., 522d.
[86] Hannah Arendt, "*Truth and Politics*," in *The Portable Hannah Arendt*, ed. Peter Baehr (New York: Penguin, 2000): 545–75, 547.
[87] Ibid., 547.
[88] Plato, *Apology*, ed. John M. Cooper, trans. G.M.A. Grube, *Plato: Complete Works* (Indianapolis: Hacket, 1997), 32e.

reverses himself in such a way, we must pause and ask whether his position is as it seems in *either* of the two speeches. As Bartsch puts it, "it is precisely the inconsistencies that give rise to the problem of Maternus' sincerity in his final speech that also explain the *need* for the final speech at all."[89] That is to say, Maternus' first speech could not have been his only speech for *prudential* reasons. Despite his unwillingness to compromise, he shows the need – perhaps too late – to do so through his second speech.

If Maternus echoes Socrates, Aper's conception of oratory is reminiscent of the favorable and conventional depictions of oratory in the *Gorgias*: It is linked to persuasion in certain contexts, namely "judges in a law court, councilors in a council meeting, and assemblymen in an assembly or in any other political gathering that might take place."[90] For Gorgias, Polus, and Callicles, the ability to speak persuasively brings with it power, rewards, and esteem, as it does for Aper. Just as Polus and Callicles contrast the life of the orator with that of Socrates and the philosopher, Aper contrasts his own active and practical life with the inactive and impractical life of the poet Maternus, a man who, like Socrates, is quite unable to defend himself and is without power because he neglects oratory. Maternus, like Socrates, goes against conventional opinions, turning upside down normal ways of seeing things with respect to oratory. In particular, Maternus (like Socrates) would be quite unable to defend himself due to his ignorance of oratory.

By contrast, Maternus, like Socrates, questions the moral status of rhetoric: It is useful chiefly in front of those who do not know, and rather than aim at what is actually good, it aims at the merely pleasant and seemingly fit. In addition to questioning its moral status, Socrates argues that without injustice, rhetoric has little use or purpose, just as medicine is unnecessary among the healthy. Indeed, rhetoric (conventionally conceived) is most useful in escaping just punishment.[91] An individual armed with rhetoric may well avoid suffering injustice, insofar as he commits himself to flattering those with power, but he is quite likely to commit injustice. By contrast, the philosopher who avoids the dirty hands of the rhetorician may well suffer injustice, but his own moral innocence is – like that of the poet for Maternus – his best defense against committing injustice.

---

[89] Shadi Bartsch, *Actors in the Audience: Theatricality and Doublespeak from Nero to Hadrian* (Cambridge: Harvard University Press, 1994), 114.
[90] Plato, *Gorgias*, 452e.
[91] Ibid., 481b.

Yet Maternus, unlike Socrates, is concerned not only with avoiding injustice, but with protecting his physical security, a concern that is thwarted with tragic irony. Trusting to his innocence, Maternus is in danger because he is not innocent; he intentionally sets out to anger those with power, going so far as to undermine not only his claims in his second speech with the presence of orators in his well-constituted state, and to reverse his depiction of the present as corrupt in his first speech. In seeking to avoid the perils of the forum, Maternus simply replaces them with the perils of poetry.

Maternus' desire is self-defeating given his practice; he is almost woefully imprudent. Moreover, he confuses cooperation with cooptation: There were not just two options – either activity or inactivity. We ought, perhaps, to be more sympathetic to Aper than many readers are. Perhaps it is not without justice that Aper upbraids Maternus for failing to pursue oratory despite its benefits, namely the ability "to make friendships and preserve them, to form extended connections, and to take whole provinces under his wing." Aper accuses Maternus of turning "his back on a profession than which you cannot imagine any in the whole country more productive of practical benefits," let alone the pleasures of satisfaction and the production of reputation and renown.[92] For Aper, Maternus is being irresponsible; as Goldberg writes:

For Maternus to repudiate the oratorical enterprise itself, which is what he does in preferring silence to the clamor of litigants at his door (12.1), is therefore to turn his back not just on vanity and avarice but on the very obligations of his class to society.[93]

Is the choice simply between seemingly safe poetry and morally bankrupt oratory? Certainly, the answer is no: Not all orators were *delatores*, and the functioning of the principate relied on the participation of skilled individuals like Agricola, as we shall see, no less than orators like Aper. Moreover, poetry and oratory are not so dichotomous as Maternus would have us believe.[94] Perhaps the lines between the life of the poet and the life of the orator, between integrity and independence, on the one hand, and obsequy, on the other, were less sharply delineated than they might seem, and the ability to navigate between extremes was required, an ability summed up as prudence.

---

[92] Tacitus, *A Dialogue on Oratory*, 5.4.

[93] Goldberg, "Appreciating Aper: The Defense of Modernity in Tacitus' *Dialogus De Oratoribus*," 230.

[94] On this point, see William J. Dominik, "Tacitus and Pliny on Oratory," in *A Companion to Roman Rhetoric*, ed. William J. Dominik and Jon Hall (Oxford: Blackwell, 2007), 323–38, 324.

VI. PRUDENCE AND THE ACTIVE LIFE
IN TACITUS' *AGRICOLA*

If Maternus provides us with someone who seems not just naïve, but insufficiently prudent – even foolish – we see in Agricola, the central figure of Tacitus' *Agricola*, someone who is very different – along with a very different attitude toward and understanding of the active life and acting with integrity. In his magisterial treatment of Tacitus, Ronald Syme writes of the *Agricola*: "Tacitus speaks not only for Agricola or for himself. The *Agricola* expounds the moral and political ideals of the new aristocracy."[95] This was an aristocracy (unlike the aristocracy of old) devoted to serving Rome through their service to a powerful individual. Competition for the favor of one, not the many, was the imperative.

In this work of biography, Tacitus commemorates his father-in-law, and in doing so, holds him forth as an *exemplum* to be imitated by future generations.[96] The example of Agricola shows that great men can live – and thrive – even under bad rulers, but only if they possess certain virtues: "submission and moderation [*obsequiumque ac modestiam*], if animation and energy go with them."[97] History's records will preserve what is admirable from Agricola's life, and because of this, "Agricola, whose story here is told, will outlive death, to be our children's heritage."[98] By preserving aspects of Agricola's life and the virtues he exemplified, Tacitus not only commemorates Agricola but instructs his readers, providing in his commemorated father-in-law a model that might be imitated by future Romans.

What virtues enable Agricola to succeed – and to survive – despite Domitian's vices and malicious efforts? Agricola operates in a murky realm between extremes of behavior: "neither casual … nor yet indolent," he hoped for "nothing in bravado," and turned "from nothing in fear," being possessed of "caution and yet eager." Thus, while in charge of public games "he kept a mean between thrift and lavishness."[99] But Agricola is something more than a figure of Aristotelian moderation; he is eminently prudent, a

---

[95] Syme, *Tacitus*, 26.
[96] On its biographical status, see Tacitus, *De Vita Agricolae*, ed. R.M. Ogilvie and Ian Richmond (London: Oxford University Press, 1967), 11.
[97] Tacitus, *Agricola*, 42.3.
[98] Ibid., 46.4.
[99] Ibid., 5.1, 6.4.

necessary adjustment to his times, "trained to habits of deference [*obsequi*], and skillful in tempering duty with expediency [*utilia honestis miscere*]."[100]

Balance and moderation, tempered with prudence – these traits describe Agricola's character: His virtues are revealed both in dealing with and in the exercise of authority. In administering Roman Britain, "he was satisfied generally with penitence [*paenitentia*] instead of punishment," and while he certainly was capable in combat, "by his clemency, after he had overawed [the rebellious British population] sufficiently, he paraded before them the attractions of peace [*pacis*]."[101] Faced with a widely dispersed and uncivilized population, he sought to habituate them "by comfort to peace and quiet" (*quieti et otio per voluptates adsuescerent*). So successful was he that "rivalry for his compliments took the place of coercion."[102]

Though highly successful himself, Agricola was happy to let others have their due in success. Nor was he a dissembler – "his anger left no secret resentment behind it, and no man had cause to fear his silence: he thought it more honorable to hurt than to hate."[103] He was thus readily legible. In this regard, he stands in great contrast to Domitian, who greeted Agricola's own success "with affected pleasure and secret disquiet."[104] While Domitian resented Agricola's victories, he hesitated to act lest he provoke the people or the army; instead, an opportunity for his ill-gotten vengeance presented itself. Trouble came to Agricola in the end through no misdeeds of his own, but rather because of "the glory of the man, and those worst of enemies, the people who praise you."[105] Agricola was simply too prominent for his own good.

Faced with an emperor "unfriendly to high qualities," Agricola survives, as we have seen, because of his *moderatio* and *prudentia*; in doing so, he avoided ruin by not seeking renown with a "fatuous parade of independence [*libertatis*]."[106] Those individuals who had done so – they "made gestures of senatorial independence and self-respect" – often paid with their lives.[107]

---

[100] Ibid., 8.1.
[101] Ibid., 19.3, 20.2.
[102] Ibid., 21.1.
[103] Ibid., 22.4.
[104] Ibid., 39.1.
[105] Ibid., 41.1.
[106] Ibid., 41.1, 42.3.
[107] W. Liebeschuetz, "The Theme of Liberty in the *Agricola* of Tacitus," *The Classical Quarterly* 16, no. 1 (1966), 126–39, 128.

Morford suggests that those individuals who were executed were Stoic-inspired politicians – not philosophers per se, who were generally exiled instead. The threat of Stoicism, if taken too far, was clear: "the Stoic veneration of the younger Cato would make any ruler nervous, for Cato was the paragon of liberty, defined in this context as the refusal to accept the rule of a tyrant."[108] Tacitus has little use for such public acts of resistance; as Pagán puts it, "He does not consider opposition to the imperial regime a worthy endeavor; he harshly criticizes those senators who actively engage in such attempts." We should note, though, as we are beginning to see with Agricola, that "the alternative, abject submission, is equally odious."[109] One needed to tread with caution between dangerous extremes – undignified obsequy and foolish displays of liberty – guided by prudence.

Suspected by Domitian through no fault of his own, many urged Agricola not to seek a new province (Asia), praising quiet and ease – the very devices by which he reduces the Britons to subjection – as opposed to the unpleasant activity (and risk) to which he might be subjected.[110] Agricola asked to be excused from his duty; "with ready hypocrisy assumed with an official air," Domitian gave in to Agricola's request, allowing "himself to be thanked for it: the sinister favor brought him no blushes."[111] Why had Agricola "tried to avoid" prominence?[112] Perhaps he was simply not interested in glory, a man so duty bound that he, like Cato the Younger, simply eschewed it.[113] Or perhaps there was something more, a reflection of Agricola's prudence and the changed reality of a Rome ruled by a *demens princeps*.[114] Whatever else we may say about Agricola, his virtues are suited to his times. They might not have served him so well during the height of the republic, with its combative politics conducted in the public eye; indeed, his precarious situation is akin to what Cicero laments about his own status in his letter to

---

[108] Mark Morford, *The Roman Philosophers from the Time of Cato the Censor to the Death of Marcus Aurelius* (London: Routledge, 2002), 191.

[109] Victoria E. Pagán, "Distant Voices of Freedom in the *Annales* of Tacitus," *Studies in Latin Literature and Roman History, Collection Latomus* X (2000), 358–69, 359.

[110] Tacitus, *Agricola*, 42.1.

[111] Ibid., 42.2.

[112] Ibid., 41.4.

[113] Plutarch writes "that to which Cato gave least thought was his in greatest measure, namely, esteem, favor, surpassing, honor, and kindness" during his service as a military tribune. Plutarch, *Life of Cato the Younger*, trans. Bernadotte Perrin, *Plutarch's Lives* (Cambridge: Harvard University Press, 1967), 9.4.

[114] On Domitian as *demens*, cf. Pliny, *Panegyricus*, 33.3–4.

Plancius. The power of the *princeps* had to be reckoned with, as did the institutional changes the principate brought with it; this required moderation and prudence as well as realism.

VII. CONCLUSION

Where Agricola succeeded, despite the perils of public life and a vicious *princeps*, Maternus failed, notwithstanding his exit from the tumult of the forum. Agricola's virtues – moderation and discretion, coupled with submission – are not evident in Maternus' desire to write his *Thyestes*, despite his professed desire for security. Mayer writes that the two works:

may be regarded as [Tacitus'] attempt to come to terms with and describe for others the emptiness he himself found at the end of the traditional paths to glory and prestige in Rome, paths which he and his father-in-law had so successfully trodden in their different ways.[115]

But this reading does not exhaust the possibilities: As we have noted, Aper may not be as unsympathetic as he seems. Agricola, moreover, is active and praised because of his activity. Nor is it clear that Tacitus agrees with Maternus, or even unambiguously endorses the thesis that oratory has declined. While Maternus may echo Socrates of the *Gorgias*, we are not presented with the well-ordered regime of the *Republic* in Maternus' speech or the potential true statesman of the *Gorgias*; the sheer presence of orators and oratory, diminished as they might be in their role and magnitude, went to show that Rome was not a perfect society, that the emperor was not Plato's philosopher-king, and that orators still had work to do. Oratory still had a place, then, substantially altered, to be sure, but it was not dead precisely because the principate was not perfect.

Moreover, without eloquence – in this case, the eloquence of the historian – Agricola's example to posterity would not just be of little use, but not even extant. Agricola is relatively safe, and indeed he succeeds, but he can only go so far, and without Tacitus, all his efforts would be for naught – he would not be remembered. The reality Cicero laments – a false and limited *dignitas*, a mere shadow of the past – is a reality facing Agricola: Absent a good *princeps*, there might be little scope for acting with integrity. The present may have

---

[115] Tacitus, *Dialogus De Oratoribus*, ed. Roland Mayer (Cambridge: Cambridge University Press, 2001), 2.

been peaceful, then, but it was not a peace produced through the eloquence of the orator. Rather, it was the peace of monarchy.

Both the *Dialogue* and *Agricola*, moreover, problematize peace and quiet, questioning their value from the perspective of integrity and liberty. Simply put, the absence of overt violence is not the same thing as peace, and it certainly falls short of the peace that Cicero connected to eloquence. Tacitus' discussion of Sparta is of particular importance in this regard. Part of Maternus' argument, as we have seen, involves the positive invocation of Sparta and Crete as examples of well-ordered polities. The harmony that prevails in Sparta is precisely the sign of its being well-governed, or possessing εὐνομία.[116] Indeed, as Winton puts it, idealized representations of Sparta saw it "as a polis that transcends politics, a polis the perfection of whose institutions obviates the possibility of conflict and the need for change."[117]

Sparta's εὐνομία obviates the need for eloquence because it lacks – at least in idealized representations – an antagonistic context. For Cicero, however, well-ordered states were fertile territory for oratory to blossom; he praises, as we have seen, Athens for just such reasons. And he writes in the *Brutus* that "Upon peace and tranquility eloquence attends as their ally, it is, one may say, the offspring of well-established civic order [*bene constitutae civitatis quasi alumna quaedam eloquentia*]."[118] Tacitus, however, valorizes Sparta because it lacks eloquence in the *Dialogue*; his invocation of Sparta, along with Crete and Macedonia, is highly pointed – as Bartsch notes, "a Roman *princeps* would prefer to *dissociate* his regime from states mostly synonymous with despotism."[119] Sparta was no despotism, but it was no Athens, either, lacking the tumults and raucousness of its democratic rival, embodying a kind of peace and quiet that were absent in Rome's own participatory past.

Tacitus contrasts well-ordered, stable, and peaceful polities with little political agitation and turmoil, with tumultuous, poorly ordered, and unstable polities. Given Maternus' apparent praise for Sparta (not known for its

---

[116] Rawson writes, "Sparta regarded herself, and was regarded, as an embodiment of *eunomia*." Elizabeth Rawson, *The Spartan Tradition in European Political Thought* (Oxford: Clarendon Press, 1969), 14.

[117] Richard Winton, "Herodotus, Thucydides and the Sophists," in *Cambridge History of Greek and Roman Political Thought*, ed. Christopher Rowe and Malcolm Schofield (Cambridge: Cambridge University Press, 2000), 89–121, 101.

[118] Cicero, *Brutus*, 45. For the *bene constitutae civitatis* formula, see also *Brutus*, 6. Cf. Cicero, *Orator*, 141.

[119] Bartsch, *Actors in the Audience*, 111.

oratory) and Crete, well-ordered constitutions linked in the minds of many classical thinkers, as well as his description of the pre-oratory age of poetic innocence as a Golden Age, it would appear that Tacitus takes the side of the philosophers against the orators and Cicero. Whereas Cicero saw (true) oratory as productive of community and linked to peace, Maternus views oratory writ large as destructive of community and linked to conflict.[120] But we might need to identify Tacitus with Maternus to sustain this reading, an identification we should resist, and the choice is not simply between activity and withdrawal: The peacful reality was more ambiguous.

Cicero, for one, was certainly aware of the ambiguity of *pax*, writing in his second *Philippic* that "the name of peace is sweet and is itself a healthful thing; but there is a great difference between peace and servitude" – *et nomen pacis dulce est et ipsa res salutaris; sed inter pacem et servitutem plurimum interest.*[121] Not all peace is equal. For whatever else Cicero meant by peace when linking it to oratory, it did not entail the absence of political conflict or the rule of one; without the conflict of the forum and the courts, oratory would have had little practical purpose, as seen in *On the Ideal Orator* 1.32–4 and 3.59, and without dispersed power, Ciceronian oratory had little use. Peace did not emerge through unilateral action or imposition; it emerged through interaction, between speakers and audiences, in public. Nor would there be any use in oratory's ability "to have a hold on human minds, to win over their inclinations, to drive them at will in one direction, and to draw them at will from another," were it not for diversity of opinion and disagreement.[122] In describing free communities as peaceful, Cicero surely did not mean by *pax* what it meant in the *Agricola* or *Dialogue* – the enervating absence of overt armed conflict due to rule by one.

The conditions of peace were ambiguous, just as the situation facing an elite Roman was ambiguous and potentially risky. Ambiguity and risk required prudence. If the context had changed, and if there was peace – peace secured by means quite different from Cicero's vision of peace secured through the active and vigorous efforts of the orator-statesman – this does not mean, however, that the life of action was without value. Eloquence

---

[120] Saxonhouse reads the dialogue as "ultimately Platonic," with Tacitus holding forth a vision of a well-governed state that parallel's Plato's *Republic*. Saxonhouse, "Tacitus' *Dialogue on Oratory*: Political Activity under a Tyrant," 54.

[121] Cicero, *Philippics*, trans. Walter C.A. Ker (Cambridge: Harvard University Press, 1938), 2.113.

[122] Cicero, *On the Ideal Orator*, 1.30.

and political activity were not entirely dead, any more than the only choice was between servility and withdrawal (or futile opposition). The peace of the present is a function of the apparent absence of social antagonism, an absence that creates different challenges and problems for the active life – especially the cultivation of prudence.

One could hardly speak independently if subject to a *dominus*; but one could hardly write and speak in a fitting way if reduced to flattery. One needed, in short, to be prudent if one was to act and speak in a way that was both safe and honorable. Yet there was a mode of writing that would enable its practitioner to continue to perform the *functions* of oratory without producing Maternus' ill-advised poetic compositions: history. History, as I will argue in the next chapter, could serve a didactic purpose as well as an epideictic function, holding forth to rulers the blame of future generations as punishment for their wickedness; without history, moreover, an individual like Agricola would scarcely be remembered.

6

TACITUS' MORAL HISTORIES

I. INTRODUCTION

In the prior chapter, I developed a reading of Tacitus' *Agricola* and *Dialogue on Orators* as negotiating the tensions between contumacy and obsequiousness. Tacitus seeks to find some middle ground between foolish and futile outspokenness, on the one hand, and cooptation and sycophancy, on the other. At the same time, while facing an ambiguous peace and present, he tries to find an active alternative to withdrawal from public life – the tactic of Maternus – that entails integrity and not abject flattery. In this regard, then, Agricola provided a prudent model to imitate and study, unlike Maternus who, despite his second exculpatory speech, seemed naïve to the realities of moving in the public eye under an emperor.

These realities reflected the concentration of power in the hands of a single ruler, an individual whose behavior and character were of great importance in setting the conditions of the active life in politics. Understanding the character of the ruler is central to understanding whether and when one might or might not be interfered with, or whether one might or might not speak with relative freedom. Behavior that might be appropriate under Nerva or Trajan might be inappropriate under Nero or Domitian, for example. If character was of such great importance, it became imperative to find a way to read the ruler and to develop the ability to read and react rightly to rulers. This posed a particular problem for those who sought glory through eloquence – written or spoken – and whose writings portrayed and criticized rulers. One needed to do this in such a way that one did not anger the ruler by being overly forthright, and also without trying to please the ruler so much that one's writings would have no teeth. One needed to be noticed without being overly conspicuous.

In this regard, Hobbes – whose attitude toward eloquence we encountered in Chapter 2 – has a distinctive take on what it means to avoid unwelcome attention under a monarch. In *On the Citizen*, when comparing the advantages and disadvantages of monarchy and democracy, Hobbes admits that monarchy entails dangers but emphasizes that "all the acts of Nero are not essential to monarchy."[1] Monarchs may well – and often do – engage in cruel behavior toward individual subjects, but "kings are only severe against those who either trouble them with impertinent counsels, or oppose them with reproachful words, or control their wills."[2] It is not difficult to live a peaceful and quiet life under a monarch; it merely requires being inconspicuous: "Whosoever therefore in a monarchy will lead a retired life, let him be what he will that reigns, he is out of danger" – this was the ostensible goal of Maternus.[3] The problem is that being a competent and successful practitioner of eloquence – or a successful general, as in the case of Agricola – makes one conspicuous; the great orator lives in the public eye and attracts attention; glory is her reward. So, too, does the great historian.

For Cicero, as noted in Chapter 2, history was the domain of the orator; matters were less clear for Tacitus' contemporary, the orator and writer Pliny. In a letter to Titinius Capito, answering the latter's request that he write history, Pliny confesses that the idea intrigues him "because the saving of those who deserve immortality from sinking into oblivion, and spreading the fame of others along with one's own, seem to me a particularly splendid achievement." For Pliny himself, the "love and longing for a lasting name" is the greatest attraction, and "man's worthiest aspiration."[4] This claim is especially true if one has "nothing in him to blame and so has no fear if he is to be remembered by posterity." History is especially useful in this regard, not least because history, as opposed to poetry and oratory, gives pleasure "however it is presented," whereas poetry and oratory gain little favor without reaching the summit of eloquence. Not only is history useful for gaining fame and easier to work in than poetry or oratory; for Pliny, it was also a family tradition: He notes that his uncle and adoptive father "was a historian of scrupulous accuracy."[5]

---

[1] Hobbes, *The Citizen*, 227.
[2] Ibid., 227.
[3] Ibid., 227.
[4] On memory and the *Panegyricus*, see Gowing, *Empire and Memory*, 125–31.
[5] Pliny, *Letters*, 5.8.1–5.

Pliny delays, however, because he wants to revise his speeches "so that all the work I put into them will not perish with me for want of this last attention." Nor can he revise his speeches and write history at the same time; they are both too weighty for a single author to undertake simultaneously. And while oratory and history are similar, they differ in crucial respects: "oratory deals largely with the humble and trivial incidents of everyday life, history is concerned with profound truths and the glory of great deeds." They differ not just in topic, but also in style; alluding to Thucydides, he writes that "there is all the difference between a 'lasting possession' and a 'prize essay': the former is history, the latter oratory."[6] If he were to embark upon history while still working on oratory, Pliny fears that he might "treat one in the manner proper to the other."[7]

He leaves the choice of topic – ancient history or recent history – to Capito, though with a note of wariness. Ancient history has its risks: It "has had its historians"; a crowded field, putting together the relevant material would be "a great labor." Perhaps recent history seems more fruitful in ensuring one's own immortality as well as the immortality of others, given that "no one has handled" it. But if he works on recent history, he writes, "I shall receive small thanks and give serious offense."[8] The closer the focus of one's writing is to the present period, the closer one's history is to the immediate concerns of the audience: Those who can still be offended are potentially great in number. Moreover, there is "more to censure than to praise in the serious vices of the present day," and if one happens to find something to praise in such degenerate times, the praise one gives, no matter how effusive, seems "grudging."[9] By contrast, the blame one assigns in writing histories, no matter how small, seems "excessive." Pliny claims to have "enough courage of my convictions not to be deterred by such considerations," demurring, in the end, and suggesting to Capito that he should choose for Pliny a topic, lest Pliny find another reason not to write history when he is "ready to start at last."[10]

The historian was in a bind, for Pliny: If one chose to write about ancient history, one faced both competitors and the difficulties involved in assembling relevant source material. If, by contrast, one chose to write about

---

[6] Cf. Thucydides, *History of the Peloponnesian War*, 1.22.
[7] Pliny, *Letters*, 5.8.6–12.
[8] Ibid., 5.8.13.
[9] Ibid., 5.8.14.
[10] Ibid., 5.8.14.

recent history, one might easily give offense, even if one would have no competitors. It is hard not to attract unwelcome attention if one touches on subjects within living memory. In either situation, though, history performs a praiseworthy function: It preserves the name and memory of those who might otherwise not be remembered, while at the same time preserving one's own name and enhancing one's fame. It was an appealing outlet for ambition with a useful social function – dealing with great deeds and their commemoration.

Tacitus, as I argued in discussing the *Agricola*, turns to history both to commemorate others (such as his father-in-law, Agricola) and incidentally himself, as author. A tempting reading is to suggest that this represents his turn from oratory to history, in light of the argument of the *Dialogue*; yet we have seen that there is good reason to doubt that Tacitus straightforwardly proclaims the death of oratory in the *Dialogue* or that he is to be identified with Maternus. Indeed, Tacitus does not say in his own voice that oratory is dead, though the institutional and political changes separating republican from imperial oratory are made clear. As we saw, the task for the elite Roman was to cultivate prudence; dispositions and attitudes that would have fit the time of Cicero, during which he likened eloquence to a kind of weapon, would hardly fit the time of a Nero or Domitian.

In this chapter, which builds on the prior, I argue that Tacitus writes *rhetorical* history. In this regard, a number of classical scholars have addressed the rhetorical elements of ancient historiography, whether in the similarity of historiography to rhetoric in expectations and conventions, the role and construction of speeches in historiography, or the similarities between the techniques of the historian and the rhetorician. Rhetorical devices, techniques, and reflections are to be found in Greek historians, such as Thucydides, and in the Roman historians Sallust and Livy, as noted in prior chapters.

I argue, however, that Tacitus' histories serve a moral-political *and* rhetorical purpose, providing models of how to read and navigate particular rulers. His choice of topic (prior dynasties and *principes*) enables Tacitus to be insulated from the kind of foolhardy opposition to the principate that he criticizes in both the *Agricola* and the *Dialogue*. By concentrating on the distant past and prior dynasties, he also avoids the pitfall of flattery that lurked if he wrote of present rulers. To be openly critical of those in power was to court danger, as it might be *not* to praise them; as he puts it in his preface to *Agricola*, and in discussing the difficulties of writing under Domitian, "even though I was about to write the life of a man who was already dead, I had to seek permission which I should not have needed, had invective been my purpose; so harsh was the spirit of the age, so cynical to virtue."[11] In placing his criticisms of particular *principes* in the (often distant) past, Tacitus engages in political reflection. Tacitus affixes blame to prior *principes* and attaches praise to current and recent *principes*; in delineating particular qualities to be recognized and praised, moreover, he engages in a kind of practical theorizing suited to the cultivation of prudence.

I begin in Section II by discussing Tacitus' depiction of the principate's effect on historiography, with particular attention to the problem of bias. I then turn in Section III to his avowed purposes in his historical writings, focusing on their similarity to epideictic rhetoric in their use of praise and blame, and the way in which he reads the character of rulers. Following this discussion, I discuss in Section IV three Roman works of praise-cum-counsel – Cicero's speech *For Marcellus*, Seneca's *On Mercy*, and Pliny's *Panegyricus* – to explore the dynamics of these works and their treatment of the praiseworthy quality of mercy. With these works in mind, I turn in Section V to Tacitus' use of praise and blame, and the way in which he deploys them in depicting good and bad rulers for his readers, concluding in Section VI by briefly suggesting that Tacitus is engaged in an implicit criticism of the principate itself.

II. THE CONCENTRATION OF POWER AND THE DISTORTION OF ELOQUENCE

In discussing the *Dialogue*, we saw that insofar as the institution of the principate meant the decline of participatory and antagonistic politics, oratory was bound to change as well. Personal security and the fame of the orator were difficult to reconcile, unless the nature of oratory itself transformed. We saw a similar link between the institution of the principate and the transformation of eloquence and liberty in the *Agricola*. In the *Agricola*, and even more so with the *Histories* and *Annals*, Tacitus replaces the challenges to oratory with the challenges the principate posed to writing history. That is to say, the constraining effects of the principate made themselves felt for historians and orators.

---

[11] Tacitus, *Agricola*, 1.4.

Machiavelli provides a useful illustration – given his Roman topic – of what these constraining effects might mean in his *Discourses*. In a chapter dealing with the blameworthiness of those who set up tyrannies, he writes that no one should "be deceived by Caesar's renown when he finds writers extolling him before others."[12] Those who do so are "corrupted" by Caesar's "fortune" or the sheer fact that the empire he founded lasted so long – and which, because its rulers bore the name Caesar, "did not permit writers to speak freely of him."[13] To understand what those writers *would* have said of Caesar – had they been able to speak freely – one need only look "at what they say of Catiline," who is less blameworthy than Caesar because he did not succeed. The other tactic, Machiavelli suggests, is to "look at the praise bestowed on Brutus," Caesar's enemy.[14]

Imperial historians cannot always speak frankly, it seems, and we should be alert to distortions akin to what Machiavelli describes in the case of Tacitus. When we turn to Tacitus' account of historical writing's fate under the principate, we see just such a cause for suspicion. In the laudatory biography *Agricola*, Tacitus distinguishes between the eloquence of pre- and post-imperial historiography, though with clear emphasis on the corruptive influence of Domitian in particular. Just as in the past it was easier "to do deeds worth recording, so also there was inducement … to the most distinguished men of ability to publish such records of virtue."[15] Domitian was not amenable to such deeds; like many ancient tyrants, he was "an emperor unfriendly to high qualities."[16] Moreover, his hostility to the virtues is evident in a crucial passage (noted in the last chapter): Tacitus writes that "it was all in vain that the practice of public speaking and the glamour of the arts of peace had been silenced, if another was to usurp military glory."[17] It was necessary, in short, to silence eloquence and to diminish the glory of others in order to glorify the *princeps*. The ambitious orator thus faced a formidable obstacle in a vainglorious and paranoid *princeps*.

Thus was the effect of Domitian on historiography in the *Agricola*. In his preface to the *Histories*, Tacitus notes that historians active during the republic wrote with "equal eloquence and freedom" – *pari eloquentia ac libertate*.[18] After Actium, however, peace required that all power be conferred on one,

---

[12] Machiavelli, *The Discourses on Livy*, 135–6.
[13] Ibid., 136.
[14] Ibid., 136.
[15] Tacitus, *Agricola*, 1.2.
[16] Ibid., 41.1.
[17] Ibid., 39.2.
[18] Tacitus, *The Histories*, 1.1.

and writers of such great genius disappeared.[19] Three factors in particular contributed to the problem): "men were ignorant of politics as being not any concern of theirs; later, because of their passionate desire to flatter [*adsentandi*]; or again, because of their hatred [*odio*] of their masters."[20] The dislocation of politics from the public sphere to the palace resulted in a widespread detachment from the practice of politics; the great power of the few gave rise to bias, whether through adulation or hatred.

In the *Annals*, too, Tacitus links Augustus' institution of sole rule to the decline of historiography. Augustus had brought together a Rome exhausted by civil discord (*discordiis civilibus*) under his rule (*imperium*), taking unto himself the title *princeps*. During the reign of Augustus, "intellects of distinction were not lacking to tell the tale" of his rule, and certainly many histories had been written of the adversity and prosperity of Rome's earlier past. However, imperial historians were deterred by adulation (*adulatione*), and thus the histories of Tiberius, Caligula, Claudius, and Nero were rendered false through fear (*metum*) of the rulers while they still lived or through hatred (*odiis*) when they had but recently died.[21] It is not hard to understand the rise of elite sycophancy: Augustus had won over all through the sweetness of leisure (*dulcedine otii pellexit*); he met no resistance, qua Tacitus, for those who might have resisted were dead in battle or by proscription. By contrast, "the rest of the nobility found a cheerful acceptance of slavery the road to wealth and office, and ... stood now for the new order and safety in preference to the old order and adventure"; this is the "eerie silence" by which Eder so poignantly characterizes the beginning of Augustus' reign.[22] The dichotomy between republic and principate and its effects on eloquence given the twin dilemmas of flattery and contumacy – rooted in the power of the *princeps* – thus frames Tacitus' historical writings.

This dilemma has implications for writing truthfully. Part of what makes for truth in historiography, suggests Tacitus, is knowledge and familiarity

---

[19] Ibid., 1.1. Lucan also comments that the "interests of peace required that all power should be concentrated in the hands of one man." Lucan, *The Civil War*, trans. J.D. Duff (Cambridge: Harvard University Press, 1988), 1.125–6.

[20] Tacitus, *The Histories*, 1.1.

[21] Tacitus, *The Annals* trans. John Jackson, *Tacitus: The Histories and the Annals* (Cambridge: Harvard University Press, 1986), 1.1.

[22] Ibid., 1.2. Walter Eder, "Augustus and the Power of Tradition: The Augustan Principate as Binding Link between Republic and Empire," in *Between Republic and Empire: Interpretations of Augustus and His Principate*, ed. Kurt A. Raaflaub and Mark Toher (Berkeley: University of California Press, 1990): 71–122, 75.

with public affairs. But truth also requires, as we see in *Histories* 1.1, that the writer neither desire to flatter nor write in hatred of her rulers; this, as we saw in Pliny's letter to Capito, was precisely the dilemma of the contemporary historian. If a writer flatters her subjects, she "is subject to the shameful charge of servility [*servitutis*]," whereas if she goes out of the way to malign her subjects, this is but a false image of liberty (*falsa species libertatis inest*); Tacitus' language echoes his description in the *Agricola* (42.3) of those who engage in such behavior. Tacitus argues that it is necessary for those who profess uncorrupted honesty to speak without favor or hatred – *incorruptam fidem professis neque amore quisquam et sine odio dicendus est*.[23] Yet for Tacitus, because prior imperial historians lacked both knowledge and the proper attitude toward their rulers, there was no care (*cura*) for posterity (*posteritatis*). They thus fell short in the performance of their duties as historians. He tells us much the same thing, though this time explicitly about himself, in the *Annals*, where he depicts himself as seeking to remedy the historiographic shortcomings of his predecessors by writing of the Julio-Claudians *sine ira et studio* - "without anger and without partiality" - *quorum causas procul habeo* - "from the motives of which I stand sufficiently removed."[24]

These are rather strange passages given Tacitus' frequent hostility to particular *principes*, especially Tiberius, Claudius, Nero, and Domitian. On the face of it, it is hard to see that Tacitus is writing *sine ira et studio* when he so frequently condemns his subjects. Luce provides a fruitful suggestion:

The Greeks and Romans usually spoke of the absence of favoritism or hatred. Today the desideratum is often given as a positive and particularized virtue, "objectivity" or "impartiality," for which the ancients had no special vocabulary, speaking simply of the "truth," which could be compromised in ways other than through bias.[25]

Luce also points out that whereas we find prefatory emphases on objectivity in imperial historians writing of the near past, we do not find them in the prefaces of those writing of the distant past; he cites Livy, Dionysius of Halicarnassus, Diodorus, and Cassius Dio in this regard.

Herodotus, Thucydides, and Xenophon do not make similar claims either, though each of them writes of both distant and contemporary history. Yet they are not writing in the confines of monarchies. Luce suggests that such

---

[23] Tacitus, *The Histories*, 1.1.
[24] Tacitus, *The Annals*, 1.1.
[25] T.J. Luce, "Ancient Views on the Causes of Bias in Historical Writing," *Classical Philology* 84, no. 1 (1989): 16–31, 17.

a claim, then, "may have had its origins in the later fourth century with historians who recorded the careers of Philip II and Alexander."[26] Bias is in part a function of the historian's emotions toward his subjects, and they are the product of the "benefits one has enjoyed or hopes to enjoy and injuries one has received or fears to receive."[27] Such benefits and harms, as well as the attendant emotions, are most common in the cases of monarchs, whose great power enabled them to confer harms and benefits with ease.

We may note Polybius' *Histories* 8.8.3 by way of illustration, where he writes that because of "their regard for the kings or their fear of them," some historians gloss over Philip V's crimes against the Messenians, arguing that they "deserve no censure" but "were to be regarded as praiseworthy achievements." For Polybius, however, such actions were "in defiance of divine or human law." Indeed, many historians of Philip V wrote histories that "much more resemble panegyrics than histories."[28] Polybius recommends that writers "give an account of [kings] consistent with ... previous statements and in accord with the character of each," though admittedly this is an "exceedingly difficult thing to do."[29]

Plutarch provides an additional illustration, noting in the *Life of Pericles* that whereas it is difficult for historians writing long after events because the "lapse of time is an obstacle to their proper perception" of them, for those writing on "their contemporaries," the difficulty lies in the tendency "partly through envious hatred and partly through fawning flattery," each of which "defiles and distorts the truth."[30] The dilemma of the imperial historian – the historian writing under the eye of someone possessing great power – is to navigate between flattery and excessive criticism, just as the dilemma of the ambitious Roman seeking fame and glory was to navigate between servility and futile displays of opposition.

III. TACITUS' PURPOSES

Having explored the dilemmas of the imperial historian, we may now turn to the issue of what Tacitus seeks to achieve through his histories. That

---

[26] Ibid., 19.
[27] Ibid., 19.
[28] Polybius, *The Histories*, 8.8.6.
[29] Ibid., 8.8.7.
[30] Plutarch, *The Life of Pericles*, trans. Bernadotte Perrin, *Plutarch's Lives* (Cambridge: Harvard University Press, 1967), 13.12.

Tacitus understands his histories to have a moral and didactic function is clearly evident. In his *Agricola*, as seen previously, he describes the custom of preserving for future generations "the works and ways of famous men," a project which "our age has not yet abandoned ... even now, indifferent though it be to its own affairs."[31] The continuity of this practice is most evident when "some great and notable virtue has dominated and over-powered the vice common alike to small states and great."[32] His task, in the *Agricola*, is to commemorate the virtues of Agricola, a man whose prudence shows that one can excel under bad monarchs. Such a man, who practices moderation and discretion, might even provide a model for the future, a far more profitable model than those who have earned glory by a futile death.

In the *Histories*, Tacitus notes that unlike earlier writers, who had more freedom, he faces a difficult dilemma: Historians who seek to curry favor are quickly disregarded, but those who engage in "calumny and spite" attract a ready audience, the prior seeming to embody "servility," the latter making "a false show of independence." Tacitus' period, in the *Histories*, is "rich in disasters, terrible with battles, torn by civil struggles, horrible even in peace." Despite this, his period "was not so barren of virtue that it did not display noble examples [*bona exempla*]" – *exempla* he can hand to posterity.[33] He cites, in particular, virtuous familial behavior – mothers joining their children in flight, wives joining husbands in exile, strength on the part of other relatives, slaves who showed "a fidelity which defied even torture." To cap it off, "Eminent men met the last necessity with fortitude, rivaling in their end the glorious deaths of antiquity."[34]

Tacitus tells us in his own voice (*reor*), in Book 3 of the *Annals*, that the first function of history is not to pass over virtues in silence (*ne virtutes sileantur*) and "to ensure that merit shall not lack its record and to hold before the vicious word and deed the terrors of posterity and infamy" – *pravis dictis factisque ex posteritate et infamia metus sit*.[35] In Book 4 of the *Annals*, Tacitus again takes up the theme of history's utility in the context of a digression on the kinds of rule. The people, the first men, or single individuals rule all nations and cities; however, the precise balance between people and elites varied throughout Rome's history. When in Roman history the regime was

---

[31] Tacitus, *Agricola*, 1.1.
[32] Ibid., 1.1
[33] Tacitus, *The Histories*, 1.1, 1.2, 1.3.
[34] Ibid., 1.3.
[35] Tacitus, *The Annals*, 3.65.

either dominated by the plebs or by the patricians, it was essential to "study [*noscenda*] the character of the masses and the methods of controlling them," or else "those who had acquired the most exact knowledge [*perdidicerant*] of the temper of the senate and the aristocracy were accounted shrewd in their generation and wise." Despite the fact that Rome is now a monarchy (*unus imperitet*), "the collection and the chronicling of these details may yet serve an end," no matter how inglorious may be the effort. His histories provide events (*eventis*) by which the many, who are without innate insight, may learn (*docentur*).[36] They might provide insight into the character of the ruler in particular, just as the masses and the aristocracy were studied in the past.

Insofar as Tacitus' histories commemorate vicious and virtuous characters and actions through blame and praise, holding forth as reward future praise and future blame as punishment, they are similar to the rhetorical genre of epideictic. In chronicling the details of monarchy, and deploying praise and blame, he provides a kind of instruction to his readers, readers who, like him, lived in a world in which the character of the ruler mattered a great deal. By focusing on the character of rulers, moreover, he engages in a mode of practical political theorizing – reading, in essence, particular *principes* – apt to his times.[37]

Praise and blame feature in the writings of Sallust and Livy, to be sure; but Tacitus' statements regarding his intent, especially in the *Annals* – to hold forth the judgment of posterity on the wicked – illustrate the centrality of these devices to achieving his ends and provide a connection to epideictic. Aristotle had defined epideictic as oratory that "either praises or censures somebody."[38] Cicero takes note of the genre in *On the Ideal Orator* but says little about it; in fact, Antonius notes that it is "less essential than the other two" genres – namely, forensic and deliberative.[39] He later describes the genre in more detail, though again noting:

I excluded this whole subject because there are many kinds of speeches that are more important and of greater scope, for which barely anyone gives precepts, and because we do not generally use laudatory speeches that much.[40]

---

[36] Ibid., 4.33.
[37] On the idea of reading principes, see Patrick Sinclair, *Tacitus the Sententious Historian: A Sociology of Rhetoric in Annales 1–6* (University Park: The Pennsylvania State University Press, 1995), 62–6, 162.
[38] Aristotle, *Rhetoric*, 1358b11.
[39] Cicero, *On the Ideal Orator*, 2.43.
[40] Ibid., 2.341.

The focus of *On the Ideal Orator* is, after all, largely on the rough and tumble oratory that is connected to the institutions and practices of republican politics. Moreover, Cicero doubts in *On the Ideal Orator* both the distinctiveness and utility of epideictic in Rome: Deliberative and forensic oratory both deploy praise and blame, negating the distinctiveness of epideictic, and its Greek examples are "more for the pleasure of reading, or for glorifying a particular individual, than for the practical purposes of the forum that we are now considering."[41] Cicero's own forays into epideictic – his speeches of praise for Caesar, the speeches *For Ligarius* and *For Marcellus* – seem to demonstrate in their timing and content the political ambiguity of epideictic, since such speeches would have had little use at all had not Caesar "attained supreme power" – *summa potestate*.[42] After all, Cicero himself noted in *On Friendship* the connection between flattery – "the handmaid of vice" – and tyranny.[43]

Whereas Cicero subordinated epideictic to forensic and oratory, Quintilian elevates it, arguing that it is more useful in Rome than it is in Greece, and not only for private persons: "funeral orations are often imposed as a duty on persons holding public office … [and] the award of praise or blame to a witness may carry weight in the courts."[44] The most important work of extant imperial oratory – Pliny's *Panegyricus* – is itself an example of the genre, dealing as it does with the praise of Trajan as well as the blame of Domitian.[45]

Nor should we assume that epideictic was necessarily an impractical genre given its topic matter or Cicero's mixed attitude toward it, apparently severed from the formal decision-making institutions of the republic or flawed due to Polybius' criticisms of historiography that resembled panegyric. Aristotle thought that epideictic might in fact be a way of engaging in exhortation. In Book 1 of the *Rhetoric*, in the context of his analysis of epideictic, Aristotle writes that "To praise a man is in one respect akin to urging a course of action."[46] People are praised especially for their deeds, as "deeds are evidence

---

[41] Ibid., 2.341.
[42] Cicero, *Pro Marcello*, trans. N.H. Watts, *Cicero: The Speeches*, ed. N.H. Watts (Cambridge: Harvard University Press, 1958), 1.1.
[43] Cicero, *De Amicitia*, 89.
[44] Quintilian, *Institutio Oratoria*, 3.7.2.
[45] On the context, see Miriam Griffin, "Seneca and Pliny," in *The Cambridge History of Greek and Roman Political Thought*, ed. Christopher Rowe and Malcolm Schofield. Cambridge: Cambridge University Press, 2000: 532–58, 543.
[46] Aristotle, *Rhetoric*, 1367b36.

of the doer's character," and if deeds are strongly linked to character, we might praise someone who has not yet done a deed because "he is the sort of man who *would* do it."[47] Aristotle illustrates the claim thus: "the statement 'A man should be proud not of what he owes to fortune but of what he owes to himself' … amounts to a suggestion" as well as praise. It would be simple praise, however, if we were to phrase it thus: "Since he is proud not of what he owes to fortune but of what he owes to himself." He suggests, then, that when "you want to praise anyone, think what you would urge people to do; and when you want to urge the doing of anything, think what you would praise a man for having done."[48] Epideictic might thus have a deliberative aspect, insofar as it too could urge its hearers on toward a particular behavior.

Quintilian also notes the relationship between praise and counsel, suggesting that "panegyric is akin to deliberative oratory inasmuch as the same things are usually praised in the former as are advised in the latter."[49] Quintilian suggests that virtue may be praised, and vice dispraised, in two ways:

Some have been branded with infamy after death … even in the case of the living the judgment of mankind serves as a proof of their character, and the fairness or foulness of their fame proves the orator's praise or blame to be true.[50]

The praise or blame of the orator, in addition to providing exhortation, also helps to cement the fame – or infamy – of those they praise or blame. Those reading such writings, moreover, might learn through the examples they contain – and the praise and blame attribute to these examples – how to orient themselves as they engaged in the active life.

IV. BLURRING PRAISE AND COUNSEL

We have seen, then, that praise and counsel might be blurred, and can see this blurring of praise and counsel in three prominent Roman works of praise: Cicero's *For Marcellus*, Seneca's *On Mercy*, and Pliny's *Panegyricus*.

---

[47] Ibid., 1367b31–3.
[48] Ibid., 1368a4–8.
[49] Quintilian, *Institutio Oratoria*, 3.7.28.
[50] Ibid., 3.7.20–2.

Syme viewed these texts – especially Pliny's *Panegyricus* – with a fair amount of cynicism:

In the *Panegyricus* the type of discourse devoted to flattering the supreme power has come to perfection, with few tricks left for later practitioners to learn. The way to it led from Cicero's *Pro Marcello*, praising the glory and the clemency of Caesar the Dictator, through the *De clementia* which Seneca dedicated to Nero.[51]

Syme is wary of the praise of *clementia* in particular, and especially Caesar's *clementia*:

When Caesar the dictator paraded a merciful and forgiving spirit … he did not endear himself to all men in his class and order. Clemency depends not on duty but on choice and whim, it is the will of a master not an aristocrat's virtue. To acquiesce in the *"clementia Caesaris"* implied a recognition of despotism.[52]

This point appears to find support in Cicero's *On Duties*, where he notes that Cato chose to die rather than gaze on the visage of even a forgiving tyrant.[53] In his classic work on Roman *libertas*, Wirszubski argues that *clementia* increased in importance with "the decline of the idea that the citizen's rights have one guarantee – the law."[54] It is only when law ceased to rule, then, replaced by the will and whim of a monarch, that justice was replaced by mercy; praise of mercy was at best bittersweet, and a sign of servitude.

Cicero, too, seems to view *clementia* with a fair amount of skepticism. In a famous letter to Atticus, he describes the conflict between Antonius and Caesar, and the popularity of the latter and the fear aroused by the former, writing of Caesar that the towns "are delighted with his artful clemency [*insidiosa clementia*] and fear the other's [i.e. Antonius'] wrath."[55] Clearly, Cicero is not sanguine about Caesar's *clementia*; yet he does not seem to doubt that it is a virtue per se, but rather that Caesar is *actually* merciful. Indeed, Cicero defines *clementia* as a virtue in *On Invention*: "Clemency is a kindly and gentle restraint of spirits that have been provoked to dislike of a person of inferior rank."[56] In *On Duties*, Cicero writes that "nothing is more

---

[51] Syme, *Tacitus*, vol. 1, 95.
[52] Ibid., 414.
[53] Cicero, *On Duties*, 1.112.
[54] Wirszubksi, *Libertas as a Political Idea at Rome*, 151.
[55] Cicero, *Letters to Atticus*, trans. D.R. Shackleton Bailey (Cambridge: Harvard University Press, 1999), 8.16.2.
[56] Cicero, *De Inventione*, 2.164.

to be praised, nothing more worthy of a great and splendid man than to be easily appeased [*placabilitate*] and forgiving [*clementia*]," while nevertheless affirming that though "gentleness and forgiveness" [*mansuetudo et clementia*] may be commendable, there is a need for *severitas* when it comes to the republic, "for without that the city cannot be governed."[57]

Being merciful requires that one have the capacity to harm, a capacity rooted not just in the potential susceptibility to anger, but especially in power differentials between superiors and inferiors. Dyck suggests that "the term is naturally applied to one who possesses monarchical or quasi-monarchical powers," as for instance seen in Scipio's praise for Numa Pompilius' *clementia* in *On the Commonwealth* 2.27.[58] We need not go so far, however; nonmonarchs, such as Cicero's son, whom he advises to cultivate *clementia*, could be merciful, and in one of his letters Cicero joins *clementia* to a number of virtues that he claims to himself.[59] As Konstan argues, what people resented about Caesar's *clementia* was his superior status, and what they questioned was his sincerity; they did not question whether *clementia* was a virtue.[60]

Clementia Caesaris is a prominent theme in Cicero's *For Ligarius* and *For Marcellus*, the latter of which – mixing praise and counsel in his portrait of Caesar – will be our focus.[61] The speech *For Marcellus* is, on one level, highly disconcerting; after all, the hero of the republic who would call Caesar's death a just tyrannicide here praises the republic's destroyer for his mercy, after he forgave his former enemy Marcus Marcellus.[62] Cicero goes so far as to liken Caesar in his clemency and moderation to a god.[63] Yet Cicero is perfectly forthright in describing Caesar as having "attained

---

[57] Cicero, *On Duties*, 1.88.

[58] Andrew R. Dyck, *A Commentary on Cicero, De Officiis* (Ann Arbor: University of Michigan Press, 1996), 226.

[59] Cicero, *Letters to Atticus*, 7.2.7.

[60] David Konstan, "Clemency as a Virtue," *Classical Philology* 100 (2005): 337–46. 340–1.

[61] For a discussion of Caesar's policy of *clementia*, see Stefan Weinstock, *Divus Julius* (Oxford: Oxford University Press, 1971), 233–43.

[62] On Caesar's justifiable murder, see Cicero, *On Duties*, 3.18. Furhmann is sympathetic, suggesting that "Cicero was evidently hoping that Caesar would continue the policy of clementia, which he himself had once found suspect, and that he would have recourse even to former adversaries [like himself] in an attempt to establish a new order in the Republic that had now collapsed. He was not mistaken in this assumption." Furhmann, *Cicero and the Roman Republic*, 146

[63] Cicero, *Pro Marcello*, 3.8.

supreme power," and it is precisely because of Caesar's power that Cicero finds Caesar's moderation and clemency so striking.[64]

Cicero's praise is not without teeth: He notes that Caesar owes part of his military success to fortune, which is to say that it is not solely a reflection of his merits and efforts. Unlike his success in arms, the glory attendant on his mercy is solely due to his efforts, and hence more demonstrative of his virtues. Caesar has not simply vanquished "all other victors in civil war" by his "equity" and "compassion"; Cicero tells his audience that Caesar has "vanquished" himself by pardoning Marcellus.[65] Indeed, he has even vanquished victory, as he deliberately chooses clemency rather than exercise the right of conquest against his former enemies.

Cicero reassures Caesar (whom he represents as worried for his safety), suggesting that those foes who have not perished "have become your firmest friends" because of Caesar's pity (*misericordia*).[66] And he asks a pointed rhetorical question:

what man on earth is so ignorant of life, so unversed in politics, so utterly careless of his own well-being and that of the community, as not to realize that his own well-being is bound up in yours, and that on your sole life hangs the lives of all?[67]

The question, presumably, is intended to reassure Caesar publicly, just as it reminds those listening that their fates are intertwined with Caesar's fate, for better or worse. There is an additional level: It serves as a pointed reminder that politics is more dependent on a single person than it had been before. As others benefit from Caesar, Caesar himself will benefit and complete his work if he should "plant the constitution [*rem publicam*] firmly," by which he might "reap the chiefest fruits thereof in peace and tranquility."[68] While others may depend on Caesar for their safety, Caesar's own benefit will derive from securing the commonwealth and serving the public good. In securing the constitution, Cicero tells Caesar that he will have paid his country what he owes her.

Emphasizing the positive relationship between Caesar's virtues and the glory he will receive in memory once he is dead, Cicero tells Caesar that if

[64] Ibid., 1.1.
[65] Ibid., 4.12.
[66] Ibid., 7.21.
[67] Ibid., 7.22.
[68] Ibid., 9.27.

"this city is never to be tranquilized by your measures and your institutions, the passage of your name to the ends of the earth will be but a wayward roaming." Some will praise Caesar, to be sure, but "others perchance shall find some quality, and that the chiefest, to be lacking, should you fail to quench the fires of civil war, and thereby bring salvation to your country."[69]

Cicero urges Caesar to look toward "the verdict even of those who shall pass judgment upon you many ages hence."[70] Future generations will view Caesar's life "without partiality or interest [*sine amore et sine cupiditate*]," just as they will judge his character and deeds "without animosity or hatred [*sine odio et sine invidia*]" – Tacitus, as we have seen, echoes this language.[71] Given that the true glory of Caesar awaits him in future memory, Cicero tells Caesar "you should so bear yourself that no forgetfulness may ever dim the luster of your name."[72] While Cicero praises Caesar, then, he also exhorts him to a particular course of action (securing the republic), holding forth the potential reward of future glory (or disapprobation) as an incentive to acting in the recommended way. Such a tactic is of particular use when dealing with one who, like Caesar, was greatly concerned with how he was perceived, and especially with his glory, which Cicero here defines as "the bright and widespread fame won by great services conferred upon a man's own friends or upon his country or upon the human race at large."[73]

A similar set of tactics – the praise of a powerful individual for possessing and displaying mercy, connecting the display of mercy to glory and its absence to ignominy, and holding forth possible future reprobation for not displaying mercy (in a work aimed at public consumption) – are evident in Seneca's *On Mercy*. Seneca was not just a philosopher, but was also the tutor and adviser to Nero, a task that brought him Dio's derisive label of "tyrant teacher."[74] *On Mercy*, written in 55 CE, was designed both to bolster the new rule of Nero and to promote Nero's public image; as Griffin puts it:

The public cannot have viewed *De Clementia*, as they could other of his philosophical works, as a purely literary product unrelated to Seneca's political

---

[69] Ibid., 9.29.
[70] Ibid., 9.29.
[71] Ibid., 9.29.
[72] Ibid., 9.30.
[73] Ibid., 9.26.
[74] See Miriam Griffin, *Seneca: A Philosopher in Politics* (Oxford: Clarendon Press, 1992), 148.

activities. Nor were they meant to. When the Princeps' adviser addressed him on political subjects in public, that was an official statement.[75]

The very publicity of the work, though, brought an additional purpose: By seeking to establish Nero as marked by his *clementia*, Seneca may have been seeking to *commit* Nero to *clementia*, a virtue Nero had already praised in his criticism of Claudius' *saevitia* and which he would avow on taking power.[76]

Seneca writes the work, dedicated to the 18-year-old Nero, "as a kind of mirror, showing you to yourself on the point as you are of attaining the greatest of pleasures," which is to have done good deeds, and to be aware of one's own good deeds.[77] Seneca singles out as the greatest of Nero's attributes his mercy, the most humane of virtues. Nero is unquestionably above and superior to his subjects, and his greatness lies in the fact that he is "not only above them but also for them."[78] As Cicero argued of Caesar, Seneca writes that in Nero's safety lies the safety of Rome:

Their own safety ... is what men have at heart when for one man they lead ten legions into battle, rushing at the front line and baring their breasts to the wounds, lest their emperor's standards be overthrown. For he is the bond which holds the commonwealth together; he is the breath of life drawn by these several thousands.[79]

Unlike Cicero, however, Seneca argues that Nero is like the head of the commonwealth, without which it could not exist (and without which he could not exist as well). The very dignity of the ruler, towering above his subjects, lies in his virtuous behavior:

if he grants life and dignity to men who have risked and deserve to lose them, he does what none save a man of power can do. One can take the life of even a superior; one cannot grant it to anyone except an inferior.[80]

---

[75] Ibid., 133.

[76] Ibid., 136.

[77] Seneca, *On Mercy*, ed. John M. Cooper and J.F. Procope, *Seneca: Moral and Political Essays* (Cambridge: Cambridge University Press, 1995), 1.1.1. For a recent discussion of the "mirror for princes" genre, see Cary J. Nederman, "The Mirror Crack'd: The *Speculum Principum* as Political and Social Criticism in the Late Middle Ages," *The European Legacy* 3, no. 3 (1998): 18–39.

[78] Ibid., 1.3.3.

[79] Ibid., 1.4.1.

[80] Ibid., 1.5.6.

Despite exceeding all others in power and stature, Seneca's idealized Nero is far from free: "The slavery of being supremely great lies in the impossibility of ever becoming anything less."[81] In this constraint, Nero is akin to the gods: "They too are held bound to the heavens."

For Seneca, as with Cicero, mercy is becoming to Nero's superior personage and also to his personal security: Unlike private individuals, "For kings … the surer way to security is through gentleness, since frequent punishment, while it crushes hatred in a few, arouses it in everyone."[82] This is a lesson Seneca finds exemplified in the career of Augustus, whose "habit of mercy brought him safety and security, popularity and favor, although he had placed his hand on a Roman people that had never yet bowed its neck."[83] Augustus' mercy, however, differs from Nero's, in that Augustus' was closer to "exhausted cruelty," as it followed on years of bloodshed, whereas Nero has yet to shed the blood of a citizen.[84] Mercy, then, brings to the ruler both security and glory: "The glory of empire, it is at the same time its surest protection."[85]

Based on the importance of clemency, chiefly its status as the most humane of virtues, and the one most befitting a ruler, Seneca argues that "it is mercy which makes there be a great distinction between king and tyrant."[86] By Seneca's argument, Dionysus I of Syracuse, despite ruling outside of the laws, was no tyrant; Sulla, who laid down his power voluntarily, was a tyrant because he killed so many of his fellow citizens. Sulla is not remembered well, nor could be a ruler who frequently engages in cruelty and savage punishment; rather, "his greatest glory is to hold back his power, rescuing many from the anger of others, while exposing no one to his own."[87] A king made glorious by mercy is also an effective king, as "Men are inhibited from doing wrong by the very mercifulness of the ruler."[88] A

---

[81] Ibid., 1.8.3.

[82] Ibid., 1.8.6.

[83] Ibid., 1.10.2.

[84] Ibid., 1.11.2. On Augustus' *clementia*, see Zvi Yavetz, "The Res Gestae and Augustus' Public Image," in *Caesar Augustus: Seven Aspects*, ed. Fergus Millar and Erich Segal (Oxford: Clarendon Press, 1984): 1–36.

[85] Seneca, *On Mercy*, 1.11.4.

[86] Ibid., 1.12.3.

[87] Ibid., 1.17.3. See Cicero's account of the praise attributed to holding back anger and refraining from harm in Cicero, *On Duties*, 1.64–5. On Sulla, see Erich S. Gruen, *The Last Generation of the Roman Republic* (Berkeley: University of California Press, 1974), chapter I.

[88] Seneca, *On Mercy*, 1.22.3.

tyrant is ineffective, by contrast, and also insecure: "The cruelty of tyrants has set nations and peoples, both those afflicted and those threatened by it, to work at their destruction."[89]

Thus, we see in our first two examples of Roman works of praise that each advises its recipient while it praises and blames, locating security and fame with virtue and mercy, while displaying positive and negative examples for their audiences. Let us turn to our third, and the closest to Tacitus' time: Pliny's *Panegyricus*. In 100 CE, Pliny delivered an oration of thanks to Trajan for his consular election; in the existing version (lengthened from the original) it takes roughly three hours to recite, per Syme's estimate.[90] Certainly, Pliny does come off as rather over-eager to praise, suggesting that Jupiter himself had chosen Trajan as *princeps*; perhaps he was aware of this, as he felt the need to begin with a prayer to Jupiter so that "independence, truth, and sincerity mark my every word, and my vote of thanks be as far removed from a semblance of flattery as it is from constraint."[91] Such a prayer marks this speech off as different from what one might expect with Domitian as *princeps*, insofar as a speaker praising Domitian might well have engaged in flattery or felt constrained by the mercurial Domitian.

In a similar vein, Pliny issues an intriguing caveat:

There is no danger that in my references to his humanity he will see a reproach for arrogance; that he will suppose I mean extravagance by modest expenditure, and cruelty by forbearance; and that I think him covetous and capricious when I call him generous and kind, profligate and idle instead of self-controlled and active, or that I judge him a coward when I speak of him as a brave man.[92]

This is to say that he is not engaging in redescription or flattery; such a caveat may be warranted because of past behavior. Praise of Domitian, in retrospect, ought to have been received with a grain of salt, as one can well imagine that those who profited under him and praised him were aware that their words might not be taken literally.[93]

---

[89] Ibid., 1.26.1.

[90] Trajan was a patient ruler, according to Pliny, though we may well think with Syme that "three hours of intensive glorification would be an inhuman ordeal for the most patient of rulers." Syme, *Tacitus*, vol. 1, 94.

[91] Pliny, *Panegyricus*, 1.6.

[92] Ibid., 3.4.

[93] Saying the opposite of what one meant, and leaving it to those one was addressing or speaking about to suggest otherwise, was not an uncommon rhetorical technique. Quintilian, for

Pliny praises Trajan for a number of reasons, many of which center on his possession of *civilitas*: Trajan is "one of us – and his special virtue lies in his thinking so, as also is his never forgetting that he is a man himself while a ruler of men."[94] Though superior to all, Trajan acts as if he were an equal; as Pliny tells him, "you are one among us all, the greatest of us simply because you are the best."[95] However, Trajan is also praiseworthy for his *clementia*, as were Nero for Seneca and Caesar for Cicero. Trajan's *clementia* is evident in expelling *delatores* from Rome on boats, entrusting "vengeance over men on earth to the gods of the sea," and for showing, in his administration of justice, that "strictness [*severitas*] need not be cruel nor mercy [*clementia*] weak."[96]

With a new *civilis princeps*, Pliny suggests that the dilemma of being a member of Rome's elite, which had marked prior *principes*, has faded away. As opposed to the reign of Domitian, under Trajan "no one need purchase security with disgrace"; moreover, "foresight and prudence no longer prompt men to spend a lifetime keeping out of sight," as they had in the reign of Nero, according to the *Agricola*.[97] Though Rome is ruled by a *princeps*, virtues are rewarded "as they were in times of liberty."[98] Were it not for virtue being rewarded (and vice being punished), there would be little way to "make men bad or good," as without an equitable system, men might turn to "idleness, torpor and extravagance."[99] In his positive example to his subjects, Trajan controls their behavior more effectively than his predecessors: "by the firmness of our allegiance we are reaching the point when we shall all conform with the ways of a single man."[100] So effective a moral exemplar is Trajan that he *is* the censorship: "example is what we need more than command. Fear is unreliable as a teacher of morals. Men

instance, notes that "since the boundary between vice and virtue is often ill-defined," there might be occasions on which "it is desirable to use words that swerve a little from the actual truth, calling a rash man brave, a prodigal generous, a mean man thrifty." Quintilian doubts that the true orator, which is to say the good man (*quidem orator, id est vir bonus*) would do this, apart from "consideration for the public interest." Quintilian, *Institutio Oratoria*, 3.7.25.

[94] Pliny, *Panegyricus*, 2.4. On the attribute *civilis*, see Andrew Wallace-Hadrill, "Civilis Princeps: Between Citizen and King," *The Journal of Roman Studies* 72 (1982): 32–48.

[95] Pliny, *Panegyricus*, 21.4.

[96] Ibid., 35.1–2, 80.1.

[97] Ibid., 44.5.

[98] Ibid., 44.6.

[99] Ibid., 44.8.

[100] Ibid., 45.5.

learn better from examples, which have the great merit of proving that the advice is practicable."[101]

Much of Pliny's praise of Trajan is structured as a comparison with the deficiencies of his predecessors; this is, in fact, Pliny's avowed desire, and it provided an abundance of positive and negative *exempla*. In part, such a comparison allows Pliny to show how Trajan "is amending and reforming the character of the principate which had become debased by a long period of corruption." But the very nature of epideictic is such that praise "is best expressed through a comparison," and if Trajan's subjects are grateful for him, they ought "to attack those who are least like him: for no one can properly appreciate a good prince who does not sufficiently hate a bad man." Among the most effective of Trajan's benefits, in this regard, is "the freedom he allows us to criticize bad rulers with impunity."[102] Pliny points out that Domitian was unwilling to allow Nero to be criticized, suggesting that "anything said against one so like himself could be applied to him," and hence fearing the possible comparison.[103] Were Romans under Trajan to keep silent, however, there would be no way to say that Trajan was better than Domitian.

Pliny, like Seneca, notes the futility of Domitian's behavior:

Experience shows that the one guard which a prince can wholly trust is his own innocence … It is useless for a man to be armed with terror if he lacks the protection of love; for arms only call out more arms.

Trajan's defense is "popularity;" Domitian's was "cruelty."[104] What matters for a *princeps* is not whether he is or is not remembered; he will be, no matter what he does. Rather, the issue is *how* he is remembered – well or badly – "and this is preserved not in portraits and statutes but in virtue and good deeds."[105]

V. TACITUS' USE OF PRAISE AND BLAME

The opposition between love and fear, and the utility of each as a basis for one's position of authority, is an important topic in the works just surveyed;

---

[101] Ibid., 45.6.
[102] Ibid., 53.1–3.
[103] Ibid., 53.4.
[104] Ibid., 49.2–3.
[105] Ibid., 55. 10.

it was also a prominent topic in Cicero's *On Duties* and played an important role in Livy's conception of the ties between leader and led, giving rise to consensus. Security and glory are to be found in the love of one's subjects, not in their fear. A ruler ought to endeavor to be loved, if for no other reason than that it was befitting to his security, though in fact it was more honorable to be loved, and being loved was a function of being honorable. Having explored these works of praise, what they admire, and what they hold forth for disapprobation – and how the admirable and the blameworthy served as components of *exempla* – let us turn now to Tacitus' mode of praising and blaming *principes* while seeking to avoid the contrary extremes of servility and contumacy. These dilemmas, we have seen Tacitus suggest, are particularly the product of living under the principate.

A useful starting point is the story of Cremutius Cordus, who had been prosecuted under the reign of Tiberius for publishing a history in which he praised Brutus and called Cassius "the last of the Romans."[106] It is not difficult to imagine why such statements were dangerous, given their status as tyrannicides and violent opponents of the first Caesars. Having been accused by Satrius Secundus and Pinarius Natta, clients of Sejanus, Cordus had decided "to take his leave of life." In his defense speech, Cordus argues that he is innocent in actions, and accused in words; moreover, his words were not directed against Tiberius or Augustus. Rather, he praised Brutus and Cassius. Other historians had done the same, including Livy, friend of Augustus himself; he also cites Asinius Pollio and Messalla Corvinus. Cicero praised Cato while Caesar still ruled; Caesar merely responded with his own oration. Julius and Augustus tolerated the poems of Bibaculus and Catullus; Cordus is unsure whether to credit this to their moderation (*moderatione*) or wisdom (*sapientia*). What he emphasizes, however, is that matters disregarded (*spreta*) are forgotten, whereas if one grows angry, it will seem to be recognition (*si irascare, adgnita videntur*). That is to say, the angry reaction of one who thinks he is being mocked or blamed – even indirectly – supports the mockery or criticism, making what had been implied seem overt.

His speech reaches a crescendo when he comes to the Greeks, among whom "not liberty [*libertas*] only but license [*libido*] itself went unchastised, or, if a man retaliated, he avenged words by words."[107] Above all, though, he

---

[106] Tacitus, *The Annals*, 4.34.

[107] For a recent discussion of the strong link between free speech and democracy in Athens, see Kurt A. Raaflaub, "Aristocracy and Freedom of Speech in the Greco-Roman World," in *Free Speech in Classical Antiquity*, ed. Ineke Sluiter and Ralph M. Rosen (Leiden: Brill,

emphasizes that among the Greeks the historian "was absolutely free and immune from censure [in] the expression of an opinion on those whom death had removed beyond the range of rancor or of partiality [*odio aut gratiae exemisset*]."[108] He concludes by noting that if he is condemned, he will be remembered with Brutus and Cassius; afterwards, he starved himself to death.

His books were burned, "but copies remained, hidden and afterwards published: a fact which moves us the more to deride the folly of those who believe that by an act of despotism in the present [*praesenti potentia*] there can be extinguished also the memory of a succeeding age [*sequentis aevi memoriam*]." Rather, "genius chastised grows in authority," and those who have ruled with savagery (*saevitia*) have not escaped dishonor while giving geniuses glory (*gloriam*). In this passage, Tacitus has Cordus vindicate, and he himself indirectly vindicates, the writing of history and the futility of censorship, while at the same time asserting its moral function and service to posterity. Cordus, and hence Tacitus, is able to do, through his history, what epideictic oratory might do: praise and blame, exhort and persuade. Cordus justifies criticism of the past by emphasizing its distance from the present – an effort (though unsuccessful) to balance between contumacy and sycophancy.

This is not an easy balance to strike – we have seen this in our discussion of the three works of epideictic; their authors were all aware that their praise might seem farfetched. Tacitus, as we saw in Section II, was aware of the distorting effects of great power on eloquence. Tacitus is able to achieve this critical distance partly because his subjects have exited the stage, just as Caesar's future observers would judge him differently than those hearing Cicero give the speech *For Marcellus*. But by giving much attention to negative examples of vicious behavior, Tacitus also provides a set of moral and political cues that allow his readers to orient themselves.

Part of what Tacitus does in his histories, then, is hold out to future reprobation the misdeeds of those who have gone before him; but in addition to holding out crimes for reprobation, he holds out virtues for approbation. In

2004): 41–61. On *parrhesia* and Athenian freedom, see e.g. Kurt A. Raaflaub, *The Discovery of Freedom in Ancient Greece*, trans. Renate Franciscono (Chicago: University of Chicago Press, 2004), 223–5.

108 Tacitus, *The Annals*, 4.35. These echo precisely the motives of bias that we encountered in Cicero's *Pro Marcello*, 9.28 when future generations would judge Caesar "without partiality or interest [*sine amore et sine cupiditate*]," just as they will judge his character and deeds "without animosity or hatred [*sine odio et sine invidia*]."

particular, we see in Tacitus a number of antitheses between imperial virtues and vices, especially savagery (*saevitia*) and mercy (*clementia*). With a sufficiently *clemens princeps*, one may say what one thought with more freedom, and prudence of the kind displayed by Agricola became less essential; with a *princeps* marked by *saevitia* or *crudelitas*, however, the opposite was the case, and one had to emulate Agricola and confront the dilemmas of the *Dialogue on Orators*. In either case, it was important to read the character of the prince rightly an act facilitated by Tacitus' use of praise and blame.

Let us start with the qualities of the bad ruler in the earliest of Tacitus' writings: the *Agricola*. Domitian is marked by *saevitia*, a quality that collides with those who excel.[109] Tacitus does not hesitate to describe Domitian's rule as "our former slavery," a period whose horror further highlights the "present blessings" of Trajan's reign, who "is increasing daily the happiness of the times."[110] We see little of Nero, himself no model ruler, in the *Agricola*, though we are told of Agricola that "He read aright the reign of Nero, wherein to be passive was to be wise [*sapientia*]."[111] Our first sustained portrait of the psychology of the bad ruler occurs after Agricola's defeat of a major British rebellion. Despite Agricola's modesty in victory, Domitian was displeased: He:

greeted [the victories], as his manner was, with affected pleasure and secret disquiet: in his heart was the consciousness that his recent counterfeit triumph over the Germans was a laughing-stock.[112]

Domitian was thus insecure and, because of his insecurity, a dissimulator.

Domitian's inner insecurity causes him to suspect one whom he had no reason to suspect; in particular, he is afraid that Agricola will be more prominent than himself. And here Tacitus suggests that Domitian's hostility toward letters, noted in our discussion of Pliny, had a *political* purpose: Domitian wanted more glory for himself. Indeed, the very attributes that enable Agricola to succeed in the field are "Imperial qualities," according to Tacitus. Yet unlike his open and direct subordinate, Domitian did not give vent to his feelings, but rather decided "to treasure up his hatred" until Agricola's fame subsided.[113]

---

[109] Tacitus, *Agricola*, 3.2.
[110] Ibid., 3.3, 1.
[111] Ibid., 6.3. Cf. Pliny, *Panegyricus*, 44.5.
[112] Tacitus, *Agricola*, 39.1.
[113] Ibid., 39.3.

Domitian's own paranoia was exacerbated by the behavior of the informers, who accused Agricola of misdeeds many times. Agricola had done nothing, of course; he was the victim of "a master who leaned ever to the worst side."[114] Domitian is thus characterized by savagery, which leads to his tendency to engage in dissimulation, a manifestation of his vices and his awareness of others' virtues, along with his concomitant insecurity. His fear of those who were prominent, and the fear he inspired in the prominent, lead to his susceptibility to having his suspicions stoked by sycophants through their flattery. These combined to make him hostile to the success of others and suspicious of merit, especially in the liberal arts. All of this was amplified by the very success of Agricola, a success due in large part to his virtues, but made more palatable by his prudence and moderation.

We see similarities in Tacitus' portrayal of Tiberius as well. Tacitus portrays Tiberius as a largely vicious individual (though he degenerates over time with the increased influence of Sejanus), and among Tiberius' many vices, perhaps the most readily apparent is his dissembling. This is evident not long after his ascension: His coy behavior, it turned out, "had been assumed with the further object of gaining an insight into the feelings of the aristocracy: for all the while he was distorting words and looks into crimes and storing them in his memory."[115] Tiberius makes a habit of thinking one thing and saying another, often to act on his concealed thoughts with negative consequences. Even his manner of speaking was obscure, regardless of whether or not he had the desire "to conceal his thought."[116] Upon assuming the office of *princeps*, he desired "to bury every trace of his sentiments," and his way of speaking "became more intricate, uncertain, and equivocal than ever." This led to a strange situation for Rome's elite, as the great fear of the Senators "was that they might seem to comprehend him."[117] Thus, when he addressed the Senate on the successful military service of Germanicus, he did so "in terms too speciously florid to be taken as the expression of his inmost feelings" – even though "he was in earnest, and his language honest."[118]

To be sure, we might ask ourselves how Tacitus could know what Tiberius was thinking or feeling, but more important is Tiberius' service as a vehicle on whom Tacitus can fashion his censure of dissembling and a certain mode

---

[114] Ibid., 41.4.
[115] Tacitus, *The Annals*, 1.7.
[116] Ibid., 1.11.
[117] Ibid., 1.11.
[118] Ibid., 1.52.

of ruling.[119] Tacitus is no fan of false appearances: Witness his distaste for Tiberius' dissembling at the close of Book 1, where he describes "a servitude all the more detestable the more it was disguised under a semblance of liberty."[120] Simply put, Tiberius' spirit was not that of a citizen (*civilis animi*); what lay beneath the surface was not the same as what he manifested in speech and behavior.[121] On occasion, this could bring about wryly humorous situations, as when Gnaeus Piso asked Tiberius, prior to a vote:

> In what order will you register your opinion, Caesar? If first, I shall have something to follow: if last of all, I fear I may inadvertently find myself on the other side.[122]

But the consequences could be dangerous, as a "speaker ... had to walk a strait and slippery road under a prince who feared liberty and detested flattery."[123] Tiberius' dissembling poses a clear problem, then, for elite Romans, insofar as his behavior is unpredictable and illegible, and hence arbitrary. One would need to read rightly – and act prudently in light of this understanding – such a *princeps*, who serves as a negative *exemplum* of rule.

Tacitus' criticism of Tiberius couples with his defense of historiography and the futility of seeking to control history's telling. We have already seen Tacitus' claim, in his discussion of Cremutius Cordus, that those who rule with savagery (*saevitia*) do not escape dishonor, though they give geniuses glory (*gloriam*). In our discussion of Tiberius, it should be noted that Tacitus claims that Tiberius preferred savagery (*saevitiam*) to regret (*paenitentiam*).[124] Indeed, after the death of Agrippina, Tacitus notes that "there was no abatement of cruelty [*saevitia*]" in Tiberius' rule.[125] We see here again the benefits mercy brings to the powerful, and the security that comes from love, as

---

[119] Seager suggests that what Tacitus views as dissimulation – Tiberius' professed reluctance to take on the offices of Augustus – may, in fact, have been quite genuine, and that to deny it is "perverse": Tiberius was 54 on his ascension, and "had a long and tiring career, in the shadow of a man whose character and achievements he could never hope to emulate even if he wanted to. Now he was being called on to dedicate the rest of his life to the preservation of a political structure of which he had no reason to approve." Robin Seager, *Tiberius* (Oxford: Blackwell, 2005), 46.

[120] Tacitus, *The Annals*, 1.81.

[121] Ibid., 1.72.

[122] Ibid., 1.74.

[123] Ibid., 2.87.

[124] Ibid., 6.23.

[125] Ibid., 6.25.

was evident in our discussion of Cicero, Seneca, and Pliny. It is no wonder that many were amazed that although Tiberius knew the fame that followed mercy (*fama clementiam sequeretur*), he preferred what was "darker" (*tristiora*).[126] Not only did Tiberius prefer *saevitia* to *clementia*; he was not always amenable to others' virtues. We may note, for instance, that Tiberius suspected Lucius Arruntius because he was "rich, enterprising, greatly gifted, [and] correspondingly popular."[127] Although Tiberius was not so corrupt at this point as to prefer vice to virtue, "the best he feared as a private danger, the worst as a public scandal."[128] Tacitus thus links Tiberius to savagery and holds him up for disapprobation, showing that this behavior does not bring glory and is self-defeating.

Bad rulers are marked by cruelty, instability, dissembling; it would behoove an ambitious Roman, engaged in an active life, to learn to read the characters of the ruler and to cultivate prudence. Do we see *good* rulers in Tacitus? On one level, the answer must be yes, but more in juxtaposition to bad rulers than in detailed sketches; one might well point to Agricola, whose virtues as a ruler we have already discussed. We saw, for instance, that with Agricola's soldiers in Britain, "rivalry for his compliments took the place of coercion"; the same was the case with Germanicus' forces in Germany, who felt toward him a "debt of gratitude" for "his patience and his courtesy" in dealing with their mutiny.[129] In these instances, the perceived moral worth of a leader might inspire his inferiors to obey him, just as the moral example of Trajan, the living embodiment of the censorship, inspired obedience and morality for Pliny.[130]

Tacitus' depiction of Vespasian is similar to his depiction of Germanicus, in that he was able to check luxury though prior emperors had failed to do so through applying laws. With Vespasian, "deference to the sovereign and the love of emulating him proved more powerful than legal sanctions and deterrents"; as a result, luxury declined.[131] Not simply a moral exemplar himself, Vespasian acknowledged orators' merit, as Aper argues

---

[126] Ibid., 4.31.
[127] Ibid., 1.13.
[128] Ibid., 1.80.
[129] Tacitus, *Agricola*, 21.1; Tacitus, *The Annals*, 2.13.
[130] Not without ambiguity, however, the same Germanicus had a penchant for the histrionic: witness, for instance, his foolish effort to quell a mutiny in Germany by threatening to kill himself – "the act seemed brutal and ill conditioned," according to Tacitus, and one soldier even handed him his own sword, saying "it was sharper," 1.35.
[131] Ibid., 3.55.

in the *Dialogue on Oratory*. As opposed to those who "owe their position to the advantages they have received from" the emperor, orators have "an element which they never got from an Emperor and which is absolutely incommunicable."[132] Vespasian contrasts to other *principes*, during whose rule "virtues caused the surest ruin" as a result of suspicious *principes* and conniving informers.[133] This should not be surprising, given, for instance, Otho and Vitellius' characters: these "two men, the worst in the world for their shamelessness, indolence, and profligacy, had been apparently chosen by fate to ruin the empire."[134]

To be sure, part of Tacitus' valorization of these members of the Flavian dynasty, and his deprecation of the Julio-Claudian dynasty, can be read as a function of dynastic politics (the Flavians needed to set themselves apart from their predecessors), or even the inability to write objectively about those from whom Tacitus received benefits and who are still alive. But the emphasis on the disingenuousness and illegibility of Tiberius or Domitian, the outright vice of Otho and Vitellius, and the possession and display of opposite attributes by Vespasian, Nerva, and Trajan suggest that dynastic politics is not all that is going on. Moreover, as we saw in the *Annals*, Tacitus suggests that his histories have an educative function.

This educative function is linked to the perilous times. Thus, Tacitus has Galba tell Piso, after he adopted the latter to be his successor:

If the mighty structure of the empire could stand in even poise without a ruler, it were proper that a republic should begin with me. But as it is, we have long reached such a pass that my old age cannot give more to the Roman people than a good successor, or your youth more than a good emperor.[135]

In this passage, we see little pretense that the republic might be restored. In counseling his chosen successor on how to rule, Galba advises him, "Keep Nero before your eyes." Nero, for Galba, serves as an *exemplum* not to emulate, but to avoid. His downfall was the result of "his own monstrous character, his own extravagance": these "flung him from the necks of the people." While "Nero will always be missed by the worst citizens," Galba says, "you and I must take care that he be not missed also by the good." We might say the

---

[132] Tacitus, *Dialogue on Oratory*, 8.3.
[133] Tacitus, *The Histories*, 1.2.
[134] Ibid., 1.50.
[135] Tacitus, *The Histories*, 1.16.

same of Tiberius and Domitian, and by Tacitus' account, we may not say the same about Vespasian, Nerva, and Trajan.

Galba concludes with a wonderful Tacitean phrase: "you are going to rule over men who can endure neither complete slavery nor complete liberty."[136] This phrase, for Syme, seems to encapsulate Tacitus' thinking: "It early became evident that one man held all the power and authority. And it was not long before a theory developed, to save appearances and permit the senator to maintain his dignity: precisely the ideal of the middle path, liberty but not license, discipline but not enslavement."[137] This need to find a middle path between extremes, whether it be in oratory, historiography, or elite behavior, is a far cry from the republic of old. What mattered now above all else was the character of the ruler: A good ruler might make Rome something like what it had been; a bad ruler, one who was fearful, hostile to virtue, and prone to cruelty and dissembling, peeled away the façade.

Good or bad, though, it was necessary – and prudent – to read them rightly. But rulers, even the most vicious, want to be remembered well and to be loved. And so when the inhabitants of further Spain wanted to erect a temple to Tiberius, Tiberius demurred; he was "sturdily disdainful of compliments" and had already had a temple dedicated to him in the East. Rather, Tiberius sought to have "my temples in your breasts," and he believed that being well thought of required "modesty"; Tacitus chalks this up to "a contemptuous rejection of ... divine honors," as well as "self-distrust [and] degeneracy of soul." Tacitus sees in Tiberius that "in the scorn of fame was implied the scorn of virtue."[138]

VI. CONCLUSION

In this chapter, I have read Tacitus as engaging in a kind of practical political theorizing in his historical writings. Through his reading of particular *principes*, and the way in which he deployed praise and blame in their depictions, Tacitus provides models of imperial character that enable his readers to better cultivate prudence – prudence that was essential to engaging in the public life, as I argued in Chapter 5. Rulers marked by *saevitia*, such as Domitian and Tiberius, needed to be recognized, and their character needed

---

[136] Tacitus, *The Histories*, 1.16.
[137] Syme, *Tacitus*, vol. II, 548.
[138] Tacitus, *The Annals*, 4. 37–8.

to be navigated in prudent ways. Moreover, Tacitus' practice of praising and blaming imperial character echoes the practice of the orator engaging in epideictic, providing a kind of reward and punishment in future generations for the behavior and character of *principes*.

Through projecting his criticism backward – and onto prior dynasties – Tacitus can engage in behavior that might otherwise prove imprudent and dangerous. He does not emulate Maternus, whose subject matter is too obvious, and whose pleas of innocence – if they did not ring hollow – would hardly have the teeth to fend off informers. Nor does he go the route of the toady, flattering those who rule, though he does say good things about Nerva and Trajan. Tacitus engages in criticism of particular *principes* – Tiberius, Caligula, Claudius, Nero, Domitian, among others. But he does so in a way that does not explicitly criticize the principate, and makes recent rulers – such as Nerva and Trajan – look better by comparison. The problem is that each of the monarchs that Tacitus criticized – such as Tiberius and Domitian – had a character which was deficient; the problem was not that each was monarch in the first place – at least not overtly. Tacitus' tactic seems, then, to echo Hobbes' statement: "all the acts of Nero are not essential to monarchy."[139]

Yet we might go somewhat further in interpreting Tacitus. Insofar as he needed to project his criticism into the past, faced with the twin dilemmas of obsequiousness and contumacy in speaking of the present, we might say that he mounts an implicit criticism of the principate itself. That speaking freely becomes increasingly difficult when power is concentrated, and that the safest vehicle for criticism is to project this criticism backwards: Both point toward a subtle critique of the principate, affirming both the unfreedom of those who are subject to domination and the subversive power of rhetoric. One may accept that there is no going back to the republic, a past that Tacitus does not idealize, and hope for a good monarch. But placing one's hope in the character of the monarch – and keeping in mind the importance of prudence – is a far cry from placing one's hopes in one's own abilities as an orator as practiced in the institutions of the republic. Tacitus seems to proclaim the death of oratory, yet he does not do so in his own voice; he seems to suggest that criticism and dissent are futile, but engages in criticism and dissent. In doing so, he deploys rhetoric, recalling the republic and its liberty in an ironic and poignant way.

[139] Hobbes, *The Citizen*, 227.

EPILOGUE

It is fitting to end our discussion with Tacitus, who both displays the connection between rhetoric and liberty in Roman political thought and at the same time highlights the tensions and conflicts this connection entailed. If, as we saw in Chapter 1 and throughout this book, rhetoric and liberty may go hand in hand, guiding decisions, cultivating judgment, and fostering community, rhetoric might undermine liberty and political community. Similarly, the practice of rhetoric, though it might be a manifestation of liberty and foster judgment, might also be a manifestation of license and smother judgment. Tacitus echoes the arguments and criticisms of Plato, and prefigures the concerns of Hobbes. In Tacitus' writings, we see not only the case for rhetoric and liberty, but also their critique.

Despite the apparent dangers of rhetoric – its potentially harmful relationship to political community, its incompatibility with peace, and its connection to misunderstood liberty – I suggested that Tacitus should not be identified with Maternus, per se. If Tacitus serves to highlight the relationship between rhetoric and liberty in part through his seeming opposition to Cicero, he also provides us with warnings about the problems entailed in the absence of rhetoric. A kind of peace may have characterized the principate, but it was a peace brought about by the rule of one. For rhetoric not to have a place in the community, we would need an ideal society – just as we would need a perfectly healthy population for medicine to have no place. The presence of rhetoric, limited as it was, invites us to explore the contradictions and ambiguities not just in Maternus' speeches, but in Tacitus' writings as a whole. These contradictions and ambiguities highlight the salience of prudence, just as they mimic and appropriate the rhetorical practice of arguing *in utramque partem*, itself linked to prudence.[1] They also invite us to explore how Tacitus used his writing to engage in a mode of historiography and critique that did not fall into the traps of either contumacy or obsequiousness. Tacitus emphasizes the importance of prudence, and the need to navigate between extremes of behavior: foolish outspokenness, servile acquiescence, and outright withdrawal. Through his delineation of good and bad character in Rome's rulers – those marked by *saevitia*, and those marked by *clementia* – he engaged in a kind of practical political theorizing for his readers, who were in need of signposts by which they might cultivate and practice prudence.

In this regard, Tacitus – like Sallust and Livy – serves as a resource for reflecting upon contemporary concerns with republicanism and rhetoric. The preservation of republican liberty and civic virtue, the boundaries of republican communities, the role of rhetoric in political conflict, the relationship between rhetoric, conflict, and liberty – each of these writers wrestled with these problems in different ways. Sallust depicted a Rome that seemed to be pulled apart by conflict and antagonism after the restraining effects of external fear had been removed. An attachment to the particular institutions and practices of the Roman republic seemed insufficient to foster the dispositions required to support it, an outcome that seemed to suggest that a thicker conception of civic virtue was required if Rome's citizens were to retain the right orientation to the community.

Yet this problem pointed, as I argued, to the antagonism and competition that lay beneath the surface of Sallust's Rome, antagonism that had been checked, but not eliminated, by the *metus hostilis*. Rather than seek to snuff out the antagonisms that threatened to boil over following the destruction of Carthage, or to reach a thicker and deeper form of civic agreement, I argued that the practice of rhetoric by outstanding individuals held out hope for treating and channeling antagonism. Antagonistic rhetoric between such individuals offered both a resource for treating conflict between social forces. Sallust's antagonistic republic, then, highlights the ways in which the antagonism embedded in the practice of rhetoric can help to foster republican community and to contain the antagonisms of republican citizenship.

Livy navigated the dilemmas of conflict and contestation through the rhetorical construction of leadership. Rhetoric, and the devices of ethos and

---

[1] On arguing *in utramque partem*, see Remer, "Hobbes, the Rhetorical Tradition, and Toleration."

pathos, became mechanisms that mediated the interactions between mass and elite. Authority was not a top-down relationship, but rather a relationship based on negotiation and consensus, held together by the display of character and its observation and relying on the voluntary adherence of the many. The centrality of morals to Livy's understanding of the republic highlights the role of affect, consensus, and approbation in the maintenance of republican communities. Just as contemporary theorists view rhetoric as a source for cultivating trust and thus fostering the conditions of liberty, the rhetorical construction of leadership and consensualism fostered a health political community for Livy.

Tacitus' writings reflect a way of thinking about rhetoric, liberty, and conflict that both echoed and subverted themes we saw in earlier writers, and especially Cicero. Yet in his appropriation and critique of Ciceronian arguments about oratory that seem to be misapplied in the imperial present, he highlighted the centrality of prudence, itself a trait that was central to the effective practice of oratory. Tacitus shows that prudence is necessary in navigating the dilemmas of domination, while also using the tools of rhetoric – especially the praise and blame of the epideictic orator – to show his audience how to read their rulers and holding out the prospect of future praise and blame through his writings.

I read each of these writers with Cicero, albeit in different ways, and it is fitting that we return to Cicero by way of conclusion. We saw in Cicero the close connection between rhetoric and liberty, the potential for the prior to support and to subvert the latter, and the changed conditions in oratory that accompanied changed political conditions. All of these themes have been salient in discussing Sallust, Livy, and Tacitus, just as they are salient in contemporary accounts of rhetoric and republicanism. Cicero held forth the possibility of a free and participatory mode of politics rooted in the judgments and opinions of the many, a politics that entailed consensus in the face of antagonism. In reading Sallust, Livy, and Tacitus with Cicero and other ancient writers, as well as contemporary republican and rhetorical scholarship, we have seen the ways in which the politics of the republic were ultimately contested, how rhetoric and liberty moved together and gave structure to historical treatments of the republic, and how these relationships were remembered and theorized in Roman historiography. Exploring their writings in light of contemporary concerns in political theory provides resources for theorizing the relationship between liberty, rhetoric, and conflict in political communities.

BIBLIOGRAPHY

Abizadeh, Arash. "On the Philosophy/Rhetoric Binaries: Or, Is Habermasian Discourse Motivationally Impotent?" *Philosophy and Social Criticism* 33, no. 4 (2007): 445–72.

Ad C. Herennium De Ratione Dicendi. Translated by Harry Caplan. Cambridge: Harvard University Press, 1964.

Adcock, F.E. *Roman Political Ideas and Practice.* Ann Arbor: University of Michigan Press, 1964.

Allen, Danielle S. *Talking to Strangers: Anxieties of Citizenship since Brown v. Board of Education.* Chicago: University of Chicago Press, 2006.

Arendt, Hannah. *Truth and Politics.* In *The Portable Hannah Arendt*, edited by Peter Baehr. New York: Penguin, 2000: 545–75.

Aristotle. *The "Art" of Rhetoric.* Translated by John Henry Freese. Cambridge: Harvard University Press, 1947.

Nicomachean Ethics. Translated by Terrence Irwin. Indianapolis: Hackett, 1985.

Politics. Edited by C.D.C. Reeve. Indianapolis: Hackett, 1998.

Rhetoric. Translated by W. Rhys Roberts. Edited by Jonathan Barnes. Vol. II, *The Complete Works of Aristotle.* Princeton: Princeton University Press, 1984.

Astin, Alan E. *Cato the Censor.* Oxford: Oxford University Press, 1978.

Austin, J.L. *How to Do Things with Words.* Edited by J.O. Urmson and Marina Sbisa. Cambridge: Harvard University Press, 1975.

Bailyn, Bernard. *The Ideological Origins of the American Revolution.* Cambridge: Harvard University Press, 1967.

Bartsch, Shadi. *Actors in the Audience: Theatricality and Doublespeak from Nero to Hadrian.* Cambridge: Harvard University Press, 1994.

Batstone, William W. "The Antithesis of Virtue: Sallust's *Synkrisis* and the Crisis of the Late Republic." *Classical Antiquity* 7, no. 1 (1988): 1–29.

Berlin, Isaiah. "Two Concepts of Liberty." In *The Proper Study of Mankind: An Anthology of Essays*, edited by Henry Hardy and Roger Hausheer. New York: Farrar, Straus and Giroux, 1997: 191–242.

Boesche, Roger. "The Politics of Pretence: Tacitus and the Political Theory of Despotism." *History of Political Thought* VIII, no. 2 (1987): 189–210.

Brink, C.O. "Can Tacitus' *Dialogus* Be Dated? Evidence and Historical Conclusions." *Harvard Studies in Classical Philology* 96 (1994): 251–80.

Briscoe, J. "The First Decade." In *Livy*, edited by T.A. Dorey. London: Routledge and Kegan Paul, 1971: 1–20.

Brown, Robert. "Livy's Sabine Women and the Ideal of Concordia." *Transactions of the American Philological Association* 125 (1995): 291–319.

Brunt, P.A. "*Libertas* in the Republic." In *The Fall of the Roman Republic and Other Related Essays*. Oxford: Clarendon Press, 1988: 281–350.

Burke, P. "Tacitism." In *Tacitus*, edited by T.A. Dorey. New York: Basic Books, 1969: 149–71.

Cato. *Les Origines: Fragments*. Edited by Martine Chassignet. Paris: Société d'Édition "Les Belles Lettres," 1986.

Chaplin, Jane D. *Livy's Exemplary History*. Oxford: Oxford University Press, 2000.

Chrissanthos, Stefan G. "Freedom of Speech and the Roman Republican Army." In *Free Speech in Classical Antiquity*, edited by Ineke Sluiter and Ralph M. Rosen. Leiden: Brill, 2004: 341–67.

Cicero. *Brutus*. Translated by G.L. Hendrickson, *Cicero: Brutus and Orator*. Cambridge: Harvard University Press, 1952.

De Amicitia. Translated by William Armistead Falconer, *Cicero: De Senectute, De Amicitia, De Divinatione*. London: William Heinemann, 1923.

De Inventione. Translated by H.M. Hubbell, *Cicero: De Inventione, De Optimo Genere Oratorum, Topica*. Cambridge: Harvard University Press, 1960.

De Lege Agraria. Translated by John Henry Freese, *Cicero: Pro Publio Quinctio, Pro Sexto Roscio Amerino, Pro Quinto Roscio Comoedo, De Lege Agraria*. Cambridge: Harvard University Press, 2000.

De Legibus. Translated by Clinton Walker Keyes, *Cicero: De Republica and De Legibus*. Cambridge: Harvard University Press, 2000.

De Officiis. Translated by Walter Miller. Cambridge: Harvard University Press, 1997.

De Oratore. Translated by E.W. Sutton. Cambridge: Harvard University Press, 1987.

De Re Publica: Selections. Edited by James E.G. Zetzel. Cambridge: Cambridge University Press, 1995.

De Republica. Translated by Clinton Walker Keyes, *Cicero: De Republica and De Legibus*. Cambridge: Harvard University Press, 2000.

Letters to Atticus. Translated by D.R. Shackleton Bailey. Cambridge: Harvard University Press, 1999.

Letters to Friends. Translated by D.R. Shackleton Bailey. Cambridge: Harvard University Press, 2001.

On Duties. Edited by M.T. Griffin and E.M. Atkins. Cambridge: Cambridge University Press, 1991.

On the Commonwealth. Edited by James E.G. Zetzel, *On the Commonwealth and on the Laws.* Cambridge: Cambridge University Press, 1999.

On the Ideal Orator. Translated by James M. May and Jakob Wisse. Oxford: Oxford University Press, 2001.

Orator. Translated by H.M. Hubbell, *Cicero: Brutus and Orator.* Cambridge: Harvard University Press, 1952.

Philippics. Translated by Walter C.A. Ker. Cambridge: Harvard University Press, 1938.

Pro. M. Marcello. Translated by N.H. Watts, Cicero: Orations. Cambridge: Harvard University Press, 1958.

Pro Sulla. Translated by C. MacDonald, *In Catilinam I–IV, Pro Murena, Pro Sulla, Pro Flacco.* Cambridge: Harvard University Press, 1989.

Tusculan Disputations. Translated by J.E. King. Cambridge: Harvard University Press, 1966.

Coby, J. Patrick. *Machiavelli's Romans.* Lanham: Lexington Books, 1999.

Cohen, Joshua. "Deliberation and Democratic Legitimacy." In *Deliberative Democracy: Essays on Reason and Politics,* edited by James Bohman and William Rehg. Cambridge: MIT University Press, 1997: 67–91.

Connolly, Joy. *The State of Speech: Rhetoric and Political Thought in Ancient Rome.* Princeton: Princeton University Press, 2007.

Cox, Virginia. "Machiavelli and the *Rhetorica Ad Herennium:* Deliberative Rhetoric in *The Prince.*" *The Sixteenth Century Journal* XXVIII, no. 4 (1997): 1109–41.

Dahl, Robert A. *A Preface to Democratic Theory.* Chicago: The University of Chicago Press, 2006.

Damon, Cynthia. "Rhetoric and Historiography." In *A Companion to Roman Rhetoric,* edited by William J. Dominik and Jon Hall. Oxford: Blackwell, 2007: 439–50.

The Digest of Justinian. Edited by Theodor Mommsen, Paul Krueger, and Alan Watson. Vol. I. Philadelphia: University of Pennsylvania Press, 1985.

Dominik, William J. "Tacitus and Pliny on Oratory." In *A Companion to Roman Rhetoric,* edited by William J. Dominik and Jon Hall. Oxford: Blackwell, 2007: 323–38.

Downs, Anthony. *An Economic Theory of Democracy.* New York: Harper and Row, 1957.

Dyck, Andrew R. *A Commentary on Cicero, De Officiis.* Ann Arbor: University of Michigan Press, 1996.

Earl, D.C. *The Political Thought of Sallust.* Cambridge: Cambridge University Press, 1961.

"Prologue-Form in Ancient Historiography." *Austfieg und Niedergang der Romischen Welt: Geschichte und Kultur Roms im Spiegel der Neueren Forschung* 1, no. 2 (1972): 842–56.

Eckstein, Arthur M. *Moral Vision in the Histories of Polybius.* Berkeley: University of California Press, 1995.

Eder, Walter. "Augustus and the Power of Tradition: The Augustan Principate as Binding Link between Republic and Empire." In *Between Republic and Empire: Interpretations of Augustus and His Principate*, edited by Kurt A. Raaflaub and Mark Toher. Berkeley: University of California Press, 1990: 71–122.

Edwards, Catharine. *The Politics of Immorality in Ancient Rome.* Cambridge: Cambridge University Press, 1993.

Elster, Jon. "The Market and the Forum: Three Varieties of Political Theory." In *Foundations of Social Choice Theory*, edited by Jon Elster and Aanund Hylland. Cambridge: Cambridge University Press, 1986: 103–32.

Fantham, Elaine. "The Contexts and Occasions of Roman Public Rhetoric." In *Roman Eloquence: Rhetoric in Society and Literature*, edited by William J Dominik. London: Routledge, 1997: 111–28.

"Imitation and Decline: Rhetorical Theory and Practice in the First Century after Christ." *Classical Philology* 73, no. 2 (1978): 102–16.

The Roman World of Cicero's De Oratore. Oxford: Oxford University Press, 2004.

Fontana, Benedetto. "Sallust and the Politics of Machiavelli." *History of Political Thought* XXIV, no. 1 (2003): 86–108.

"Tacitus on Empire and Republic." *History of Political Thought* XIV (1993): 27–40.

Fontana, Benedetto, Cary J. Nederman., and Gary Remer. "Introduction: Deliberative Democracy and the Rhetorical Turn." In *Talking Democracy: Historical Perspectives on Rhetoric and Democracy*, edited by Benedetto Fontana, Cary J. Nederman, and Gary Remer. University Park: The Pennsylvania State University Press, 2004: 1–25.

Furhmann, Manfred. *Cicero and the Roman Republic.* Translated by W.E. Yuill. Oxford: Basil Blackwell, 1992.

Galinsky, Karl. *Augustan Culture: An Interpretive Introduction.* Princeton: Princeton University Press, 1996.

Garsten, Bryan. *Saving Persuasion: A Defense of Rhetoric and Judgment.* Cambridge: Harvard University Press, 2006.

Garver, Eugene. *Aristotle's Rhetoric: An Art of Character.* Chicago: The University of Chicago Press, 1994.

Goldberg, Sander M. "Appreciating Aper: The Defense of Modernity in Tacitus' *Dialogus De Oratoribus.*" *Classical Quarterly* 49, no. 1 (1999): 224–37.

Gowing, Alain. *Empire and Memory: The Representation of the Roman Republic in Imperial Culture.* Cambridge: Cambridge University Press, 2005.

Griffin, Miriam T. "Seneca and Pliny." In *The Cambridge History of Greek and Roman Political Thought*, edited by Christopher Rowe and Malcolm Schofield. Cambridge: Cambridge University Press, 2000: 532–58.

Seneca: A Philosopher in Politics. Oxford: Clarendon Press, 1992.

Gruen, Erich S. *The Hellenistic World and the Coming of Rome.* Vol. 1. Berkeley: University of California Press, 1984.

The Last Generation of the Roman Republic. Berkeley: University of California Press, 1974.

Habermas, Jürgen. "Reconciliation through the Public Use of Reason: Remarks on John Rawls's *Political Liberalism.*" *The Journal of Philosophy* 92, no. 3 (1995): 109–31.

The Theory of Communicative Action, Volume 1: Reason and the Rationalization of Society. Translated by Thomas McCarthy. Boston: Beacon Press, 1981.

"Three Normative Models of Democracy." In *Democracy and Difference: Contesting the Boundaries of the Political,* edited by Seyla Benhabib. Princeton: Princeton University Press, 1996: 21–30.

Hamilton, Alexander. *Federalist 1.* In *The Federalist Papers,* edited by Clinton Rossiter. New York: The New American Library of World Literature, 1961.

Hammer, Dean. *Roman Political Thought and the Modern Theoretical Imagination.* Norman: University of Oklahoma Press, 2008.

Hardie, Alex. *Statius and the Silvae: Poets, Patrons and Epideixis in the Graeco-Roman World.* Liverpool: Francis Cairns, 1983.

Hartz, Louis. *The Liberal Tradition in America: An Interpretation of American Political Thought since the Revolution.* New York: Harcourt, Brace and World, 1955.

Hellegouarc' h, J. *Le Vocabulaire Latin Des Relations Et Des Partis Politiques Sous La Republique.* Paris: Société d'Édition "Les Belles Lettres," 1972.

Herodotus. *The Histories.* Translated by Aubrey de Selincourt. New York: Penguin, 1996.

Hobbes, Thomas. *The Citizen.* Edited by Bernard Gert, *Man and Citizen (De Homine and De Cive).* Indianapolis: Hackett, 1991.

Leviathan. Edited by Richard Tuck. Cambridge: Cambridge University Press, 1996.

Of the Life and History of Thucydides. Edited by David Grene, *The Peloponnesian War: The Complete Hobbes Translation.* Chicago: University of Chicago Press, 1989.

Hölkeskamp, K.J. "The Roman Republic: Government of the People, by the People, for the People?" *Scripta Classica Israelica* 19 (2000): 203–33.

Homer. *The Iliad.* Translated by Richard Lattimore. Chicago: University of Chicago Press, 1951.

Honohan, Iseult. *Civic Republicanism.* London: Routledge, 2002.

Hornblower, Simon. *A Commentary on Thucydides.* Vol. 1. Oxford: Oxford University Press, 1991.

Hornqvist, Mikael. *Machiavelli and Empire.* Cambridge: Cambridge University Press, 2004.

Isocrates. *Areopagiticus.* Translated by George Norlin, *Isocrates II* . New York: William Heinemann, 1929.

On the Peace. Translated by George Norlin, *Isocrates II*. London: William Heinemann, 1929.

Javitch, Daniel. *Poetry and Courtliness in Renaissance England*. Princeton: Princeton University Press, 1978.

Kahn, Victoria. *Rhetoric, Prudence, and Skepticism in the Renaissance*. Ithaca: Cornell University Press, 1985.

Kant, Immanuel. *The Critique of Judgement*. Translated by James Creed Meredith. Oxford: Clarendon Press, 1952.

Kapust, Daniel J. "Cato's Virtues and *The Prince*: Reading Sallust's *War with Catiline* with Machiavelli's *The Prince*," *History of Political Thought* 28, no. 3 (2007): 433–448.

——— "Between Contumacy and Obsequiousness: Tacitus on Moral Freedom and the Historian's Task." *European Journal of Political Theory* 8, no. 3 (2009): 293–311.

——— "On the Ancient Uses of Political Fear and Its Modern Implications." *Journal of the History of Ideas* 69, no. 3 (2008): 353–73.

Kennedy, George A. *The Art of Persuasion in Greece*. Princeton: Princeton University Press, 1963.

——— *The Art of Rhetoric in the Roman World, 300 B.C.–A.D. 300*. Princeton: Princeton University Press, 1972.

Konstan, David. "Clemency as a Virtue." *Classical Philology* 100 (2005): 337–46.

Kraus, C.S., and A.J. Woodman. *Latin Historians*. Oxford: Oxford University Press, 1997.

Leeman, Anton D., Harm Pinkster, and Jakob Wisse. *M. Tullius Cicero, De Oratore Libri III: Kommentar.* Vol. 4. Heidelberg: C. Winter, 1981.

Levene, D.S. "Sallust's Jugurtha: An 'Historical Fragment.'" *The Journal of Roman Studies* 82 (1992): 53–70.

——— "Sallust's Catiline and Cato the Censor." *The Classical Quarterly* 50, no. 1 (2000): 170–91.

Liebeschuetz, W. "The Theme of Liberty in the *Agricola* of Tacitus." *The Classical Quarterly* 16, no. 1 (1966): 126–39.

Lintott, Andrew. *The Constitution of the Roman Republic*. Oxford: Oxford University Press, 1999.

——— "The Crisis of the Republic: Sources and Source-Problems." In *The Cambridge Ancient History, Volume IX: The Last Age of the Roman Republic, 146–43 B.C.*, edited by J.A. Crook, Andrew Lintott, and Elizabeth Rawson. Cambridge: Cambridge University Press, 1994: 1–15.

Livy. *From the Founding of the City*. Translated by B.O. Foster. Cambridge: Harvard University Press, 1922.

Long, A. A. *Hellenistic Philosophy: Stoics, Epicureans, Sceptics*. Berkeley: University of California Press, 1986.

Long, A.A., and D.N. Sedley. *The Hellenistic Philosophers*.Vol. 1. Cambridge: Cambridge University Press, 1987.

Lucan. *The Civil War*. Translated by J.D. Duff. Cambridge: Harvard University Press, 1988.

Luce, T.J. "Ancient Views on the Causes of Bias in Historical Writing." *Classical Philology* 84, no. 1 (1989): 16–31.

Livy: The Composition of His History. Princeton: Princeton University Press, 1977.

Lucretius. *De Rerum Natura*. Translated by W.H.D. Rouse. Cambridge: Harvard University Press, 1992.

Machiavelli, Niccolo. *The Discourses on Livy*. Edited by Bernard Crick. New York: Penguin, 1983.

MacIntyre, Alasdair. *After Virtue*. Notre Dame: Notre Dame University Press, 1984.

Madison, James. *Federalist 10*. In *The Federalist, or the New Constitution*, edited by Max Beloff. London: Basil Blackwell, 1987.

Manin, Bernard. "On Legitimacy and Political Deliberation." *Political Theory* 15, no. 3 (1987): 338–68.

Markovits, Elizabeth. *The Politics of Sincerity: Plato, Frank Speech, and Democratic Judgment*. University Park: The Pennsylvania State University Press, 2008.

Mason, Sheila M. "Livy and Montesquieu." In *Livy*, edited by T.A. Dorey. London: Routledge and Kegan Paul, 1971: 118–158.

May, James M. "Cicero as Rhetorician." In *A Companion to Roman Rhetoric*, edited by William J. Dominik and Jon Hall. Oxford: Blackwell Publishing, 2007: 250–63.

McCormick, John P. "Machiavelli against Republicanism: On the Cambridge School's 'Guicciardinian' Moments." *Political Theory* 31, no. 5 (2003): 615–43.

"Machiavellian Democracy: Controlling Elites with Ferocious Populism." *American Political Science Review* 95, no. 2 (2001): 297–313.

McGushin, P. *Bellum Catilinae: A Commentary*. Leiden: E.J. Brill, 1977.

Miles, Gary B. *Livy: Reconstructing Early Rome*. Ithaca: Cornell University Press, 1995.

Millar, Fergus. *The Crowd in Rome in the Late Republic*. Ann Arbor: University of Michigan Press, 1998.

Momigliano, Arnaldo. "Camillus and Concord." *The Classical Quarterly* 36, no. 3/4 (1942): 111–20.

Mommsen, Theodor. *History of Rome*. Translated by William Purdie Dickinson. New York: Charles Scribner's Sons 1911.

Morford, Mark. *The Roman Philosophers from the Time of Cato the Censor to the Death of Marcus Aurelius*. London: Routledge, 2002.

Morstein-Marx, Robert. *Mass Oratory and Political Power in the Late Roman Republic*. Cambridge: Cambridge University Press, 2004.

Mouritsen, Henrik. *Plebs and Politics in the Late Roman Republic*. Cambridge: Cambridge University Press, 2001.

Mulhall, Stephen, and Adam Swift, eds. *Liberals and Communitarians*. Blackwell: Oxford, 1996.

Murphy, Cullen. *Are We Rome? The Fall of an Empire and the Fate of America*. New York: Houghton Mifflin Company, 2007.

Narducci, Emanuele. "*Brutus*: The History of Roman Eloquence." In *Brill's Companion to Cicero: Oratory and Rhetoric*, edited by James M. May. Leiden: Brill, 2002: 401–25.

Nederman, Cary J. "The Mirror Crack'd: The *Speculum Principum* as Political and Social Criticism in the Late Middle Ages." *The European Legacy* 3, no. 3 (1998): 18–39.

——. "Rhetoric, Reason, and Republic: Republicanisms – Ancient, Medieval, and Modern." In *Renaissance Civic Humanism: Reappraisals and Reflections*, edited by James Hankins. Cambridge: Cambridge University Press, 2000: 247–69.

Nelson, Eric. *The Greek Tradition in Republican Thought*. Cambridge: Cambridge University Press, 2004.

Ogilvie, R.M. *A Commentary on Livy Books 1–5*. Oxford: Oxford University Press, 1965.

Oratorum Romanorum Fragmenta Libera Rei Publicae. Edited by Henrica Malcovati. Milan: Aug. Taurinorum, 1955.

Pagán, Victoria E. "Distant Voices of Freedom in the *Annales* of Tacitus." *Studies in Latin Literature and Roman History*, Collection Latomus X (2000): 358–69.

Petronius. *Satyrica*. Translated by R. Bracht Branham and Daniel Kinney. Berkeley: University of California Press, 1996.

Pettit, Philip. "Discourse Theory and Republican Freedom." In *Republicanism: History, Theory and Practice*, edited by Daniel Weinstock and Christian Nadeau. London: Frank Cass Publishers, 2004: 62–82.

——. "The Freedom of the City: A Republican Ideal." In *The Good Polity: Normative Analysis of the State*, edited by Alan Hamlin and Philip Pettit. Oxford: Basil Blackwell, 1989: 141–67.

——. "Keeping Republican Freedom Simple: On a Difference with Quentin Skinner." *Political Theory* 30, no. 3 (2002): 339–56.

——. *Republicanism: A Theory of Freedom and Government*. Oxford: Oxford University Press, 1997.

——. "Reworking Sandel's Republicanism." In *Debating Democracy's Discontent: Essays on American Politics, Law and Public Philosophy*, edited by Anita L. Allen and Milton C. Regan, Jr. New York: Oxford, 1998: 40–59.

——. *A Theory of Freedom: From the Psychology to the Politics of Agency*. Oxford: Oxford University Press, 2001.

Plato. *Apology*. Translated by G.M.A. Grube. Edited by John M. Cooper, *Plato: Complete Works*. Indianapolis: Hacket, 1997.

Gorgias. Translated by Donald J. Zeyl. Indianapolis: Hackett, 1987.

Phaedrus. Translated by Christopher Rowe. Warminster: Aris and Phillips, 1986.

Republic. Translated by C.D.C. Reeve. Indianapolis: Hackett, 2004.

Pliny. *Letters.* Translated by Betty Radice, *Pliny: Letters and Panegyricus* I, Cambridge: Harvard University Press, 1969.

Panegyricus. Translated by Betty Radice, *Pliny: Letters and Panegyricus II.* Cambridge: Harvard University Press, 1969.

Plutarch. *Life of the Younger.* Translated by Bernadotte Perrin, *Plutarch's Lives.* Cambridge: Harvard University Press, 1967.

Life of Cicero. Translated by Bernadotte Perrin, *Plutarch's Lives.* Cambridge: Harvard University Press, 1967.

Life of Marcus Cato. Translated by Bernadotte Perrin, *Plutarch's Lives.* Cambridge: Harvard University Press, 1967.

Life of Pericles. Translated by Bernadotte Perrin, *Plutarch's Lives.* Cambridge: Harvard University Press, 1967.

Pocock, J.G.A. *The Machiavellian Moment.* Princeton: Princeton University Press, 1975.

Polybius. *The Histories.* Translated by W.R. Paton. Cambridge: Harvard University Press, 1929.

Quintilian. *Institutio Oratoria.* Translated by H.E. Butler. Cambridge: Harvard University Press, 1963.

Raaflaub, Kurt A. "Aristocracy and Freedom of Speech in the Greco-Roman World." In *Free Speech in Classical Antiquity,* edited by Ineke Sluiter and Ralph M. Rosen. Leiden: Brill, 2004: 41–61.

The Discovery of Freedom in Ancient Greece. Translated by Renate Franciscono. Chicago: University of Chicago Press, 2004.

"From Protection and Defense to Offence and Participation: Stages in the Conflict of the Orders." In *Social Struggles in Archaic Rome,* edited by Kurt A. Raaflaub. Berkeley: University of California Press, 1986: 198–243.

"The Conflict of the Orders in Archaic Rome: A Comprehensive and Comparative Approach." In *Social Struggles in Archaic Rome,* edited by Kurt A. Raaflaub. Berkeley: University of California Press, 1986: 1–51.

Rawson, Elizabeth. *Intellectual Life in the Late Roman Republic.* London: Duckworth, 1985.

The Spartan Tradition in European Political Thought. Oxford: Clarendon Press, 1969.

Remer, Gary. "Hobbes, the Rhetorical Tradition, and Toleration." *The Review of Politics* 54, no. 1 (1992): 5–33.

"Humanism, Liberalism, & the Skeptical Case for Religious Toleration." *Polity* 25, no. 1 (1992): 21–43.

"The Classical Orator as Political Representative: Cicero and the Modern Concept of Representation." *Journal of Politics* 72, no. 4 (2010): 1063–82.

Riley, Patrick. "Rousseau's General Will: Freedom of a Particular Kind." *Political Studies* XXXIX, no. 1 (1991): 55–74.

Robbins, Caroline. *The Eighteenth-Century Commonwealthman: Studies in the Transmission, Development and Circumstance of English Liberal Thought from the Restoration of Charles II until the War with the Thirteen Colonies.* Cambridge: Harvard University Press, 1959.

Robin, Corey. *Fear: The History of a Political Idea.* Oxford: Oxford University Press, 2004.

Rodgers, Daniel T. "Republicanism: The Career of a Concept." *The Journal of American History* 79, no. 1 (1992): 11–38.

Romilly, Jacqueline de. "Eunoia in Isocrates or the Political Importance of Creating Good Will." *The Journal of Hellenic Studies* 78 (1958): 92–101.

Rousseau, Jean-Jacques. *Of the Social Contract.* Edited by Victor Gourevitch, *Rousseau: The Social Contract and Other Later Political Writings.* New York: Cambridge University Press, 1997.

Rutledge, Steven. *Imperial Inquisitions: Prosecutors and Informants from Tiberius to Domitian.* New York: Routledge, 2001.

———. "Oratory and Politics in the Empire." In *A Companion to Roman Rhetoric,* edited by William J. Dominik and Jon Hall. Oxford: Blackwell, 2007: 109–21.

Sallust. *The Histories.* Translated by P. McGushin. Vol. 1. Oxford: Clarendon Press, 1992.

———. *War with Catiline.* Translated by J.C. Rolfe, *Sallust.* Cambridge: Harvard University Press, 1985.

———. *War with Jugurtha.* Translated by J.C. Rolfe, *Sallust.* Cambridge: Harvard University Press, 1985.

Sallustius. *Historiarum Reliquiae.* Edited by Bertoldus Maurenbrecher. Stuttgart: Teubner, 1967.

Saxonhouse, Arlene W. "Tacitus' *Dialogue on Oratory*: Political Activity under a Tyrant." *Political Theory* 3, no. 1 (1975): 53–68.

Scanlon, Thomas F. *The Influence of Thucydides on Sallust.* Heidelberg: Carl Winter, 1980.

Schofield, Malcolm. "Cicero's Definition of *Res Publica.*" In *Cicero the Philosopher: Twelve Papers,* edited by J.G.F. Powell. Oxford: Clarendon Press, 1995): 63–83.

Schumpeter, Joseph A. *Capitalism, Socialism, and Democracy.* New York: Harper and Row, 1950.

Seager, Robin. *Tiberius.* Oxford: Blackwell, 2005.

Seneca. *On Favors.* Edited by John M. Cooper and J.F. Procope, *Seneca: Moral and Political Essays.* Cambridge: Cambridge University Press, 1995.

———. *On Mercy.* Edited by John M. Cooper and J.F. Procope, *Seneca: Moral and Political Essays.* Cambridge: Cambridge University Press, 1995.

Sinclair, Patrick. *Tacitus the Sententious Historian: A Sociology of Rhetoric in Annales 1–6.* University Park: The Pennsylvania State University Press, 1995.

Skinner, Quentin. *Hobbes and Republican Liberty*. Cambridge: Cambridge University Press, 2008.

"The Italian City-Republics." In *Democracy: The Unfinished Journey, 508 B.C. to A.D. 1993*, edited by John Dunn. New York: Oxford University Press, 1992: 57–69.

Liberty before Liberalism. Cambridge: Cambridge University Press, 1998.

"Machiavelli's *Discorsi* and the Pre-Humanist Origins of Republican Ideas." In *Machiavelli and Republicanism*, edited by Gisella Bock, Quentin Skinner, and Maurizio Viroli. Cambridge: Cambridge University Press, 1990: 121–41.

"On Justice, the Common Good and the Priority of Liberty." In *Dimensions of Radical Democracy: Pluralism, Citizenship, Community*, edited by Chantal Mouffe. London: Verso, 1992: 211–24.

Reason and Rhetoric in the Philosophy of Hobbes. Cambridge: Cambridge University Press, 1996.

"The Republican Ideal of Political Liberty." In *Machiavelli and Republicanism*, edited by Gisella Bock, Quentin Skinner, and Maurizio Viroli. Cambridge: Cambridge University Press, 1990: 293–309.

Southern, Pat. *Domitian: Tragic Tyrant*. Bloomington: Indiana University Press, 1997.

Steel, Catherine. *Roman Oratory*. Cambridge: Cambridge University Press, 2006.

Suetonius, *Domitian*. Translated by J.C. Rolfe, Vol. II *Suetonius*. Cambridge: Harvard University Press, 1992.

Syme, Ronald. "Livy and Augustus." *Harvard Studies in Classical Philology* 64 (1959): 27–87.

The Roman Revolution. New York: Oxford University Press, 1939.

Sallust. Berkeley: University of California Press, 1964.

Tacitus. Vol. I and II. Oxford: Oxford University Press, 1958.

Tacitus. *Agricola*. Translated by M. Hutton and W. Peterson, *Tacitus: Dialogus, Agricola, Germanicus*. Cambridge: Harvard University Press, 1963.

The Annals. Translated by John Jackson, *Tacitus: The Histories and the Annals*. Cambridge: Harvard University Press, 1986.

De Vita Agricolae. Edited by R.M. Ogilvie and Ian Richmond. London: Oxford University Press, 1967.

A Dialogue on Oratory. Translated by W. Peterson and M. Winterbottom, *Tacitus: Dialogus, Agricola, Germania*. Cambridge: Harvard University Press, 1958.

Dialogus De Oratoribus. Edited by Roland Mayer. Cambridge: Cambridge University Press, 2001.

The Histories. Translated by Clifford H. Moore. Cambridge: Harvard University Press, 1925.

Thucydides. *History of the Peloponnesian War*. Translated by Rex Warner. New York: Penguin, 1972.

Thucydidis. *Historiae*. Edited by Henry Stuart Jones. Vol. I. Oxford: Clarendon Press, 1955.

Trenchard, John. *Cato's Letters; or, Essays on Liberty, Civil and Religious, and Other Important Subjects.* Vol. 1. New York: Russell and Russell, 1969.

Vasaly, Ann. "Personality and Power: Livy's Depiction of the Appii Claudii in the First Pentad." *Transactions of the American Philological Association* 117, no. 1987 (1987): 203–26.

Viroli, Maurizio. *Republicanism.* Translated by Antony Shugaar. New York: Hill and Wang, 2002.

Walker, William. "Sallust and Skinner on Civil Liberty." *European Journal of Political Theory* 5, no. 3 (2006): 237–59.

Wallace-Hadrill, Andrew. "Civilis Princeps: Between Citizen and King." *The Journal of Roman Studies* 72 (1982): 32–48.

Walsh, P.G. *Livy.* Oxford: Oxford University Press, 1974.

——— *Livy: His Historical Aims and Methods.* Cambridge: Cambridge University Press, 1961.

Ward, Allen M. "How Democratic Was the Roman Republic?" *New England Classical Journal* 31, no. 2 (2004): 101–19.

Weinstock, Stefan. *Divus Julius.* Oxford: Oxford University Press, 1971.

Weithman, Paul. "Political Republicanism and Perfectionist Republicanism." *Review of Politics* 66, no. 2 (2004): 285–312.

Whidden, Christopher. "Cyrus's Imperial Household: An Aristotelian Reading of Xenophon's Cyropaedia." *Polis* 25, no. 1 (2008): 31–62.

Whitfield, J.H. "Machiavelli's Use of Livy." In *Livy*, edited by T.A. Dorey. London: Routledge and Kegan Paul, 1971: 73–96.

Wiedemann, Thomas. "Reflections of Roman Political Thought in Latin Historical Writing." In *The Cambridge History of Greek and Roman Political Thought*, edited by Christopher Rowe. Cambridge: Cambridge University Press, 2000: 517–31.

Williams, Gordon. *Change and Decline: Roman Literature in the Early Empire.* Berkeley: University of California Press, 1978.

Winterbottom, M. "Quintilian and the *Vir Bonus.*" *The Journal of Roman Studies* 54 (1964): 90–7.

Winton, Richard. "Herodotus, Thucydides and the Sophists." In *The Cambridge History of Greek and Roman Political Thought*, edited by Christopher Rowe and Malcolm Schofield. Cambridge: Cambridge University Press, 2000: 89–121.

Wirszubksi, Chaim. *Libertas as a Political Idea at Rome.* Cambridge: Cambridge University Press, 1950.

Wisse, Jakob. "*De Oratore*: Rhetoric, Philosophy, and the Making of the Ideal Orator." In *Brill's Companion to Cicero: Oratory and Rhetoric*, edited by James M. May. Leiden: Brill, 2002: 375–400.

Wood, Gordon S. *The Creation of the American Republic 1776–1787.* Chapel Hill: University of North Carolina Press, 1969.

Wood, Neal. "Sallust's Theorem: A Comment on 'Fear' in Western Political Thought." *History of Political Thought* XVI, no. 2 (1995): 174–89.

Woodman, A.J. *Rhetoric in Classical Historiography*. London: Croom Helm, 1988.

Yack, Bernard. "Rhetoric and Public Reasoning: An Aristotelian Understanding of Political Deliberation." *Political Theory* 34, no. 4 (2006): 417–38.

Yavetz, Zvi. "The Res Gestae and Augustus' Public Image." In *Caesar Augustus: Seven Aspects*, edited by Fergus Millar and Erich Segal. Oxford: Clarendon Press, 1984: 1–36.

INDEX

Agricola (Tacitus), 122, 134–7, 144, 146, 150, 165–6, 168
Allen, Danielle, 18–19, 55, 79, 84, 110
Annals (Tacitus), 147–8, 150–1, 163–4, 166–8, 170
Arendt, Hannah, 131
Areopagiticus (Isocrates), 87
Aristotle
  on epideictic oratory, 151, 153
  on *ethos*, 85
  on freedom, 112
  on goodwill, 86
  on *pathos*, 86
  on political friendship, 83
  on redescription, 57–8
  on tyranny, 104
  on virtue and vice, 57–8
auctoritas, 4, 96–7
  and *libertas*, 4
  senatus auctoritas, 45
Austin, J.L., 18
avaritia. *See* Livy, on *avaritia*; *See* Sallust, on *avaritia*

Bartsch, Shadi, 132
Batstone, William, 75
benevolentia. *See* Livy, on *benevolentia*; *See* Cicero, on *benevolentia*; *See* Rhetoric to Herennius, *benevolentia* in
Berlin, Isaiah, 9

Book of the Courtier (Castiglione), 117
Brunt, P.A., 3, 96, 112
Brutus (Cicero), 1, 138

Carthage, 41. *See* Sallust, on Carthage
Castiglione, Baldessare, 117
Catiline, L. *See* Sallust, on Catiline; *See* Hobbes, Thomas, on Catiline
Cato the Elder
  and the destruction of Carthage, 39, 41
Cato the Younger. *See* Sallust, on Cato the Younger
Cato's Letters (Trenchard), 112
Cicero
  on Atticism, 36
  on *benevolentia*, 87–8, 102, 105
  on *clementia*, 154–7
  on *concordia*, 73, 83
  on *dignitas*, 118
  on eloquence's relationship to peace, 37
  on epideictic oratory, 151
  on flattery, 103, 107, 112
  on friendship, 102
  on Hortensius, 1
  on love and fear, 104–5
  on mercy and leadership, 154–7
  on Numa Pompilius, 73, 155
  on *prudentia*, 62
  on redescription, 62
  on Romulus, 73

Cicero (*cont.*)
  on social and political conflict, 76
  on Socrates, 116
  on Tarquinius, 104
  on the development of Rome, 73
  on the Gracchi, 107
  on the honorable and the
    advantageous, 62–3
  on the lion and the fox, 106
  on the perfect orator, 78
  on the place of eloquence in
    the republic, 1, 27
  on the political role of the orator, 114–18
  on the *rector rei publicae*, 101
  on the relationship of eloquence
    to wisdom, 116
  on the tasks of the orator, 34
  on tyranny, 104
  on *verecundia*, 101
Cincinnatus. *See* Livy, on Cincinnatus
clementia. See Sallust, on *clementia*; *See*
  Cicero, on *clementia*; *See* Seneca, on
  clementia; *See* Pliny, on *clementia*; *See*
  Tacitus, on *clementia*
concordia, 86. *See* Livy, on *concordia*; *See*
  Cicero, on *concordia*; *See* Sallust, on
  concordia
Conflict of the Orders, 76, 94
Connolly, Joy, 21, 29, 44, 76–7
*Considerations of the Causes of the Greatness
  of the Romans and their Decline*
  (Montesquieu), 28
contio, 44
Cox, Virginia, 61

Dahl, Robert, 14
deliberative democracy, 14
deliberative oratory, 47, 61–5
  and the conflict between the honorable
    and the advantageous, 61
Dialogue on Orators (Tacitus), 3, 123–9,
  132–3, 169
dignitas, 46, 66, 118, 137
  and *libertas*, 46

Discourses on the First Ten Books of Livy
  (Machiavelli), 82–3, 146
Domitian, 119–20. *See* Pliny, on Domitian;
  See Tacitus, on Domitian; *See*
  Suetonius, on Domitian
Domitian (Suetonius), 119
Downs, Anthony, 14
Dyck, Andrew, 155

epideictic oratory, 151–3
exempla, 23, 92, 102
  Agricola as *exemplum*, 134
  Cato's use of, 70
  in rhetoric, 93
  in Tacitus' *Histories*, 150
  Livy's use of, 92

Fantham, Elaine, 123
fear. *See* Sallust, on collective fear; *See*
  metus hostilis; *See* Livy, on collective
  fear; *See* political fear; *See* Polybius,
  on political fear
Federalist 1 (Hamilton), 4
flattery. *See* Pliny, on flattery; *See* Cicero,
  on flattery; *See* Plato, on flattery; *See*
  Tacitus, on flattery
  and servitude, 112
Fontana, Benedetto, 44
For Marcellus (Cicero), 155–7
For Sulla (Cicero), 112
forensic oratory, 47
friendship. *See* Cicero, on friendship;
  See Aristotle, on political
  friendship
From the Founding of the City (Livy),
  89–90, 92–103, 107–9

Garsten, Bryan, 20–1, 56, 79
Garver, Eugene, 86
Goldberg, Sander, 123
goodwill. *See* Isocrates, on goodwill; *See*
  Livy, on goodwill; *See* Cicero, on
  benevolentia; *See* Livy, on *benevolentia*;
  See Rhetoric to Herennius, *benevolentia* in

and leadership, 105–6
Gorgias (Plato), 20, 130–1
Gracchi. *See* Tacitus, on the Gracchi; *See*
  Cicero, on the Gracchi; *See* Sallust,
  on the Gracchi
Griffin, Mirriam, 157

Habermas, Jurgen, 14–16
Hammer, Dean, 26, 82
Hamilton, Alexander, 4
Herodotus
  on the function of history, 22
Histories (Herodotus), 22
Histories (Polybius), 23, 39, 149
Histories (Sallust), 49–50
Histories (Tacitus), 122, 147–8, 150, 169–70
History of the Peloponnesian War
  (Thucydides), 23, 40–1, 80
Hobbes, Thomas
  his attitude towards rhetoric, 33
  his reading of Sallust, 25, 32–4
  on Catiline, 33
  on collective fear, 43
  on eloquence and logic, 37
  on Nero, 171
  on rhetoric and tumult, 33
Hortensius, 1

in utramque partem, 78, 173
Institutes (Quintilian), 56–7, 121, 152, 160
Isocrates, 86–7
  on goodwill, 86–7

Javitch, Daniel, 117

Kant, Immanuel
  on rhetoric, 17
Konstan, David, 155

Levene, D.S., 70, 77
Leviathan (Hobbes), 32, 43
libertas
  and *auctoritas*, 4
  and Cremutius Cordus in Tacitus'

Annals, 163
  and *dignitas*, 46
  and *eloquentia* in Tacitus' *Histories*, 146
  and free speech, 3
  and rule of law, 99
  and the example of Agricola, 135
  Camillus' invocation of, 107
  in Tacitus' *Dialogue on Orators*,
    125, 128
  love of the people for, 44
  the Gracchi and, 46
Life of Marcus Cato (Plutarch), 41
Life of Pericles (Plutarch), 149
Livy
  compared to Machiavelli, 82–3
  compared to Sallust, 90–1
  on history as a visual monument, 92
  influence of, 6–7
  on Alexander, 94
  on *avaritia*, 91
  on *benevolentia*, 97
  on Brutus, 99
  on Camillus, 89–90, 95
  on Capitolinus, 107
  on Cincinnatus, 91–2
  on collective fear, 94
  on *concordia*, 83, 89–90, 93, 95–6, 109
  on goodwill, 97
  on goodwill and the observation of
    character, 95–9, 108
  on *imperium*, 96–7
  on love and fear in political
    relationships, 98
  on *luxuria*, 91–2, 100, 102
  on Menenius Agrippa, 95, 108
  on *mores*, 89, 108
  on Numa Pompilius, 100–1
  on piety, 100
  on shame and fear, 96
  on Tarquinius, 98
  on the Appii Claudii, 96
  on the body politic, 95
  on Valerius, 102–3
  his use of *exempla*, 92

love and fear in political relationships, 98, 153–62
Luce, T.J., 91, 148–9
luxuria. See Sallust, on *luxuria; See* Livy, on *luxuria*

Machiavelli, Niccolo
  compared to Livy, 82–3
  on Caesar, 146
  on Catiline, 146
MacIntyre, Alisdair, 9
Madison, James, 29
Manin, Bernard, 16–17
Maternus. *See* Tacitus, on Maternus
  compared to Socrates, 132–3
Mayer, Roland, 137
metus hostilis, 38–43, 91, 93, 95. *See also* political fear; *See also* Sallust, on collective fear; *See also* Livy, on collective fear
Millar, Fergus, 4
moderatio. See Tacitus, on *moderatio*
Momigliano, Arnaldo, 83
Mommsen, Theodor
  on Sallust, 34
Montesquieu, Charles de Secondat
  Considerations of the Causes of the Greatness of the Romans and their Decline, 28
mores. See Livy, on *mores*

Nelson, Eric, 13
Nicomachean Ethics (Aristotle), 57–8
Numa Pompilius. *See* Cicero, on Numa Pompilius; *See* Livy, on Numa Pompilius

On Duties (Cicero), 2, 104, 106
On Friendship (Cicero), 102, 105, 107, 112
On Invention (Cicero), 62–3
On Mercy (Seneca), 157–60
On the Agrarian Law (Cicero), 4
On the Citizen (Hobbes), 33, 37, 142, 171
On the Commonwealth (Cicero), 28, 71–3, 83, 101–2, 104

On the Ideal Orator (Cicero), 5, 27, 34–7, 61, 76, 78, 87–9, 93, 114–18, 152
On the Laws (Cicero), 96
On the Peace (Isocrates), 87
Orator (Cicero), 36, 88–9
Origins (Cato), 39

Pagán, Victoria, 136
Panegyricus (Pliny), 120, 160–2
pathos. See Aristotle, on *pathos*
Pettit, Philip, 109
  on common interests, 21
  on republican liberty, 11
  on servility, 113
  on the common good, 13
Phaedrus (Plato), 59
Plato, 19
  attitude toward conventional rhetoric, 19
  on flattery, 131
  on redescription and moral corruption, 59
  on the contrast between philosophy and rhetoric, 130
Pliny, 142–4, 160–2
  on *clementia*, 160–2
  on Domitian, 160–2
  on flattery, 160
  on history and oratory, 142–4
  on love and virtue, 162
  on Trajan, 161–2
Plutarch
  on Cato and Scipio Nasica, 41
  on Cato the Younger, 136
  on the difficulties of writing history, 149
Pocock, J.G.A., 28
political fear, 38–43
Politics (Aristotle), 104
Polybius
  on flattering history, 149
  on political fear, 39–40
  on the function of history, 23
  on the Roman constitution, 39–40

Posidonius, 38–9
   on the fall of Carthage, 38
prudentia. *See* Cicero, on *prudentia*; *See*
   Tacitus, on *prudentia*

Quintilian, 56–7, 61, 160
   on epideictic oratory, 152–3
   on redescription, 57

redescription. *See* Aristotle, on
   redescription in; *See* Cicero,
   on redescription; *See* Rhetoric
   to Herennius, redescription; *See*
   rhetoric, redescription; *See* Plato, on
   redescription and moral corruption;
   See Quintilian, on redescription
Remer, Gary, 78
Republic (Plato), 59
republican political thought, 8–13
   and Roman political thought, 9–11
   civic virtue in, 11–12, 29–30
   common good in, 12
   corruption in, 28
   liberty in, 9–11
   perfectionist and political virtue in,
     29, 51
   republican revival and, 8
rhetoric
   Allen on rhetoric and trust, 19, 56
   and antagonism, 76
   and goodwill, 85–9, 105
   and political theory, 13–21
   and Roman historiography, 22–3
   and Roman liberty, 3
   deliberative oratory, 47, 61–5
   epideictic oratory, 151–3
   ethos, 85
   exempla in, 93
   forensic oratory, 47
   Garsten on rhetoric and judgment,
     20–1, 56
   Hobbes's attitude towards, 33
   Kant's attitude toward, 17
   pathos, 86

Plato's attitude toward conventional,
   19
   redescription in, 56–8, 63–5
Rhetoric (Aristotle), 57–8, 85–6, 112, 152
Rhetoric to Herennius, 63–5
   benevolentia in, 87
   on the honorable and the advantageous,
     63–5
   redescription in, 63–5
Roman political thought
   revived interest in, 8
Romilly, Jacqueline de, 86
Romulus, 76. *See* Cicero, on Romulus
Rousseau, Jean-Jacques, 16

saevitia. *See* Tacitus, on *saevitia*
Sallust
   Cato and Caesar's debate, 65–70
   compared to Cicero's view of history,
     35–6
   compared to Thucydides, 47
   contrasted to Livy, 90–1
   his comparison of Cato and Caesar,
     73–4
   his relationship to Caesar, 34
   his relationship to Hobbes, 25
   his relationship to Thucydides, 36
   influence of, 6–7
   on antagonism, 25, 31, 43–7, 74–7
   on *avaritia*, 42, 50, 60, 69
   on Caesar, 66–8, 73–4
   on Carthage, 30–1, 46–50
   on Catiline, 37, 45, 77–8
   on Cato the Younger, 68–70, 73–4
   on *clementia*, 66
   on collective fear, 42, 48–50
   on *concordia*, 42, 45–6, 48–50
   on Fortune, 43
   on G. Memmius, 44–5
   on *luxuria*, 69
   on moral corruption, 47, 49
   on parties and factions, 46
   on the breakdown of dichotomies,
     48–50

Sallust (*cont.*)
  on the corruption of language, 45, 50
  on the expulsion of Rome's kings, 29
  on the Gracchi, 46
Schofield, Malcolm, 104
Schumpeter, Joseph, 14
Second Philippic (Cicero), 139
Seneca, 157–60
  on Augustus, 159
  on *clementia*, 157–60
  on love and *clementia*, 157–60
  on Nero, 158–9
  on the distinction between emulation
    and fear, 161
Skinner, Quentin
  on redescription, 57
  on republican liberty, 9–10
  on republican virtue and corruption, 12
  on the common good, 12
Socrates, 130. *See* Cicero, on Socrates
  compared to Maternus, 132–3
Suetonius
  on Domitian, 119
Syme, Ronald, 5, 75, 90, 134, 154

Tacitus
  his comparison of Aper to Maternus,
    132
  exempla in *Histories*, 150
  history as providing markers, 26
  influence of, 6–7
  on Agricola, 134–7, 168
  on Aper, 124–5, 133
  on Athens, 128
  on *clementia*, 168
  on Cordus, 163–4
  on Domitian, 135–6, 144, 146, 165–6
  on finding a middle path, 170
  on flattery, 167

  on history as judgment, 26
  on Maternus, 3, 123–9
  on *moderatio*, 134
  on Nerva, 122
  on poetry and eloquence, 125
  on *prudentia*, 26, 135
  on reading the character of rulers, 151,
    170–1
  on *saevitia*, 166–7
  on Sparta and Crete, 138–9
  on the context of eloquence, 126–9
  on the dilemmas facing historians, 146–8
  on the Gracchi, 129
  on the principate and historiography,
    146–7
  on Tiberius, 166–8, 170
  on Vespasian, 168
  on writing history, 149–51
  tensions in speeches of Maternus, 132
Thucydides
  Diodotus, 66, 68, 80
  his relationship to Sallust, 36
  on political fear, 40–1
  on the Corcyrean stasis, 40
  on the distortion of language, 41
  on the function of history, 22
Tiberius. *See* Tacitus, on Tiberius
Trenchard, John, 112
Tusculan Disputations (Cicero), 123
tyranny, 104–5

War with Catiline (Sallust), 42–3, 45–6,
    48–9, 60, 65–71, 73–4, 79
War with Jugurtha (Sallust), 43–4, 46,
    48–9, 60
Weithman, Paul, 30, 51
Wiedemann, Thomas, 24
Wirszubski, Chaim, 96, 154
Wisse, Jakob, 117

Made in the USA
Las Vegas, NV
19 June 2022

50418805R00120